THREE
PSYCHOTHERAPIES
A Clinical Comparison

Three Psychotherapies
A Clinical Comparison

By
CLEMENS A. LOEW, Ph.D.,
HENRY GRAYSON, Ph.D.
and
GLORIA HEIMAN LOEW, Ph.D.

WITH CONTRIBUTIONS BY

Yael Danieli, Ph.D., Rainette Eden Fantz, Ph.D., Herbert Fensterheim, Ph.D., Melvyn Hollander, Ph.D., Michael Kriegsfeld, Ph.D., Arnold A. Lazarus, Ph.D., Miriam Polster, Ph.D., Leo J. Reyna, Ph.D., Leon Salzman, M.D., Bennett Simon, M.D., Paul Stark, Ph.D., Joseph C. Zinker, Ph.D.

BRUNNER/MAZEL Publishers • New York

SECOND PRINTING

Library of Congress Cataloging in Publication Data

Loew, Clemens A   1937-

Three psychotherapies.

Includes bibliographies.
1. Behavior therapy. 2. Gestalt therapy. 3. Psychoanalysis. I. Grayson,
Henry, 1935-   joint author.   II. Loew, Gloria, 1941-   joint author.
III. Danieli, Yael.   IV. Title.   [DNLM: 1. Psychotherapy—Case studies.
WM420 L825t] RC480.5.L58 1975   616.8'91   74-81152 ISBN 0-87630-098-0

*To the Memory of My Father
and to the Courage
of My Mother and Uncle.*
C. A. L.

Introduction

The field of psychotherapy encompasses a variety of useful treatment approaches. There has always been much controversy as to which is the *best* technique. We feel that it is now obvious that no approach is successful in helping *every* individual with any type of difficulty. Some are more effective than others for some kinds of people with some kinds of problems.

The purpose of this book is to explore some of the most representative psychotherapeutic modalities to compare similarities and differences of theory, technique and approach.

To cover a representative sample of problems treated, we have chosen three cases: obsessive-compulsive personality, schizoid personality, and the sexual disorder of frigidity. A behavior therapist, a Gestalt therapist and a psychoanalytic therapist were asked to respond to each case. Thus there are nine different basic contributions. In addition, in regard to the frigidity case we asked three additional therapists to present their views. The purpose of the latter contributions was to illustrate comparisons not only *between* different treatment approaches, but also *within* the modalities.

All of the therapists were given a case description based on intake interviews, along with a set of guidelines to use in writing about the case. The therapists were basically asked to speculate about how they would go about treating this individual if he or she were seeking help in their office.

Following the chapters by the three contributors on each case, the editors have written a comparative chapter highlighting conceptual and technical similarities and differences.

The purpose of these editorial chapters is to provide the reader with some essential variables with which to compare these three approaches. The reader may further speculate as to the effectiveness and suitability of these therapies for the particular case under consideration.

We have also attempted to project ourselves into the probable experiential world of both the therapist and the patient, in order to help the reader in formulating comparisons. The end result, hopefully, will be that the reader will be more familiar with and open to the theories presented. Further, we hope the reader will explore these concepts for future use and appropriately integrate them into his therapeutic work.

We purposely did not write a comparative chapter on the second set of authors—Salzman, Zinker, and Hollander—on the frigidity case. The purpose of these contributions was to provide the reader with some basis to compare and contrast therapists from the *same* schools. As an exercise we leave it to the reader to speculate on this intra-school comparison.

We found it most interesting and stimulating to see how different people from different therapies help the same individual. In writing the chapters, each of us tried to maintain a sense of objectivity and to avoid using language biased toward one approach. One obvious pitfall which we found difficult—but not impossible—to avoid was to view one theory from the standpoint of another theory. Each must be viewed in its own right. Each theory has its own conceptual framework, employs its own vocabulary to explain the personality and pathology of the patient, and uses its own tools. Comparing one theory in terms of another theory usually according to a preconceived bias precludes a full understanding of what is actually happening in therapy.

The comparative approach of this book will encourage firsthand observation and insight into the workings of these three therapies. It is also expected that this work will contribute to the attainment of optimal therapeutic outcome.

CONTENTS

vii

EDITORS AND CONTRIBUTORS

HENRY GRAYSON, Ph.D.
Co-Founder and Executive Director, National Institute for the Psychotherapies; Associate Professor, Brooklyn College of The City University of New York.

CLEMENS A. LOEW, Ph.D.
Co-Founder and Director of Clinical Services, National Institute for the Psychotherapies; Supervisor, Dept. of Psychology, Postgraduate Center for Mental Health; Private practice, individual and group psychotherapy.

GLORIA HEIMAN LOEW, Ph.D.
Private practice with children and adults, New York City and New Jersey.

YAEL DANIELI, Ph.D.
Full time faculty, Department of Psychology, Brooklyn College of The City University of New York.

RAINETTE EDEN FANTZ, Ph.D.
Co-Chairman of the Postgraduate Training Faculty, Gestalt Institute of Cleveland.

HERBERT FENSTERHEIM, Ph.D.
Clinical Associate Professor, Cornell University Medical College; Head, Behavior Therapy Treatment and Research, Payne Whitney Clinic and New York Hospital.

MELVYN HOLLANDER, Ph.D.
Coordinator, Graduate Behavior Modification Program, Queens College of The City University of New York; Director, Behavior Therapy Institute, White Plains, New York; Coordinator, Behavior Therapy Services, National Institute for the Psychotherapies.

ix

MICHAEL KRIEGSFELD, Ph.D.
Executive Director, Gestalt Psychotherapy Assoc., N.Y.

ARNOLD A. LAZARUS, Ph.D.
Professor and Director, Psy. D. Program in Clinical Psychology, Graduate School of Applied and Professional Psychology, Rutgers University.

MIRIAM POLSTER, Ph.D.
Co-Director, Gestalt Training Center, San Diego, Calif.

LEO J. REYNA, Ph.D.
Professor of Psychology, Boston, University; Associate Editor of the *Journal of Behavior Therapy and Experimental Psychiatry;* Co-Editor with Joseph Wolpe and Andrew Salter of *The Conditioning Therapies.*

LEON SALZMAN, M.D.
Deputy Director, Bronx Psychiatric Center; Clinical Professor of Psychiatry, Albert Einstein Medical College.

BENNETT SIMON, M.D.
Faculty, Boston Psychoanalytic Institute; Assistant Clinical Professor of Psychiatry, Harvard Medical School (at the Cambridge Hosp.) ; Consultant, Harvard U. Health Services; Private practice, Psychiatry and Psychoanalysis.

PAUL STARK, Ph.D.
Director of the Westchester Center for the Study of Psychoanalysis and Psychotherapy; Training Analyst and Supervisor, Postgraduate Center for Mental Health.

JOSEPH C. ZINKER, Ph.D.
Associate Professor of Psychology, Lake Erie College; Chairman, Postgraduate Prog., Gestalt Inst. of Cleveland.

Foreword

LEWIS R. WOLBERG, M.D.

A spinster in a depression consulted a fortune teller who spread Tarot cards in front of her and predicted good fortune and a happy marriage in the near future. The depression, which had paralyzed the woman for years, melted away to a point where assertively aggressive and ultimately fulfilling relations with people were resumed. The 22 cards comprising the "Greater Arcana," a relic of the 14th Century, manipulated by an uneducated "diviner," had achieved what a trained psychiatrist had failed to accomplish in months of treatment.

A man overcame without any formal psychotherapy a speech problem that had plagued him since childhood. The cure was due, he insisted, to out-of-the-body experiences during which his spiritual self floated away for daily rendezvous with the spiritual self of a psychoanalyst. His material body then benefited without the inconvenience of leaving his apartment or paying a fee.

A young female adult was initiated in rites of witchcraft and overcame a serious problem of frigidity after both psychoanalysis and behavior therapy had merely succeeded in increasing her handicap.

These cases, and many others who had benefited from a motley assortment of measures, ranging from astrology to black magic, from contact with poltergeists to adjustments by chiropractors, had come to my office for what they considered minor difficulties, such as the hypnotic control of smoking or overeating. I never doubted the sincerity of their convictions nor belittled the substantial benefits they derived from their unconventional therapeutic resources. The question that concerned me was whether the measures they extolled were valid phenomena or the manifestations of a perennial human gullibility.

Utilizing hypnosis, I have had more than my share of miracle cures, perhaps less spectacular than those of Lourdes or Oral Roberts, but surely as beneficial to the paralyzed and debilitated victims who had pinned their hopes on my suggestive talents. Faith has great curative powers and, irrespective of how unscientific or intrinsically worthless the treatment process may be, it can work wonders if it is accepted at face value by both therapist and patient.

But faith alone has serious limitations. For the great majority of persons, particularly those imbedded in a serious neurosis, faith must be backed up by something more substantial than hope. Testimonials from grateful patients are of little value in appraising the scientific merit of any therapeutic measure. What is essential is that we additionally attempt to validate our findings through careful observational scrutiny and experimental testing. This necessitates open-mindedness and sufficient flexibility to challenge the very assumptions on which we structure our therapeutic systems.

An eminent scientist once approached Albert Einstein and asked how he happened to discover the theory of relativity which revolutionized our conventional ideas of time and space. "The first thing I did," replied Einstein, "was to challenge an axiom." One should certainly expect from a scientist this kind of mobility. On July 18, 1876, Louis Pasteur, speaking before the French Academy of Medicine, uttered these memorable words: "Preconceived ideas are like searchlights which illumine the path of the experimenter and serve as a guide to interrogate nature. They become a danger only if he transforms them into fixed ideas; that is why I should like to see these profound words inscribed on the threshold of all the temples of science: 'The greatest derangement of the mind is to believe in something because one wishes it to be so.' "

A deep pessimism like a black cloud has enveloped the helping professions in the mental health field and has caused many professionals and the public to doubt the efficacy of psychotherapy. Perhaps this is what has caused the invasion of weird practices and quasi-scientific methods by undisciplined drum beaters, gurus and charlatans who hold out promises of undaunted success. How much of this plight is the result of our own impotence, the product of an inability to modify our theories and alter our methods in line with the realities of a changing world? Are we so burdened by our training concepts that we cannot break out of ossified ideologies that no longer apply to contemporary conditions?

This does not mean that we must abandon the lessons of our past experience. It may mean that for greatest effectiveness we may have to adapt our procedures to special situations in the culture. Because the nature of individual psychopathology relates itself to idiopathies in the sub-culture, modifications of technique have been introduced to deal more directly with the prevailing vicissitudes. Specifically, in our present-day acting-out subculture, where there are limited barriers to immediate impulse expression, to sexuality and aggression, to the postponement of gratifications in favor of future pleasures, patients will be more attuned to expressive, behaviorally oriented techniques than to verbal interviewing. Procedures that involve emotional flooding, psychodramatics, encounter, and conditioning maneuvers have been found to make more sense to such patients than classical tactics aimed at insight.

Actually, in the face of our current social problems and needs, we are witnessing a drift toward greater therapeutic flexibility. Symptomatic of this are the responses to a recent questionnaire sent out to members of the American Academy of Psychoanalysis, the majority of whom had been in practice for over 15 years. No less than three-quarters of the respondents saw their patients fewer than 3 times weeky (i.e., once or twice weekly). A sitting rather than couch position was employed most of the time. The majority prescribed drugs and saw other members of the patient's family when necessary. Some utilized group therapy and behavior therapy as part of their armamentarium (*The Academy*, Vol. 17, No. 1, Feb. 1973). Among non-analysts there are many who are incorporating dynamic concepts to give them a better understanding of what is happening in the therapeutic relationship. While we are still far from achieving a synthesis of contemporary views, definite changes in our designs of therapy are nevertheless taking place.

The past decade has witnessed a number of "innovations" in psychotherapy. These embrace bold, imaginative and challenging techniques that differ from traditional forms. No matter how frivolous some methods may seem, they certainly invite serious, albeit critical, review and testing to substantiate their validity. Most of the innovations are really based on old and discarded ideas, if not consisting of replications of the original premises. The practice of putting old wine in new bottles is, of course, not restricted to the psychotherapies. Copernicus, for example, in undermining the current idea of a geocentric universe, in what he considered his original discovery, fished out of oblivion the ancient heliocentric theory of the Pythagoreans. Darwin did not discover the theory of evolution, he merely revived an ancient theory by adding to it his discoveries on natural selection. There are many aspects of Einstein's theory of relativity that were speculated on with great lucidity by the early Greeks. And Freud's ideas about the unconscious were really not new. He packaged the speculations of philosophers and scientists before him in a delightfully literate way. Many of the so-called "new" approaches in Gestalt therapy, behavior therapy, rational therapy, Primal therapy, encounter therapy, etc. were essentially in use at the turn of the century. The fact that they have been revived need not detract from their usefulness under proper conditions. But one certainly should expect from practitioners of these methods a quality of modesty with which some members of the helping professions are, unfortunately, not too liberally endowed.

The past decade has also seen a deterioration of the prestigious place of psychoanalysis in American psychiatry. There are many reasons for this. The family quarrel that has been going on in the field of analysis has tended to discredit it in the eyes of both the profession and the public. Although Freud presented his ideas as tentative offerings, and even revised many of his theories extensively within his lifetime, some of his followers have resisted revisions in classical theory, some of which Freud himself later advanced. Such rigidity is obviously a disservice to Freud as a scientist who, in a brilliant exposition, belabored those who set psychoanalysis up as a panacea that laid claim to the performance of miracles. "The future," Freud wrote, "will probably attribute far greater importance to psychoanalysis as the science of the unconscious than as a therapeutic procedure."

Nonetheless, riding on the coattails of Freud's genius, a coterie of professionals, fluent in the catchwords of classical psychoanalysis and impregnating themselves with power, have punished as heresy what they considered to be egregious deviations into science. It is against this self-appointed nobility that much of the current resentment has been directed. This has resulted in a splintering of the psychoanalytic movement, with some of the splinter groups banding together in a rival organization which has been roundly attacked by the original group.

Nor have the classical psychoanalysts been the only offenders. Many of the revolutionaries, breaking away from what they consider to be a crippling orthodoxy, have violated their own eloquent consecration to science by presenting their "non-freudian" or "ego-analytic" or "neo-freudian" or "transactional" or "dynamic" formulations in an atmosphere of liturgical decorum that has become as rigid and unshakable as the orthodox credenda.

This practice of freighting themselves with wisdom is certainly not unique to the practitioners of psychoanalysis. We witness entrenched and intolerant attitudes among the authorities in many fields, even such basic ones as physics and chemistry, who, establishing themselves as the arbiters of truth, speak of their contributions in perpetual hyperbole. One is reminded of the phrase in Francis Bacon's *Of Followers and Friends*: "It is good discretion not to make too much of any man at the first, because one cannot hold out that proportion." Freud was no god, and his writings are not carved in stone. But it is a sad sight to witness his body incessantly being dug up and disemboweled amidst the joyous shouts of his dissenters.

While many of Freud's clinical observations are as true today as they were when he originally documented them, the theoretical cement that binds his ideas together has undergone considerable alteration. This is particularly true of the theory of instincts. It is difficult to account for the manifold physiological, intrapsychic, interpersonal and social transactions of the individual in classical terms of energy interchange. It appears more fitting at our present stage of knowledge to consider man as a complex of multiple systems whose behavior is so reticular than we can deal only with the interface properties of these systems, examining them within the framework of an ecological phenomenology.

Psychoanalysis, nevertheless, has had a profound and perhaps permanent influence on our concepts of human behavior and on our treatment approaches. The dynamic nature of repression and other psychological defenses, the importance of psychic determinism, the goal-directed nature of behavior, the relation of psychosocial development to personality evolution, the relationship between abnormal mental symptoms and normal mental processes, the role of anxiety in symptom formation, the nature of symbolism, the significance of dreams, and the phenomena of transference and resistance—these have proved themselves of revolutionary significance and have provided us with a means of investigating and dealing with intrapsychic and interpersonal activities.

But the lesson to be learned from old or newly introduced therapies is that no theory or treatment method is sacrosanct or applicable to all problems. There are multiple approaches to the woes of mankind, and these, if the therapist is flexible and skilled, must be adapted to the needs of the patient, not the patient to the method. The danger in any of the psycho therapies is that they are too eagerly over-exploited, and applied uncritically to the entire psychopathological spectrum. There is no special magic about psychoanalysis or Gestalt therapy or behavior therapy, nor do any of them occupy a preferred place in the vestibule of science. Each may serve a useful role in the armamentarium of the psychotherapist if it is utilized conservatively as one method in a world of methods that must of necessity, with continued observation and experiment, undergo change. The willingness of psychotherapists to subject their concepts and assumptions to the methods of science is more than a mark of courage. It is the sole means by which we can lift psychotherapy out of the morass of speculation to that of ordered structure. If psychotherapy is to develop beyond an art and to establish itself as a reliable research and therapeutic tool, it must expose itself to this discipline.

Psychotherapy, then, needs an arena for constructive empirical disputation. It would be a monotonous world indeed if we were in accord on all issues. Disagreement with, constructive criticism of, and challenges to established and new ideologies are the lifeblood of the scientific spirit. It is in this light that the present volume may serve a truly constructive purpose.

The host of available therapies poses many problems for patients and their therapists. What should determine the choice of method? Is it the type of symptom or syndrome from which the patient suffers? Is it the personality structure and characterologic peculiarities of the individual seeking treatment? Is it the conviction of the administrating professional that his special type of interventions cannot fail to bring help? Or are there other, more significant variables?

Many attempts have been made to answer these questions. Indeed the mental health field is inundated with books and articles applying themselves to this crucial issue in an abstract way. The present volume stands out in sharp contrast to most of this diffuse literature.

The authors have taken upon themselves the task of attempting to compare and contrast how therapists, skilled in the techniques of different schools, operate when presented with the same case material. Each is given a brief history of a patient, and invited to outline a treatment plan. In order to do so, a design must be formulated, predicated on the theoretical model of one's personal system. Manifestly, the actual treatment process, were the therapist confronted with the flesh and blood patient, would, more or less, be modified in accordance with the more exhaustive material provided by the interview situation. But in a way we are fortunate in not having too extensive data available since this allows the participants free range in speculations, fantasies and hypotheses. We are provided with a vivid panorama of what goes into theorizing and treatment planning. We are thus enabled to compare the inferences of therapists of the same school and also to contrast them with the expositions of those of different orientations.

The reader will obviously disagree with some (or many) of the ideas of the participants. Hopefully he will not discard them too readily, but will allow them to pose some challenge for him. Nothing is more deadly to empirical progress than adherence to a unique system that admits of no change. If one maintains an open mind despite the seeming naivete of some concepts, one may, perhaps surprisingly, discover that in practice they are not as artless as they seem. One may even discover that he has been enriched by approaches that deal with problems from another point of reference.

One would expect that men reared under the muse of science would blend trust in their beliefs with tolerance toward the credos of their fellow practitioners. Evidence that we are moving toward this goal comes from a variety of sources which indicate that therapists of different persuasions are more ready now than ever before to enter into a meaningful dialogue with each other. It is hoped that this book will contribute toward the goal of better understanding among therapists of diverse orientations, and illuminate a path to more efficient therapeutic interventions.

Guidelines for Contributors

Please describe how you would approach treating this person if he (she) came to you for help. We understand that this is a hypothetical case for you, and that there might be other information which you would normally seek to know if this were a real patient in your office. Nevertheless, please use the enclosed case material as a means of conceptualizing your understanding of this patient and your treatment procedure for this particular case. Feel free to wonder what relevant new material or information might emerge as a result of your intervention.

Below is a list of issues which should be included in the body of your text. These are not intended as limitations on your writing, but as guidelines with which the various approaches could be compared and integrated.

- What is your explanation and formulation of the development of this problem? Is this important for the treatment?

- Is it important for the patient to have this knowledge? How much and at what point in treatment?

- How long would you expect treatment to last?

- What would be the frequency of sessions?

1

- What themes or material do you expect to emerge in the course of treatment? How would you use it to help the patient?

- What aspects of the patient would you expect to focus on? In what order?

- Describe the nature of the relationship between you and the patient. How do you view your role as a therapist (e.g. teacher, model, neutral, etc.)?

- What importance do you assign to the therapist?

- What changes in the patient would you expect as a result of successful treatment?

- How is the decision for termination determined?

Part I

BACKGROUND AND ORIENTATION

YAEL DANIELI, Ph.D.,
CLEMENS A. LOEW, Ph.D.,
and HENRY GRAYSON, Ph.D.

For a fuller understanding of the different approaches used in helping the three cases presented here, we will first discuss the conceptual-theoretical frameworks within which the techniques were generated.

We have compared behavior, gestalt and psychoanalytic psychotherapy according to: a) their conception of what is wrong with the individual; b) what brought it about; c) what the goal of therapy should be; and d) how to go about achieving that goal. The reader should recognize that underlying each of the three schools, there is a distinct philosophical view of the nature of man that affects what the therapist *thinks* and *does*.

1

Behavior Therapy

*"One must learn by doing the thing."**

The school of behavior therapy conceptualizes psychopathological behaviors as learned, involuntarily acquired, undesirable habits of responding to environmental stimuli. Accordingly, the goals of behavior therapy are to rid the patient of these habits and/or replace them by more effective ones. Some behavior therapists assume, further, that when the person can behave more effectively, it may also be stated that he has achieved a positive change in personality, and that his feeling of mastery over his former problem will generalize to his life.

The therapeutic techniques proposed by this school are applications of conditioning methods. Whereas Wolpe's techniques are based mainly upon the classical conditioning paradigm, those developed by Skinner's followers are anchored upon the operant conditioning model (see below). What is common to all of these and unique to the behavioral therapies is that the therapeutic purpose is always specific and precise, while the method adapted to the particular problems of each patient is executed in a planful and controlled fashion.

---

* *"... for though you think you know you cannot know for certain until you try."* — Sophocles, *Trichanae.*

Because of the conviction of the behavior therapist that neurotic behavior is neither more nor less than learned behavior, the responsibility for the patient's recovery belongs to the therapist. Failure of a patient to recover, including his failure to cooperate by doing what he is asked, is seen as the therapist's fault—wrong analysis, incorrect technique, or, sometimes, the absence of any sufficient technique.

Accordingly, whatever the difficulty and whatever the technique used to overcome it, the behavior therapist does not moralize to his patient, but rather tries to teach him that his difficulties are the result of learned habits. The patient is introduced to behavior therapy by "short didactic speeches" or a series of discussions. For example, the role of neurotic fear (anxiety) may be explained to him. He may be reassured by being told that he is not mentally ill and will not go insane, that all of his reactions can be explained in terms of previous learning (Wolpe and Lazarus, 1966).*

We will turn now to a description of the major technique based upon the classical conditioning paradigm, namely Wolpe's *counter conditioning* technique.

Counter conditioning is based on the assumption that many persistent troubling thoughts or behaviors are anxiety-based, and that treatment of these problems should consist of treatment of anxiety. One frequently used treatment for anxiety is termed *reciprocal inhibition*. This technique is based on the notion that, if a response which inhibits anxiety can be made to occur in the presence of anxiety-evoking stimuli, it will weaken the connection between these stimuli and the anxiety.

At the beginning of therapy the therapist initially obtains accurate information concerning the difficulties of the patient, particularly attempting to identify what exactly brings about

---

* References to Part I appear on pages 34-36.

the condition of which the patient complains, what exactly seems to make the condition worse, what exactly seems to make it better. The therapist may want to ask what the family is like and how the family rewards and disciplines its members. He further inquires into the patient's educational, occupational, interpersonal and sexual history. If the patient is literate, he may answer a Life History Questionnaire. In addition, information from family members and associates may increase knowledge of the patient's life. Questionnaires such as "Willoughby's Neuroticism Schedule" and Wolpe and Lang's "Fear Survey Schedule" (Wolpe and Lazarus, 1966) may be used.

When the gathering of information has been completed, the therapist tells the patient what may be hoped for from the therapy. Advice or reassurance is immediately useful. Generally, priority is given to the problem that is of the greatest immediate concern to the patient. For example, the therapist first treats a school phobia so that a child can return to class before the more fundamental family relationships are explored. It is considered highly important to show empathy to the patient and to establish a relation of trust. If the patient first needs to confide in the therapist or to be enlightened or reassured by him, it is often preferred to delay specific measures of counter conditioning until these needs are satisfied.

If it is established during the initial phase of therapy that the patient's symptoms are related to his inability to assert his feelings in interpersonal situations, the effective counter conditioning technique may be *assertive training*. With this technique, the therapist explains to the patient that he should express his resentment, for instance, openly, and that this will inhibit anxiety; also that repeated expressions of resentment should lead to a cumulative conditioned inhibition of the anxious responses that have been causing him pain. He instructs the patient how to show his resentment in various situations.

Easy assignments might precede difficult ones, until the patient gains confidence that he can openly express anger. There is always the test question: would this expression of resentment seem appropriate to the circumstances as viewed by an objective observer? If so, then it is judged as self-assertion and not aggression.

The therapist who wants to teach self-assertion paints a word-picture of the inhibited person who evades life by enduring injustices and encouraging self-punishment. This word-picture usually arouses enough resentment in the patient to overcome his fear of self-expression. Moralistic patients may need logical argument to convince them to stand up for their rights. Furthermore, they are taught that by spontaneous and appropriate responses they can avoid their own over-reactions that generally follow prolonged bottling-up of resentment.

In the course of such directed self-assertion, the patient keeps careful notes of his encounters with other persons and discusses them with the therapist. The therapist, in turn, identifies the harmful inhibitions and stresses the assertive responses that might be helpful. *Behavior-rehearsal* may be undertaken. This is play-acting, in which patient and therapist re-enact scenes in order to teach the patient to respond more effectively. The therapist may also assume the role of the patient to demonstrate to him the desired behavior, in which case he will use *modeling* as a technique. (The latter was explicitly introduced as a technique by Bandura, 1965).

Most of the patients trained in self-assertion become increasingly aware of their self-restraint and the painful consequences. This awareness leads to tentative, often clumsy attempts at self-assertion. If these attempts are satisfactory, the likelihood that they will become habits increases.

When the patient's excessive anxiety and symptoms relate to physical situations and non-human objects rather than to interpersonal situations, i.e., when he has a phobia, then *systematic desensitization* is the treatment of choice.

Systematic desensitization is usually coupled with a physiological state incompatible with anxiety, namely that of relaxation. Therapy starts with the therapist teaching the patient how to relax. During the relaxation training, the patient is taught to become aware of the tensions in his major muscles; each group of muscles in the body is relaxed in systematic order, lesson by lesson, until the patient can quickly relax his entire body. Also included in this technique is the construction of an "anxiety hierarchy": a "graded list of stimuli incorporating different degrees of a defined feature that evokes anxiety." An example of this hierarchy can be given for the fear of heights. The patient might be afraid of elevators, mountains, steep stairs, and roof-tops. Usually the list is complex and not confined simply to fear of height. But if the fears are graded more or less uniformly from lesser to greater, they can be dealt with similarly, for they comprise a "subjective anxiety scale."

If the patient has learned to relax successfully, the procedure of desensitization then begins. Should the relaxation procedure prove insufficient to diminish anxiety, drugs may be used. Often desensitization takes place under hypnosis. In any case, the therapist tries to create as deep a state of relaxation as possible. When the patient is not anxious in the therapeutic setting, he is asked to imagine scenes that evoke anxiety, but of the low degree. As soon as he is able to relax while imagining such a scene, the therapist suggests additional scenes that evoke slightly more anxiety on the subjective scale of the patient. So the procedure continues, perhaps with relapses and perhaps with some overlearning, until anxiety is mastered as much as possible. Parameters such as the duration of the imagined scenes, the intervals between the scenes, and the total number of sessions must be considered. The spacing of the sessions, usually two or three a week, seems relatively unimportant.

Anxiety that causes a partial inhibition of sexual responses can be relieved by the appropriate use of sexual arousal, since this arousal counteracts anxiety. Thus far, the direct use of sexual responses to eliminate anxiety related to sex has been undertaken mainly with men. The therapist encourages the anxious man initially to lie near his partner, who has been informed of the course of the therapy. He must perform only those sexual behaviors which he can perform confidently even though they are accompanied by anxiety. Since he may do little more than caress his partner, sexual arousal becomes easier and this resultant pleasure inhibits anxiety. Gradually, he approaches coitus, but never undertakes more than he is sure he can do. He may be instructed in ways to give pleasure to his partner, and when he can center on giving pleasure, he is distracted from his own problem.

Whereas the counter conditioning techniques are based mainly upon the classical conditioning paradigm, the following methods are anchored upon the operant conditioning model. In changing behavior by operant conditioning, the methodological emphasis is upon the successive positive reinforcement ("rewarding") of small segments of response which approximate the behavior ultimately desired to be established or omitted. When the desired behavior is finally conditioned, its maintenance depends upon how often and how much it is reinforced. This is the method of *successive approximation,* or shaping. The method of *aversive training* assumes that a response will eventually be avoided if it is negatively reinforced. *Response chaining* is another technique whereby two or more discrete responses can be put into sequence with each other through the contingency of reinforcement (Ullman and Krasner, 1965). An additional technique is that of *"negative practice"* whereby the undesirable response is deliberately encouraged without reinforcement and repeated to the extent that it recurs spontaneously less and less often until it subsides.

In order for most of these techniques to control behavior, under the basic principles of operant conditioning, it is necessary to control and manipulate effectively the environment of the subject. Consequently, these techniques have in the main been applied to patients where the environment can be controlled as completely as possible. In fact, even in regard to traditional therapies, Skinner maintains that, "In practice all these ways of changing a man's mind reduce to manipulating his environment, verbal or otherwise." (Skinner, 1964).

Applications of the principles derived from Skinner's work are numerous (Ullman and Krasner, 1965; Franks, 1969). These experiments have proved to be most fruitful in institutional settings with persons who have been unresponsive to the evocative therapies. These applications involve specific work with alcoholics, stutterers, bed-wetters, phobic patients, children who cannot control their behavior in school settings or who have trouble with toilet training; the most significant contributions are with people who suffer from anorexia nervosa and brain damage, with hyperactive and autistic children, and with chronic institutionalized patients. Operant techniques have successfully aided some autistic children to: 1) eliminate atavistic behavior which blocks normal responsiveness; 2) reinstate behavior presumably extinguished in their early life; 3) introduce cooperative behavior that leads to rewarding consequences; and 4) build up a more complex behavioral repertoire based on their initial response level (Azrin, 1956; Ferster, 1961; Mednick, 1958; Mowrer, 1952; Rimland, 1964; Shelton, 1961).

A dramatic example of the application of these techniques, on a large scale, is Ayllon and Azrin's program of instituting a "token economy" in a ward for women patients at Anna

Illinois State Hospital (1969). Administrators of other wards were asked to select patients who had been uncooperative and unresponsive to treatment. The age of the patients exceeded 50 years and the variety of diagnoses included schizophrenic classifications of various types, depression, and physiological disorders.

The experimenters assumed that a typical hospital ward reinforced passivity and that withdrawn behavior resulted from this situation. They searched for reinforcers which might be used to establish more desirable and functional behaviors of the patients by determining what they desired. Not all patients were responsive to the same reinforcers; however, they discovered that privacy, ground passes, movies, TV, attendance at religious services, psychotherapy, cigarettes, canteen purchases, trips to town, and purchases from a mail order catalog were reinforcing in various combinations to all of the patients. Under the principles of Skinner's techniques, it is stated that a reinforcer must be immediately contingent upon the performance of a desired behavior in order to establish that behavior. Since these reinforcers could not always be delivered immediately, tokens which had a fixed exchange value were used as conditioned reinforcers to bridge this gap in time. Tokens also provided automation of many reinforcers, e.g. token-operated TV and cigarette machine.

The patients earned the tokens in two ways: all patients were given a small number of tokens for self-care, which were barely enough for minimal purchases. All patients were encouraged to accept various jobs by which they might earn a larger supply of tokens. The jobs involved both on and off ward duties and required periods of time which ranged from a few minutes to as much as six hours per day for their performance. Patients were initially offered their jobs verbally. If they accepted the offer, they began at once and were paid daily at the task. If they declined the verbal offer, techniques were developed, based on the principles of shaping and chaining, to induce the patient to try new behaviors. For some patients, these techniques were necessary in order to induce them to try the reinforcers (reinforcer exposure and reinforcer sampling), as well as to induce them to initiate self-care or try a new job (response exposure and response sampling).

The experimenters took precautions to prevent the manipulation and exploitation of these patients. Only patients conducted tours of the ward and explained the procedures to visitors. Patients were not allowed to learn or perform jobs essential to the hospital operation unless they were already skilled at such jobs, thus preventing the postponement of discharge in the name of institutional efficiency.

The results of the experiment were astounding. No patient was completely unresponsive, although some never progressed beyond the minimal stage of earning tokens through self-care. The atmosphere of the ward became more pleasant and the level of self-initiating activity was increased. Three patients from this group, all of whom were assumed to be permanently hospitalized, were discharged during the two-year experiment. During this experiment, when the patients were given a week-long "paid vacation," receiving their tokens without any work, it was necessary to double the number of attendants in order to maintain the basic operations on the ward.

Behavioral therapies (especially in their *theoretical* principles) are basically deterministic and mechanistic in their philosophy of man. In their conservative positions, cognitive processes such as insight are not directly dealt with and, if recognized as therapeutic variables, are seen as the result, not the cause, of behavioral change. They attempt to treat *symptoms* or modify *behaviors*, taking full responsibility for the outcome. Accordingly, they view the *therapist* as the active agent who either directly promotes change in the patient or educates the patient in methods of self-control. The proponents of this school consider it the only scientific psychotherapy, since it rests upon principles of learning established in the experimental laboratory and relies heavily on precise measurement. According to them, the strengths of their approach may be found in its common sense interpretation of psychopathology, its provision for accurate measures of progress, and its ability to be translated and taught to non-professionals.

2

Gestalt Therapy

"Lose your mind and come to your senses."

FRITZ PERLS

Being an essential mainstream within the Human Potential Movement, the "third force" in psychology, Gestalt therapy sees itself as drawing from three main roots: (1) Existential-Phenomenological-Zen philosophical views; (2) Gestalt psychology principles in perception generalized to motivation and action and translated to describe man in relation to and with himself, others and his environment; and (3) some psychoanalytic observations, especially W. Reich's concept of character armor and formulation of repression as essentially a somatization phenomenon. Naranjo (1971) comments:

> The uniqueness of Gestalt therapy does not lie in a theory of personality or of the neurosis; nor, for that matter does it lie in theory at all. It is essentially a nonverbal creation, an approach to people in the therapeutic situation which has developed out of understanding, experience, and intuition, and continues to be transmitted nonverbally."

In the same vein, Fagan and Shepherd (1971) write:

> Also, Gestalt therapy, with its emphasis on the here and now, the immediacy of experience, and nonverbal expres-

15

siveness, and its avoidance of "aboutism" or overuse of the mental "computer," tends to correct our tendencies toward wordiness and abstractions rather than to encourage the manipulation of words necessary for the writing of books. Thus most Gestalt therapists tend to be doers rather than sayers."

Indeed, the fragmentary nature of this school's theoretical formulations makes it difficult to derive clarity from them. Thus, our discussion demands readjustment in its presentation of Gestalt therapy. Rather than get involved in theoretical abstractions, we will attempt to follow what we perceive to be the spirit of Gestalt therapy as a direct attempt to implement values and ideals of living.

Naranjo (1971) cites the "moral injunctions of Gestalt therapy" as follows:

1. Live now. Be concerned with the present rather than with past or future.

2. Live here. Deal with what is present rather than with what is absent.

3. Stop imagining. Experience the real.

4. Stop unnecessary thinking. Rather, taste and see.

5. Express rather than manipulate, explain, justify, or judge.

6. Give in to unpleasantness and pain just as to pleasure. Do not restrict your awareness.

7. Accept no *should* or *ought* other than your own. Adore no graven image.

8. Take full responsibility for your actions, feelings, and thoughts.

9. Surrender to being as you are.

Subsumed under more general principles, these are:

1. Valuation of actuality: temporal (present versus past or future), spatial (present versus absent), and substantial (act versus symbol).

3. Valuation of awareness and the acceptance of experience.

3. Valuation of wholeness, or responsibility.

The Gestalt therapists do not see these statements as decrees of duty but as statements of truth, as unavoidable facts. Thus, they view the mentally healthy person as

one in whom awareness can develop without blocking, whenever his organismic attention is drawn. Such a person can experience his own needs and the environmental possibilities fully and clearly from moment to moment, accepting both as given and working toward creative compromises. He still has his full share of inner conflicts of needs and environmental frustrations, but, being in close touch with these developing needs and the environment, he is capable of achieving reasonably adequate solutions quickly and does not magnify his real problems with fantasy elaborations.

Since he is carrying around much less of a filtering cloud of thought-fantasies to obscure the world, his sensual world is vivid and colorful, and his interpersonal world relatively uncontaminated with projections and unreal expectations. He can perceive and respond to others much more as they are and become from moment to moment, rather than as fixed stereotypes. He has a clear sense of the relative importance of things and can do what has to be done to finish situations. Since unfinished business does not pile up, he is free to do and be quite fully and intensely whatever he is doing or being, and people around him often report a sense of his being much more *with* them when he is with them. Seeing people reasonably clearly and without excessive fantasy, it is easy for him to be quite direct with others and appreciate them for what they are. Again, he has his share of conflicts with others, but he can resolve those conflicts that are resolvable, and let go of those that are not. (And he can usually tell the difference!) He is self-respecting in every sense, including an appreciation and enjoyment of his body with consequent physical grace." (Enright, 1970)

The neurotic, in contrast, has the inner as well as outer awareness blocked, rendering him unable to remain effectively in contact with his organismic needs and the relevant environmental possibilities of satisfying them. His continuous experience is clogged by unfinished businesses locked in the past and clouded by fantasies of the future. In his self-regulation, certain forces are impeded from exerting their full effect on organismic contact with the environment in that (a) his perceptual contact with large parts of his environment and of his body is either poor or blocked completely, which results in an inability to see the obvious; (b) open expression of needs is blocked, the end result being that the need continues to interfere with other needs that might organize the field in a clear-cut and coherent way; (c) repression, in which impulse unawareness is maintained by chronic muscular contractions, becomes habitual and prevents resolving conflicts and the formation of good gestalten. Thus, in the neurotic, parts of his personality and his potentials are disowned and unavailable to him, creating voids and holes in his existence. A sense of self-alienation and powerlessness is the result.

Perls (1970) sees the neurotic's tendency to avoid the "awareness continuum" as aiming at maintaining the status quo of holding onto the concept of self as a child, thereby reflective of fear or unwillingness to take one's responsibility for one's life in the here and now. He holds that in the neurotic the process of maturation, i.e., of the development from environmental support to self-support, did not adequately take place. Therefore, he will use his potentials not for self-support but to act out phony roles in order to manipulate and mobilize the environment for support instead of mobilizing his own potentials. (These manipulations can take the forms of acting/feeling helpless, playing stupid, asking questions, wheedling, flattering).

Structurally, Perls (1970) conceives of these roles as the external layer in neurosis, the first out of five layers that usually unfold in the process of successful Gestalt therapy (becoming authentic). He names these layers respectively: the phony layer, the phobic one, the impasse, the implosive layer and the explosive layer.

According to Perls' description, the *phony layer* is the one where we play games and roles, where we act as if we were actualizing concepts and ideals instead of who and what we are—"like an elephant who had rather to be a rose bush, and a rose bush that tries to be a kangaroo" (p. 20). An example typical of the games played at this layer is the "top-dog/under-dog" game that can take place internally or (projected) interpersonally. This is a mutually frustrating struggle to control between a bullying, moralizing, authoritarian role of the "top-dog" whose typical statements are: "I (You) should," 'I (You) ought to," "Why don't you (I)?", "Come on now, live up to that ideal," and a passively controlling "under-dog" that gives nominal acquiescence and excuses such as "tomorrow," "I promise," "Yes, but . . . ," "I'll try . . ." and goes on preventing the top-dog from being successful. Upon awareness of the phoniness of game playing comes the resistance to discovering who we really are. This is the *phobic layer*, where one is faced with catastrophic fantasies and fears of taking the risk of being oneself. Here a typical statement is, "If I am as I am, what will happen to me? Society will ostracize me. . . ."

Getting behind the phobic layer leads to the *impasse point*. This is what the Russian literature calls the "sick point." The impasse is a situation in which one experiences loss of environmental support, and the patient is, or believes himself to be, lacking the support of his own resources; therefore he feels incapable of coping with life on his own. The characteristic feeling within the impasse is that of being stuck, of deadness and nothingness. Awareness of the impasse leads to the next—*implosive layer*, which Perls also characterized as a catatonic state. Here one is faced with the fear of being dead, where one's energy is invested in keeping tense, rigid and frozen. It is only when the implosive state gets dissolved that one will get to the *explosive layer*, when the pent-up compressed energies will be freed and expressed. The four types of explosions that typically occur are: explosion into joy, into grief, into orgasm, and into anger. The expression and reassimilation of those energies awaken the individual to reorganize himself to feel more real, to function better and to enjoy life more, from the perspective of his inner world or stage that now replaces the former dominance of the external world or stage. Indeed, already in 1948 Perls formulated "The ultimate goal of the treatment" as: "We have to achieve that amount of integration which facilitates its own development." (p. 12)

Consonant with the school's goals of therapy and living, the "rules" adhered to by Gestalt therapists are based on the principles of direct communication that is present-centered and focuses on the awareness continuum between active and responsible participants. Thus, communication is always directed at a specific person (the "I-Thou" dimension), and "gossiping" is not allowed. Questions, especially when they disguise statements or demands for support from another person, are translated into statements starting with the word "I"; the promotion of "now" awareness is encouraged by focusing on present tense communications. Questions are related to "how" and "what" right now, rather than "why" and "then," and to verbal as much as nonverbal communications. Heavy emphasis is also put upon semantic clarifications (for instance, changing "it" language to "I" language, as in "My hand is trembling"—"I am trembling").

Most of the Gestalt work is done in groups rather than individually. The therapist is not bound by the "games" experiments common in the school's tradition. In fact, he is encouraged to be spontaneous and creative with his parents.

The following account of experimental games relies heavily on Levitsky and Perls (1970, pp. 145-149) and on Yontef (1971, pp. 26-29).

1. *Games of Dialogue.* When a split within a person is observed, the therapist suggests that the patient experiment by taking each part of the conflict in turn and having a dialogue. This can be done with any split, e.g., aggressive versus passive, masculine versus feminine, topdog versus under-dog, or with another person who is significant and absent, in which case the patient addresses the person as if he were there, imagines the response, replies to the response, etc.

2. *Making the Rounds.* During individual work in the group, a theme or a feeling involving others in the group may arise. The patient will then be encouraged to express it to each member in the group.

3. *Unfinished Business.* Whenever unresolved and incompletely expressed feelings are identified, the patient is asked to complete them. This applies to past experiences that are re-enacted in the present, as well as to feelings toward members of the group.

4. *The "I take responsibility" Game.* This game involves asking the patient to add after each statement, ". . . and I take responsibility for it." Since Gestalt therapy considers every behavior (including perceiving, feel-

ing, thinking) an act that can be frequently disowned by the patient, this exercise aims at his recognition of it.

5. *"I have a secret."* In this game the group members are asked to think of a personal secret. They are instructed *not* to share the secret itself, but to imagine (project) how they feel others would react to it.

6. *Playing the Projection.* When the patient imagines another person has a certain feeling or trait, he is asked to see whether it is a projection by experimenting with experiencing himself with that feeling or trait, or by playing the role of that person.

7. *The Game of Reversals.* When the therapist thinks the patient's behavior may be a reversal of a latent impulse, he may ask the patient to play the role opposite to that which he has been playing.

8. *The Rhythm of Contact and Withdrawal.* Here the natural inclination toward withdrawal from contact, which the patient will experience from time to time, is not dealt with as a resistance to be overcome but as a rhythmic response to be respected. The patient is asked to be aware of when and how he withdraws and when he stays in contact.

9. *"Rehearsal."* According to Perls, a great deal of our thinking consists of internal rehearsal and preparation for playing our accustomed social roles. The experience of stage fright simply represents our fear that we will not conduct our roles well. The group therefore plays the game of sharing rehearsals with each other.

10. *The Exaggeration Game.* This game applies to body language as well as to verbal communications, when the patient seems to be unaware of the meaning of the impact of a gesture or a statement. He is then asked to repeat and exaggerate or amplify it.

11. *The "May I feed you a sentence" Game.* When the therapist infers an unstated or unclear message, he may

phrase it into a sentence and ask the patient to say the sentence aloud, repeat it, in short to "try it on for size."

12. *"Of course" and "It is obvious that" Game.* These phrases are used for patients who fail to use and trust their senses.

13. *"Can you stay with this feeling?"*

Perls considers *dreams* as an existential message that is telling what a person's life is and how to come to one's senses —to awaken and take one's place in life. Since each part of the dream is regarded as a projection, each fragment of the dream—person, prop or mood—is considered an alienated part of the individual. In therapy the patient acts out the dream. He takes each part—and an encounter ensues between the divided parts of the self. Such an encounter frequently leads to integration.

Although Gestalt therapists are active and directive, the attitude they hold toward the patient is one of respect and appreciation for his self-reliance and responsibility. They may be open with the patient in sharing feelings and values. This is in keeping with the notion of the therapist as a model for living the "moral injunctions" and actualizing them in his own experience.

3

Psychoanalysis

"He who cannot remember history is compelled to repeat it."

GEORGE SANTAYANA

Classical psychoanalysis conceptualizes psychological difficulties as maladaptive and unsuccessful resolutions of "instinctual) conflicts of childhood, which were rooted in real or fantasied involvements with the significant people in the child's environment. These conflicts were too painful, unacceptable and anxiety-provoking for the child's ego to handle effectively at the time. Thus, he felt no choice but to defend himself against them: namely, by pushing them from awareness, or repressing them.

Repressing conflictual wishes, fantasies and memories, however, does not "get rid of them." The unconscious elements and processes stay alive, and press for expression and gratification. Although out of awareness, they are both active and dynamic, exerting a directive influence on the person's behavior (verbal and non-verbal), feelings, perceptions, and ways of dealing with people and situations. Much of the unconsciously determined behavior and experience is involuntary, compelled, repetitive, and rigid. In other words, it is not under the person's ego's adequate and realistic control, and he cannot comprehend its meaning. Since the uncon-

24

scious parts of the person (both the repressed components and the defenses employed against them) are sealed off from his conscious reality, they cannot be modified by the feedback of reality (Klein, 1967). These parts do not mature alongside the rest of the personality, but remain infantile. Despite the person's conscious "freedom" from the repressed infantile conflictual parts of his personality, he is actually tyrannized by them in a situation of pseudosecurity.

Psychoanalytic theory views psychopathology from six perspectives, the first five of which are unique to psychoanalysis: (1) Psychosexual *genetic* fixation; (2) The continuous *dynamic* struggle between the instinctual impulses which propel the organism toward gratification in favor of survival, security and self-esteem; (3) The resulting *topographic* restriction of consciousness (due to pushing the conflictual material out of awareness) ; (4) *Economically,* the person's ego is depleted of the energies consumed by both the unconscious struggle and the efforts at maintaining the defenses against his unacceptable instinctual impulses; (5) In terms of the *structural* viewpoint of psychoanalytic theory, the ego is thereby unable to master adequately the demands of the id and the superego, as well as those of reality; thereby his active (6) *adaptation* to reality is impaired.

The goals of psychoanalysis are to undo the repressions and to "make the unconscious conscious," thereby freeing the patient from its tyranny. Through helping the patient unlock the unconscious meanings of his repetitive, self-defeating, and self-deceptive behaviors and symptoms, and helping him to gain insight into their infantile origins, the previously fixated portions of his psyche will then become free to participate in the full development of the personalty. "Thus," Freud wrote, "psychoanalytic treatment acts as a second education of the adult, as a corrective to his education as a child" (1926, p. 268). From the economic point of view, Freud wrote: "We seek to enrich him from his own internal sources, by putting at the disposal of his ego those energies which, owing to repression, are inaccessibly confined in his unconscious, as well as those which his ego is obliged to squander in the fruitless task of maintaining these repressions" (1927, p. 256). This redistribution will bring about an enrichment of energies now available to the ego for more active and effective living. Through the insight gained into the dynamics and meanings of the patient's neurotic resolutions, he will attain the *freedom* to choose and decide upon resolutions other than the neurotic ones. As an adult who knows and understands himself, he can make decisions which satisfy his needs in reality. He can enjoy mature love relationships, and be constructive and productive at work.

The resulting structural changes in personality, which extend the power, mastery and sovereignty of the ego over both the more liberated and mature id and the more tolerant and reasonable superego, are intended to be permanent. Also, the ego can now readily handle the external world in a more secure, autonomous, flexible and multifaceted manner.

Thus, psychoanalytic treatment aims at profound recovery and welcomes most those patients "who ask (the analyst) to give them complete health, insofar as that is attainable . . ." (Freud, 1913, p. 131).

We will turn now to a description of the method (s) devised by psychoanalysis to attempt to reach its goals and to explicate the rationale for the different aspects of its treatment process.

Psychoanalysis usually requires a much longer time than other modes of treatment (an average of three to five years) and intensive contact with the analyst (two to five sessions per week), with a resulting deep, long-term commitment as well as a high financial investment.

The extensive number of visits, the physical conditions of

the orthodox psychoanalytic situation (Stone, 1961), and the psychoanalytic "rules" are intended to facilitate the goal of uncovering the patient's unconscious. In this situation the patient reclines on a couch in the customarily dimly-lit office, while the analyst sits behind the patient, out of his sight. The supine posture of the patient encourages relaxation. Combined with the seeming inactivity of the analyst, this facilitates a condition whereby fantasies and memories from early and infantile experiences are activated and made accessible to consciousness. The situation is relatively devoid of external stimuli and structures, and very conducive for the critical experience of regression.

At the beginning of the therapeutic contact or "contract" (Menninger, 1958), after the patient's presentation of his difficulties and history, the analyst tells the patient to follow *"the fundamental rule of psychoanalytic technique,"* that of *free association.* To quote one of Freud's versions of it (1913, p. 135):

> One more thing before you start. What you tell me must differ in one respect from an ordinary conversation. Ordinarily you rightly try to keep a connecting thread running through your remarks and you exclude any intrusive ideas that may occur to you and any side-issues, so as not to wander too far from the point. But in this case you must proceed differently. You will notice that as you relate things various thoughts will occur to you which you would like to put aside on the ground of certain criticisms and objections. You will be tempted to say to yourself that this or that is irrelevant here, or is quite unimportant, or nonsensical, so that there is no need to say it. You must never give in to these criticisms, but must say it in spite of them—indeed, you must say it precisely *because* you feel an aversion to doing so. Later on you will find out and learn to understand the reason for this injunction, which is really the only one you have to follow . . . say whatever goes through your

mind. Act as though, for instance, you were a traveller sitting next to the window of a railway carriage and describing to someone inside the carriage the changing views which you see outside. Finally, never forget that you have promised to be absolutely honest, and never leave anything out because, for some reason or other, it is unpleasant to tell it.

The rule of free association, which in essence asks the patient to renounce consciously as much as he can of his conscious censorship of his thoughts and feelings, provides a mode of access to the unconscious. It is based on the hypothesis that the repressed and its derivatives constantly seek discharge. When one surrenders his usual controls against the intrusion of such material, it will become observable to both analyst and patient. "Obeying" the rule also depends upon the extent to which the patient has established rapport and trust with his analyst, referred to by Zetzel (1956) as the "therapeutic alliance."

Despite the patient's conscious motivation for change, stemming as it does from his suffering and from his conscious alliance with the analyst, the same unconscious forces in him that formerly participated in defending against the conflictual material operate in opposition to positive change in treatment. These forces, named *resistance,* obstruct free association. In treatment they appear in diverse ways: silences, blockings, embarrassments, indirect and roundabout ways of expressing feelings, or "empty talk." Resistance can take the form of not showing up for a session, coming late, or not paying. In short, during the course of treatment the patient will repeat all of the different forms of defensive maneuvers he has used throughout his life to protect himself from conflict-laden material. And it is one of the critical psychoanalytic tasks to uncover and overcome these resistances (Freud, 1910a, 1910b).

The unconscious elements (both the repressed and the defences) do not manifest themselves solely in the form of the patient's verbalizations of his fantasies, memories and experiences. A major part of a person's conflict is expressed in his behavior and feelings to his analyst. *Transference* refers to the spectrum of feelings, attitudes, and expectations which the patient experiences toward the analyst, derived from his childhood relationships with significant figures. The infantile "then and there" feelings and expectations are projected and superimposed onto the person of the analyst *as if* they belonged in the "here and now." In the transference the patient reanimates old experiences in his therapeutic relationship. Transference feelings and reactions are typically automatic, uncomfortable, and ambivalent.

The analytic situation encourages transference and facilitates regression not only in mode of thinking (i.e., from secondary to primary process), but also in modes of behavior and feelings (Greenacre, 1954). The analyst's purposive frustrating inactivity in not responding to the patient's habitual modes of social behavior provokes reactions that served the patient earlier in his life (Menninger, 1958). The analyst's message is: "Know thyself, not me."

Through the course of psychoanalytic treatment, the patient, in a progressively regressive direction, exposes an elaborate system of interrelated transference reactions to the analyst that mirror his childhood relationships to critical figures in his life and the feelings and fantasies about them that ultimately gave rise to the neurotic condition (Glover, 1955). This system of transferences, which represent the central repressed interpersonal contexts that caused the neurotic conflict and its modes of resolution, is termed the *transference neurosis*. Another way of stating the function and goal of psychoanalytic treatment is that the awareness of this series of unconsciously determined reactions and comprehension of their dynamic meanings as models of relationships enable the patient to control them and choose alternative ones.

Some transference feelings ally themselves with the analyst toward the treatment goal, some with the resistance. When the transference is *positive*, i.e., when the patient feels affection and admiration for the analyst, they serve as a moving force for change and as an incentive to the analytical work. When transference is *negative*—when feelings of hostility, hatred, contempt and disgust arise—they impel the patient to thwart the analyst's work; the patient will try to defeat any therapeutic progress and at times may even leave treatment. Strong, excessive negative as well as positive feelings (especially when erotic in nature) are viewed as resistance. This is because the patient is not interested in his illness or in gaining insight, but only in the analysis (Freud, 1915).

Countertransference occurs when the analyst's responses in the treatment situation are determined by his own unconscious needs and historical interpersonal contexts. As in the case of the patient's transferential behavior, the analyst's is also inappropriate. Furthermore, it is anti-therapeutic and limiting unless the analyst becomes aware of the nature of his own distortions. It is partly because of the human possibility of the involuntary and blind reactions of countertransference that the analyst, as part of his training, must undergo his own psychoanalysis. Moreover, Freud recommended that "Every analyst should periodically—at intervals of five years or so—submit himself to analysis once more, without feeling ashamed of taking this step" (Freud, 1937).

The analyst observes the patient's verbal and nonverbal behavior. He listens to the patient, but does so in a particular way, with an "evenly hovering attention." From this vantage point, he is most open to all the nuances of the patient's verbalizations and to the emerging representations of unconscious derivatives through the patient's free associations, dreams, symptoms, slips of the tongue, and acting out.

It is not until the therapeutic alliance has been established, however, that the therapist will "analyze" the patient's material. The term *"analyzing"* is a shorthand expression which refers to insight-furthering techniques. It usually includes four distinct procedures: confrontation, clarification, interpretation, and working through (Greenson, 1967, p. 37).

Although *interpretation* is not the sole activity of the analyst (Hammer, 1968), it is the most important of the psychoanalytic procedures; all others are subsidiary, both theoretically and practically, serving as steps that lead either to an interpretation or to making it effective (Gill, 1954; Menninger, 1958). Fenichel (1945) defines interpretation as the "procedure of deducing what the patient actually means and telling it to him." He writes further: "Since interpretation means *helping something unconscious to become conscious* by naming it at the moment it is striving to break through, effective interpretation can be given only at one specific point, namely, where the patient's immediate interest is momentarily centered" (p. 25). Freud summarized "the rule" of timing (and depth) of interpretation as "we put off telling him of a construction or explanation till he himself has so nearly arrived at it that only a single step remains to be taken, though that step is in fact the decisive synthesis" (1940, p. 178). The direction of analyzing, then, is from surface to depth. Thus, defenses will be related to before what is defended against; a repeated pattern will be pointed out before it can be "re-located" in and causally connected with the past setup of relationships.

The insight sought for is emotional as well as intellectual. Moreover, even when fully experienced it does not lead to immediate change. The analytic work which facilitates the insight to lead to psychological and/or behavioral change is called "working through." Frieda Fromm-Reichmann comments:

> The process of "working through" is aimed, then, at changing awareness and rational understanding of the unknown motivations and implications of any singled-out experience into creative, that is, therapeutically effective insight. . . . Gaining this type of insight should be accompanied by understanding inhibition in the development of a patient's inherent capacities and potentialities. (1950, p. 142)

It should be noted that some of the work of working through is done by the patient outside of the analytic hour, as, for instance, in testing out new behaviors and their realistic interpersonal impact. Working through is the most time-consuming element in psychoanalytic therapy, requiring repeated interpretations to overcome the powerful forces which resist change and to establish lasting structural changes.

In the termination phase of treatment, which may take a few months, unresolved anxiety and residual unconscious conflicts are dealt with. It is most important during this phase to analyze the patient's separation anxiety or depression about terminating. Also of crucial importance is the resolution of residual negative transference as well as of the positive one. When are the goals of psychoanalysis reached? Freud wrote:

> Our aim will not be to rub off every peculiarity of human character for the sake of a schematic "normality," nor yet to demand that the person who has been "thoroughly analyzed" shall feel no passions and develop no internal conflicts. The business of the analysis is to secure the best possible psychological conditions for the functions of the ego; with that it has discharged its task (1937, p. 250).

In 1923 he also commented,

> After all, analysis does not set out to make pathological reactions impossible, but to give the patient's ego *freedom* to decide one way or the other" (p. 50, italics by Freud).

The reader may have noticed that the mere removal of symptoms without the corresponding insight into their meanings and origins was not mentioned as a goal of psychoanalysis. Freud likened the former to cosmetics, to a removal of surface manifestation, while referring to psychoanalytic treatment as surgery that addresses itself to undoing the cause of neurotic symptomatology, thereby securing its non-recurrence. Theodore Reik (1948) stated it in picturesque fashion:

> . . . the analyst is faced with the question, "Who are you?" rather than with the problem of what is the special meaning of a symptom. He will try to find the depths of personality, which are as hidden as the roots of a tree. The nature and the extent of these roots will determine the growth of the tree and what its trunk, its branches, and its flowers will be like. The roots cover more space than the branches and spread themselves wider than the crown. When we have recognized what these roots are, we shall not have many difficulties in following the growth of the tree. When analysis has penetrated deep enough, many problems that present themselves later on will be solved more easily by the knowledge now obtained. The analytic understanding of many symptoms and behavior patterns of the patient has resulted in a sufficiently clear picture of his personality, and this picture now unconsciously before my mind will help me later on to understand new symptoms and expressions true to his character. (p. 179)

At the end of psychoanalytic treatment, the patient has, hopefully, gained the same ability in relation to himself.

BIBLIOGRAPHY

AYLLON, T., and AZRIN, N. H. 1965. The measurement and reinforcement of behavior of psychotics. *Journal of the Experimental Analysis of Behavior*, 8:537-383.

AZRIN, NATHAN H. 1956. The reinforcement of cooperation between children. *Journal of Abnormal and Social Psychology*, 52:100-102.

BANDURA, A. 1965. Behavioral modification through modeling procedures. In L. Krasner & L. P. Ullman (Eds.), *Research in Behavior Modification*, pp. 310-340. New York: Holt, Rinehart and Winston.

ENRIGHT, J. B. 1970. An introduction to Gestalt techniques. In J. Fagan & I. L. Shepherd (Eds.), *Gestalt Therapy Now*, pp. 119-120. Palo Alto: Science and Behavior Books, Inc.

FAGAN, J., and SHEPHERD, I. L. 1970. *Gestalt Therapy Now*, p. vii. Palo Alto: Science and Behavior Books, Inc.

FENICHEL, OTTO. 1945. *The Psychoanalytic Theory of Neurosis.* New York: W. W. Norton & Company, Inc.

FERSTER, C. B. 1961. Positive reinforcement and behavioral deficits of autistic children. *Child Development*, 32:437-456.

FRANKS, CYRIL M. 1969. *Behavior Therapy: Appraisal and Status.* New York: McGraw-Hill Book Company.

FREUD, SIGMUND. 1910a. The future prospects of psychoanalytic therapy. In *The Standard Edition of the Complete Psychological Works of Sigmund Freud*, translated and edited by James Strachey, Vol. 11, pp. 139-152. London: The Hogarth Press Limited.

FREUD, SIGMUND. 1910b. "Wild" Psychoanalysis. In *The Standard Edition of the Complete Psychological Works of Sigmund Freud*, translated by James Strachey, Vol. 11, pp. 219-230. London: The Hogarth Press Limited.

FREUD, SIGMUND. 1913. On beginning the treatment (further recommendations on the technique of psycho-analysis, I). In *The Standard Edition of the Complete Psychological Works of Sigmund Freud*, translated by James Strachey, Vol. 12, pp. 121-144. London: The Hogarth Press Limited.

FREUD, SIGMUND. 1915. Observations on transference-love, (further recommendations on the technique of psycho-analysis, III). In *The Standard Edition of the Complete Psychological Works of Sigmund Freud*, translated by James Strachey, Vol. 12, pp. 157-171. London: The Hogarth Press Limited.

FREUD, SIGMUND. 1917. A difficulty in the path of psycho-analysis. In *The Standard Edition of the Complete Psychological Works of Sigmund Freud*, translated by James Strachey, Vol. 17, pp. 135-144. London: The Hogarth Press Limited.

FREUD, SIGMUND. 1923. The ego and the id. In *The Standard Edition of the Complete Psychological Works of Sigmund Freud*, translated by James Strachey, Vol. 19, pp. 3-63. London: The Hogarth Press Limited.

FREUD, SIGMUND. 1926. Psycho-analysis. In *The Standard Edition of the Complete Psychological Works of Sigmund Freud*, translated by James Strachey, Vol. 20, pp. 259-370. London: The Hogarth Press Limited.

FREUD, SIGMUND. 1927. The question of lay analysis. In *The Standard Edition of the Complete Psychological Works of Sigmund Freud*, translated and edited by James Strachey, Vol. 20, pp. 179-258. London: The Hogarth Press Limited.

FREUD, SIGMUND. 1937. Analysis terminable and interminable. In *The Standard Edition of the Complete Psychological Works of Sigmund Freud*, translated and edited by James Strachey, Vol. 23, pp. 209-254. London: The Hogarth Press Limited.

FREUD, SIGMUND. 1940. An outline of psycho-analysis, Chapter 6. In The *Standard Edition of the Complete Psychological Works of Sigmund Freud*, translated and edited by James Strachey, Vol. 23, pp. 172-182. London: The Hogarth Press Limited.

FROMM-REICHMANN, FRIEDA. 1950. *Principles of Intensive Psychotherapy*, p. 142. Chicago: University of Chicago Press.

GILL, M. M. 1954. Psychoanalysis and exploratory psychotherapy. *Journal of the American Psychoanalytical Association*, 2:771-797.

GLOVER, E. 1955. *The Technique of Psycho-analysis*. New York: International Universities Press.

GREENACRE, P. 1954. The role of transference: Practical considerations in relation to psychoanalytic therapy. *Journal of the American Psychoanalytical Association*, 2:671-684.

GREENSON, RALPH R. 1967. *The Technique and Practice of Psychoanalysis*, Vol. 1. New York: International Universities Press.

HAMMER, E. F. 1968. Interpretation: What is it? in Hammer, E. F. (Ed.), *Use of Interpretation in Treatment*, pp. 1-4. New York: Grune and Stratton.

KLEIN, GEORGE S. 1967. Peremptory ideation: Structure and force in motivative ideas. In Klein, George S. (Ed.), *Psychological Issues*, Vol. 5, Nos. 2-3, pp. 78-128. New York: International Universities Press.

LEVITSKY, A., and PERLS, F. S. 1970. The rules and games of Gestalt therapy. In Fagan, J., and Shepherd, I. L. (Eds.), *Gestalt Therapy Now*, pp. 145-149. Palo Alto: Science and Behavior Books, Inc.

MEDNICK, SARNOFF A. 1958. A learning theory approach to research in schizophrenia. *Psychological Bulletin*, 55:316-327.

MENNINGER, KARL. 1958. *Theory of Psychoanalytic Technique*. New York: Basic Books, Inc., Publishers.

MOWRER, O. H. 1952. Speech development in the young child. 1: The autism theory of speech development and some clinical applications. *Journal of Speech and Hearing Disorders*, 17:263-268.

NARANJO, C. 1971. Contributions of Gestalt therapy. In Otto, H., & Mann, J. (Eds.), *Ways of Growth: Approaches to Expanding Awareness*, pp. 135-136. New York: Pocket Books.

NARANJO, C. 1970. Present-centeredness: Technique, prescription, and ideal. In Fagan, J., and Shepherd, I. L. (Eds.), *Gestalt Therapy Now*, pp. 49-50. Paol Alto: Science and Behavior Books, Inc.

PERLS, F. S. 1970. Four lectures. In Fagan, J., and Shepherd, L. I. (Eds.), *Gestalt Therapy Now*, p. 20. Palo Alto: Science and Behavior Books, Inc.

PERLS, F. S. 1948. Theory and technique of personality integration. *American Journal of Psychotherapy*, 2:565-586.

REIK, THEODOR. 1948. *Listening with the Third Ear: The Inner Experience of a Psychoanalyst*. New York: Farrar, Straus & Company.

RIMLAND, BERNARD. 1964. *Infantile Autism*. New York: Appleton-Century-Crofts.

SHELTON, RALPH W., ARNDT, W., and MILLER, J. 1961. Learning principles and teaching of speech language. *Journal of Speech and Hearing Disorders*, 26:368-376.

SKINNER, B. F. 1953. *Science and Human Behavior*. New York: The Macmillan Company.

SKINNER, B. F. 1964. In Wann, T. W. (Ed.), *Behaviorism and Phenomenology*. Chicago: University of Chicago Press.

STONE, LEO. 1961. *The Psychoanalytic Situation: An Examination of Its Development and Essential Nature*. New York: International Universities Press.

ULLMAN, L. P., and KRASNER, L. 1965. *Case Studies in Behavior Modification*. New York: Holt, Rinehart & Winston, Inc.

WOLPE, J., and LAZARUS, A. A. 1966. *Behavior Therapy Techniques: A Guide to the Treatment of Neuroses*. London: Pergamon Press.

YONTEF, G. M. 1971. *A Review of the Practice of Gestalt Therapy*, pp. 26-29. Copyright by Gary M. Yontef. Dissertation, University of Arizona.

ZETZEL, E. R. 1956. Current concept of transference. *International Journal of Psychoanalysis*, 37:369-376.

Part II

OBSESSIVE-COMPULSIVE PERSONALITY

THE CASE OF MARION

Marion is 26 years old, single, and a teacher in a public school. She is a tall, fairly attractive but somewhat overweight girl with dark hair and brown, searching eyes. Her dress is neat and casual, although it seems that she could be more attractive than she allows herself to look. Her lack of poise and insecurity make her appear younger than her chronological age. She generates a quality of pressure and hyperactivity. She talks about her problems with a dramatic concern and moves restlessly.

During the initial interview there was a distinct impression of caution and timidity about her. She kept her head down, her shoulders were stooped forward, and she would periodically glance at the interviewer and scan the room. Marion talked hurriedly about herself as if a pause would cause her further anxiety. She was verbal and introspective.

The patient came for treatment because she was depressed and dissatisfied with her relationships with men, each of which had lasted for about a year. She currently was involved with a man whom she had known for about a year and recently was experiencing the same pattern of progressive dissatisfaction. She said she worried continuously about her ability to have a satisfactory involvement and felt "doomed" to repeat the same pattern for her entire life.

Marion also complained of stomachaches, blemishes on her face, and other bodily malfunctions, all of which she considered psychosomatic. The physicians she had seen attributed these symptoms to tension.

Recently, while driving to school, she had a "strange sensation" that she would lose control and die and be mangled in a car accident. She recalled experiencing this fear for the first time when she was on a blind date in college. At that time she was afraid that her date would lose control and they would both die. This fear had recurred periodically ever since.

Marion's life seemed to be characterized by control, restraint, and caution. In expressing her unhappiness, she spoke about her need to follow a routine ("I feel more secure that way."), to plan her daily activities (she kept a list), and to carefully deliberate any new moves or decisions ("It takes me hours to buy a single skirt."). She said she feels guilty most of the time, but did not know why. Her friends sometimes complain that she is "heavy" and lacks enthusiasm. She said it is "hard to let go. I always feel like I have to be in complete control; I think I am just unable to have any fun."

Socially, Marion said she got along well with people, had two good girl friends and several casual friends. In relation to women she always felt inferior and frequently found herself "lost in their shadow." When in the presence of men, she also felt inadequate and anxious. A distinctive characteristic was her need to give devotion, and to wait on men whom she really did not find attractive. She avoided "interesting" men and gravitated to those who seemed "weak." She dated infrequently until she finished college. Her first sexual experience was at the age of 21. She enjoyed sex moderately, but felt restrained and envious of the pleasures which her girl friends reported. She had no orgasm during intercourse, but did experience orgasm during masturbation.

Historically, she has a sister 3 years older, from whom she felt distant as a child. Her father, a dentist, is seen as an unambitious "shmo" who couldn't breathe without mother's permission. In contrast, the mother, also a teacher, is seen as ambitious, dominating, and controlling. She felt closer to father and as a child remembers him as carefree and fun, while mother was cautious, careful, and critical. Marion recalls many fun experiences with father in playful wrestling, teasing, and tickling. When she reached early teens, she felt uneasy with father and soon felt repulsed and disappointed by him.

She also said that her father is her dentist. She spoke about the pain she experienced when he worked on her teeth and his apparent enjoyment of it. She remembers sometimes screaming from the pain of his drilling and his teasing her about being a coward. Marion felt that he "butchered" her mouth.

Throughout her schooling Marion did well academically and afterwards she did well professionally. She was proud of this.

During the past 5 years she had had the following dream periodically: *"I see a dog's face coming at me. It is coming right at me with big, big teeth and I force myself to wake up. It was frightening."*

4

Behavior Therapy Approach
The Case of Marion

HERBERT FENSTERHEIM, Ph.D.

The first step in formulating a treatment program for any patient is to determine the target behaviors to be modified. The aim is to choose specific behaviors which, if modified, would change a wide spectrum of other behaviors and so ameliorate the presenting problems. It is only after selecting these behaviors that the appropriate techniques for instituting change can be considered.

The method I use to determine these target behaviors revolves around the *behavioral formulation*. First I define the presenting problems, their specific histories, and the conditions under which they fluctuate. I next systematically investigate behaviors that may be relevant to the person's current difficulties. Finally I place these behaviors into a formulation that indicates their probable contribution to the presenting problems. This is the general method I follow with every patient, often implicitly but more often explicitly, and it is the method I shall follow in this discussion. Each of these steps will be described at the proper time.

41

PRESENTING PROBLEMS

This young woman presents two major problems. The first is a depression of unknown intensity and duration. It is not extreme to the extent that it paralyzes her and it is characterized by feelings of guilt, of being doomed, and by an inability to have any fun. The second presenting problem concerns unsatisfactory relations with men. Her involvements with men appear to last about a year and are characterized by progressive dissatisfaction and a partial frigidity. She also tends to be compliant with them and to gravitate towards men whom she really does not find attractive.

No specific history of these presenting problems can be drawn from the information at hand. However, because of the diagnosis of obsessive-compulsive personality, it is assumed that they developed within the context of a behavior pattern "characterized by excessive concern with conformity and adherence to standards of conscience" (DSM II, 1968). She is assumed to be "rigid and overinhibited."

Other problems are evident. Among them are somatic disorders attributed to tension, a recurrent "horrific" obsession, and feelings and ruminative obsessions concerning inadequacy.

BEHAVIORAL DATA

In organizing the behavioral data concerning a patient, I tend to group them into broad categories relating to general treatment methods. Previously I had suggested four such categories (Fensterheim, 1972a) : phobias, assertive problems, lack of desired habits, and presence of undesired habits. I have since found it helpful to use two additional ones: general tension, and obsessions.

General tension: Her somatic difficulties have been diagnosed as the effects of tension. These must be reevaluated.

Unfortunately, as Wolpe has pointed out (Wolpe, 1970) and as working therapists know, all too often the attribution of psychological causation to somatic complaints is the result of inadequate medical diagnosis. In this instance I would have Marion see her family doctor again and I would contact him personally. However, there are other indications of a general state of tension and I shall assume that the previous medical diagnosis is verified.

There is one important differential diagnosis to be made concerning this state of general tension. Is Marion reacting to a high level of tension or is it really a moderate level of tension to which she reacts with passivity and helplessness? Among other ways, I would test this out through the use of the *sud* scale (Wolpe and Lazarus, 1966). This involves having Marion give numerical estimates of her tension level at various times during the interview and to estimate what this level had been in different life situations. My impression of Marion is that she tends to be passive and helpless in the face of a moderate level of general tension.

This diagnosis has therapeutic importance. It means that the primary problem is not the tension but the passivity and it is the latter that must be treated. Were it the reverse, were the primary problem a high level of tension, I might consider a psychopharmaceutical consultation. In this case such a consultation is not indicated.

Phobias: In actual practice I would survey this area systematically through the use of the Fear Survey Schedule (Wolpe and Lazarus, 1966). From the material at hand there are instances where fear or other disturbed feelings are elicited from Marion by given classes of stimuli. Two main phobic areas are obvious.

1. Fear of loss of control. Thoughts or situations involving the possible loss of control elicit a phobic reaction. However

the core of the phobia, what she is most frightened of, is not obvious. In clinical practice I would obtain this information by simply asking the patient and most often I would be told. If Marion could not give me this information, I would use the initial working assumption that it is related in some way to her expressing her own anger and resentments. This is based in part on the material provided and in part on the fact that neither anger nor resentment is mentioned anywhere in the report, while such feelings are usually present in so compliant a person.

2. Fear of men. Again the specific nature and core of the phobia is not evident and directly asking the patient is the best way of obtaining this information. The working hypothesis to be used here is that it is primarily a fear of being physically or emotionally hurt by men. She also appears to feel unable to defend herself against such potential hurts and so this phobia is exacerbated by her assertive difficulties.

Obsessions: It is important to distinguish between phobias and obsessions because, despite some superficial similarities, different mechanisms are involved and different treatment methods are indicated. Phobias are concerned with the responses of the autonomic nervous system, while in obsessions it is the cognitive apparatus that is involved. There is some evidence that the tendency towards these reverberatory thoughts may be inherited (cf. Slater and Cowie, 1971) and they may take different forms, from barely noticed ruminations to the "horrific temptations" (Solyom, Zamanzadeh, Ledwidge and Kenny, 1971) which have strong phobic component (i.e., conditioned autonomic nervous system response to the content of the obsession). These obsessive thoughts tend to fluctuate directly with the level of general tension.

Obsessive thoughts have both direct and indirect consequences of clinical importance. The direct consequences concern the content of the obsession. In Marion's case there appear to be ruminative obsessions concerned with guilt, inferiority, and inadequacy. By constantly telling herself that she is guilty, inferior, and inadequate, she tends to perpetuate these feelings in herself and these in turn influence her overt behavior. The indirect consequence of the obsessive thoughts is that their presence leads to a sense of the loss of mastery, a lowering of self-esteem, and often depression. Marion attempts to cope with this indirect consequence, attempts to gain some feeling of mastery, by establishing external loci of control through the use of routines, plans, and lists.

As noted with her general level of tension, Marion's response to these uncontrolled thoughts appears to be passivity and helplessness. These latter may be reinforced and accentuated by the strong phobic component associated with her obsession of being mangled in a car accident. The fact that she was able to establish sufficient control to do well academically and professionally may indicate that if she adopted an active attitude towards controlling her ruminative obsessions she might be able to do so.

Assertion: Assertion involves the feeling of mastery of life situations and also involves open communication with people. Marion's problems in this area are sufficiently severe to account for much of her difficulty. In actual clinical practice I would obtain more information about her behavior in this area through an Assertive Training Questionnaire (Fensterheim, 1971). If necessary, I would instruct her to keep notes of trivial interpersonal incidents where she was not satisfied with what happened, or where she felt disturbed.

One large area of assertive difficulty centers around men. Although the information provided is merely suggestive, the pattern is fairly typical. The progressive dissatisfaction, the lack of longer-term relationships, the mood difficulty and perhaps even the partial frigidity often stem from poor communication. Fensterheim (1972c) reports on a case showing somewhat similar patterns which stemmed from the communication difficulties of a married couple. With Marion, the working assumption is that at least part of the difficulty stems from her fear of expressing anger and resentment to men.

A critical differential diagnosis to be made with assertive problems is whether the person knows how to act assertively but is afraid to do so, or whether the assertive skills themselves have just never been learned. As Marion has friends and (it is assumed) got along reasonably well at school and at work, she probably has some knowledge of assertive skills. The core of her assertive difficulties are the phobias already discussed. She knows generally how to act assertively, but is afraid to do so. However, these phobias have led to a lack of practice and so these assertive skills have not developed fully. This, in turn, helps to perpetuate and exacerbate the phobias. The therapeutic implication is that the removal of the phobias will not automatically lead to assertion, but there will probably have to be supervised practice and training in this area.

Habits: Although a number of habits have been noted, all would fall into categories already discussed. There do not appear to be clinically significant autonomous undesired habits. Nor do her difficulties appear to stem in any significant manner from a lack of desired habits other than those already discussed.

BEHAVIORAL FORMULATION

Having described what appears to be the clinically important behaviors, it is necessary to determine which of these behaviors to modify. Although behavior therapy is developing new methods of assessment and new schemata for studying the functional interrelations between response patterns, "as yet, the behavior therapist has little in the way of scientifically-based procedures for deciding which element within a complex behavioral chain to attack" (Kanfer and Phillips, 1970, p. 510). Hence he operates "on the basis of his 'clinical lore' in . . . deciding where, in the complex chains of interrelated behavioral patterns of daily life, the therapist should attempt to intervene" (*ibid.*, p. 520).

My behavioral formulation makes use of "clinical lore" to hypothesize the functional relationships between the different behaviors. The aim is to identify those critical behaviors which, if modified, would alter the entire behavioral pattern in the desired direction. Formulations or working hypotheses of this type are not unique to behavior therapy; I have illustrated a similar method for use with analytically-oriented crisis interventions (Normand, Fensterheim, and Schrenzel, 1967). Small (1972, p. 112) states: "To be brief, therapy must be intentional; to be intentional, therapy must be guided by diagnosis at every stage." Hence such formulations may be a requisite for any brief therapy. Indeed, it is probably only the slower-developing treatments such as traditional psychoanalysis where such formulations are not mandatory at the very onset of therapy.

The behavioral formulation differs from other such formulations by more rigorously following the scientific principle of parsimony. It utilizes the fewest inferred mediating processes needed to form a coherent picture of the behavioral organization of that person. Although historical data may be used to help in arriving at the formulation, the picture presented is that of the behavioral organization as it is at present.

The behavioral formulation for Marion is shown in Figure 1. It may be noted that the major part of the figure represents a personality disorder, while a secondary part represents a neurotic component.

The core of the behavioral formulation is her obsessive

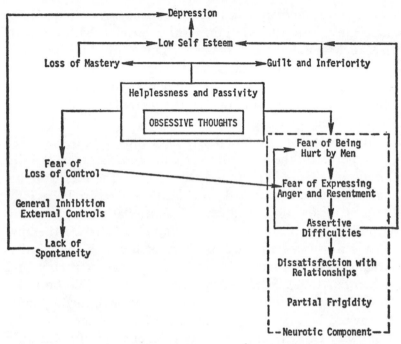

FIGURE 1. Behavioral formulation of Marion, an obsessive-compulsive personality with a neurotic component concerning her relations with men.

thoughts, her tendency towards uncontrolled, reverberatory thinking. Not very much is currently known about the processes involved in this characteristic of the cognitive apparatus, although some speculation exists. Mather (1970), for example, relates it to the stereotyped behaviors of infrahuman animals under stress. Pavlov discusses it in terms of a pathological inertness of excitation and as being "the outcome of a stress in the environment-organism interaction, with a specific preconstellation in the central nervous system" (Ban, 1964, p. 87). Such speculations, however, are little help in formulating the behavioral organization of a specific patient. Thus, although it would be nice to be able to place a series of specific biopsychological processes at the core of the formulation, we must be content with the general term of "obsessive thoughts."

In the case of Marion, there may have been an inherited predisposition towards obsessive thinking from the maternal side of her family. However, it has undoubtedly been influenced by her life experience and we do not know its specific developmental course. Nevertheless, once developed, obsessional states soon achieve a considerable degree of functional autonomy (Walton and Mather, 1964). Despite the fact that they may fluctuate with the level of general tension, the role of the obsessive thoughts in Marion's current behavioral organization is that of a precipitant of anxiety rather than as a product of anxiety. It is for this reason that this aspect of her organization is classed as a personality disorder rather than as a neurosis.

As with her level of general tension, Marion reacts to her obsessive thoughts with passivity and helplessness. These thoughts have both direct and indirect consequences, both of which have already been noted in the description of her obsessive behavior. Guilt, inferiority, and inadequacy are direct consequences, and loss of mastery and lowered self-esteem indirect consequences. A further consequence has to do with her fear of loss of control. Her awareness of the uncontrolled nature of these thoughts and their consequences constantly and understandably reinforces her fear of loss of control. This fear itself contributes to her general inhibition (for which there may already be an inherited predisposition), which in turn leads to a lack of spontaneity and to depression.

This formulation depicts the guilt, the inferiority feelings, the fear of loss of control, the lack of spontaneity, and the depression as being maintained by some defect of her cognitive apparatus which has obsessive thoughts as the obvious manifestation. This is the structure of a character disorder.

However, the subset of her behaviors dealing with men is formulated to revolve around a core of anxiety. This constitutes a neurotic component within the general framework of her personality disorder.

The core of the neurotic component is the phobia of being hurt by men. This, through her phobia of expressing anger and resentments, leads to assertive difficulties with men. These assertive difficulties, in their turn, lead to progressive dissatisfaction in her relationships on the one hand, and contribute to her low self-esteem and depression on the other hand. Her partial frigidity is formulated as part of the neurotic component, although the exact connection has not been formulated.

Two processes maintain this neurotic component and prevent it from extinguishing spontaneously. Within the neurotic component itself, her assertive difficulties, her inability to protect herself from potential hurt by men, exacerbate her fear of such hurt. Thus, the neurosis perpetuates itself. There is also a bond between the character disorder and the neurotic component. It is formulated that her fear of loss of control (which, it may be recalled, is itself constantly reinforced by actual control difficulties) reinforces her fear of expressing anger and resentment. In this manner the neurotic component is maintained by elements outside of it.

Following this formulation, there are two areas of target behaviors to modify. One concerns the personality disorder, and the other, the neurotic component. Each must be treated separately, although it is probable that a change in one would lead to at least a minimal change in the other.

To treat the personality disorder, the logical target behavior would involve the processes underlying the obsessive thoughts. Frankly, as I have already indicated, we do not know what these processes are, nor do I know how to treat the obsessiveness directly. Instead, I would focus on the helplessness and passivity in the face of the obsessions. If she can be taught an active orientation and some methods to control the obsessions, there should be a corresponding decrease in both the direct and the indirect consequences of these thoughts, as well as a decrease in her fear of losing control.

In treating the neurotic component, the target behavior would be her fear of expressing anger and resentment. This is the fear that (it has been hypothesized) reacts with the personality disorder to perpetuate the neurosis. Also, relief of this fear may well lead to a greater assertion and so disrupt the internal circuit that maintains the neurosis. If this keystone fear were relieved, there is a reasonable probability that the entire neurotic component may dissolve.

Before describing the specific therapeutic techniques to be used, two further points must be made concerning the behavioral formulation:

1. The entire formulation, although not in so much detail, would be presented to Marion. She may be able to make important corrections in it. Beyond that, it would provide her with a frame of reference for what we will be doing and with specific goals and subgoals for treatment besides the vague "relief of depression" or "better relations with men." It would also help her assume the task orientation and the advanced student thesis advisor relationship that typify the behavior therapy I conduct.

2. It must be stressed that the behavioral formulation is merely a working hypothesis and may be partially or completely incorrect. If expected behavioral changes in the life situation are not seen within several sessions (depending on the technical difficulties encountered), the formulation may have to be revised and a new treatment plan drawn up.

TREATMENT

The initial treatment of the personality disorder will center around teaching her techniques to control her obsessive thoughts and her tensions. This will encourage a generally active (as compared to her currently passive) attitude. The initial treatment of the neurotic component will center around a systematic desensitization of her fear of expressing anger towards men and around some assertive training. This last may be conducted in a group setting.

Control Techniques. Thought stoppage (Wolpe and Lazarus, 1966) will be one of the first therapeutic techniques introduced. Marion would first be taught to recognize destructive "put down" thoughts. These are the ruminative obsessive thoughts that bring feelings of guilt and inferiority in their wake. Most patients have no difficulty in recognizing such thoughts. Next she will be taught to say "STOP" to herself whenever she has such a thought and then to relax. More for supportive purposes (considering her need for external controls) than for any other reason, she will be given a hand shocker to supplement this technique.

Marion would then be instructed to use thought stoppage *as soon as* and *every time* she becomes aware of a "put down" thought in order to place it on an extinction schedule. The theory of extinction, of withdrawal of reinforcement, will be explained to her so that the procedure makes sense. The characteristics of operant extinction will also be explained: that initially the ruminative thoughts may actually increase in frequency and intensity but that once they start decreasing, progress will be rapid. She will also be cautioned that even after the thoughts are under control, an increase in general tension for any reason will cause their return. That is the time when she must really grit her teeth and use the "STOP" lest the habit be reestablished.

My prediction is that Marion would readily learn this technique and carry out her assignments. Within 3 to 4 weeks a good control over these thoughts would have been established, with a consequent change in her depressive mood. I also predict that there will be several times during the course of treatment when life situations will cause her tension level to spike, where these thoughts will return, and where she will "forget" to use this technique. However, support and instruction will quickly (24-48 hours) reestablish control.

The second control technique to be introduced would be relaxation training. Although the tension reduction that this will bring is indeed important, the primary purpose of this training is for control. The hope is to train Marion to have an active rather than a passive attitude towards her tensions.

She will be given relaxation exercises (Fensterheim, 1971) in the office and also given an audio-tape of these exercises to perform at home on a regular basis. Because people who fear loss of control often have difficulty in relaxing completely, there may be some initial difficulty. However, her demonstrated ability to follow assignments (good school work) leads to the prediction that she will master this skill through home practice.

Next she will be taught to apply relaxation to simple life situations. First she will practice attaining a relaxed state while sitting, standing and walking. Then she will apply it in a hierarchical fashion to common, trivial anxiety-provoking situations and, finally, to important anxiety-provoking interpersonal situations. This method is described within the context of a case report by Marquis (1972).

Again it must be stressed that tension reduction is merely the secondary purpose of this training. The main purpose is to develop an active attitude and increased control. Once the thought stoppage and the relaxation techniques have had a chance to be effective, I would expect a marked diminution of her depression and of her fear of loss of control, along with some increase in her spontaneity in life situations. If needed, further training in control may be given through treating her mild overweight condition or some other aspect of her life where she feels she lacks control. A therapeutic decision may eventually have to be made on whether to conduct a systematic desensitization of her fear of loss of control. However, I would tend to delay this decision and the decision concerning further control training until after the neurotic component has been treated.

Systematic Desensitization. The first step in treating the neurotic component is to conduct a systematic desensitizaion to her fear of expressing anger and resentment. With Marion, this procedure would utilize relaxation as the reciprocal inhibitor of anxiety and few technical problems (e.g., difficulties in imagining scenes or in experiencing increases in tension) are anticipated. Were she more severely obsessive, systematic desensitization using aversion relief would be the method of choice. The formulation of the proper hierarchy would be the most crucial aspect of this procedure.

There is one hierarchy I have often found useful for this fear. I would have Marion rank the names of approximately 10 people according to the degree of discomfort she would feel if she spoke up to them. I would have her imagine saying the phrase, "I don't like what you said," to each of these people. She would first imagine saying it calmly to each person, then with annoyance, and finally with anger. If indicated (and I have found it generally not to be indicated), she may imagine saying the phrase to each person in a completely uncontrolled manner. It is expected that this hierarchy would not only diminish the specific fear being treated but also the fear of loss of control and that it would also lead to some spontaneous increase in assertive behavior with men.

At best, this desensitization will break the hypothesized

link to the personality disorder and the entire neurotic component may dissipate. However, it may also become evident that the fear of being hurt by men plays a more important role in the maintenance of the neurotic behavior than had been formulated. In that case, a systematic desensitization to that phobia should be conducted.

Assertive Training. Despite the prediction of some spontaneous increase in assertive behavior, some assertive training will probably be needed. This training would follow the general lines I have described elsewhere (Fensterheim, 1972b). More specifically for Marion, she would first be taught the concept and the importance of assertion. She might be given such reading assignments as Salter (1949) and/or the assertive chapter in Fensterheim (1971). She would next be taught to recognize her own assertive problems and their consequences. This would be done by having her bring in examples of her interactions with people, analyzing each example in terms of assertion, and formulating and practicing the assertive response in selected situations.

After this initial training she would be placed in a four-session assertive training mini-group (Fensterheim, 1972b). Her task in this group would be to practice expressing anger and speaking up in other ways to men. This will improve her skill, give her greater confidence in her ability to use this skill, and provide an *in vivo* desensitization in this area. Towards the end of treatment a second such minigroup experience may be indicated.

COURSE OF TREATMENT

This treatment should be carried out in 25-40 individual sessions, with either four or eight mini-group sessions, over approximately 10 months. The number of sessions will vary according to the technical difficulties encountered, the specific hierarchies used, the rapidity of learning, and interfering, unexpected life stresses. There will be sessions, or parts of sessions, where she will discuss new conceptualizations or insights which often emerge from this kind of treatment, where she seeks counsel or guidance, or where she wants to talk about a disturbing life situation. Most sessions, however, will be devoted to the treatment program outlined.

Changes should be noted from the third or fourth treatment session as the thought stoppage and the relaxation training begin to take effect. At the end of this course of treatment, the depression should be gone, although there may be occasional depressed episodes. There should be a marked improvement in her physical symptoms and a noticeable increase in her spontaneity. Her obsessions should be gone, although returning under conditions of stress, and there should be a consequent decrease in feelings of guilt and inferiority and an increase in self-esteem. There should be a big change in her relations with men and she probably would have already dated some "interesting" men. Even without direct treatment, there is a reasonably good probability that she has become orgasmic during intercourse.

At this point it is necessary to allow her time to integrate these changes into her behavioral patterns. To achieve this, I prescribe a four to six month vacation from treatment. Marion would be instructed to contact me if there is a return of the old symptoms, the development of new symptoms, or if she needs help with a difficult life situation. Following this vacation, there would be an evaluation to determine whether further treatment is needed for the same problems, whether a new set of problems needs treatment, or whether treatment should be terminated at that point.

OUTCOME

Even if termination is indicated, Marion cannot be considered "cured." Despite the anticipated, marked improvement, two major areas of difficulty remain:

1. She has developed a number of strong habit patterns to cope with her control difficulties—patterns that inhibit her general spontaneity and lead in the direction of rigidity. These, combined with her temperamental characteristics, give rise to an entire life style. Although some of these patterns may undergo great changes as a result of treatment, the basic life style will probably remain. It is hoped that following treatment the beneficial aspects of this life style will outweigh its disruptive or limiting aspects, but some negative aspects will always be present.

2. Even more important, the core deficit of the obsessive processes remains. Treatment may have modified these to some extent, and she will have learned methods for minimizing the effects of this condition, but the basic condition continues. Although under good control in ordinary life situations, periodic difficulties will be experienced. Under stress, the control functions will probably weaken again. Obsessions will reappear although they may have a different content, a loss of mastery will occur, and she may again become depressed. New phobias may be learned and lead to the formation of new neurotic components. She should be alerted to all these possibilities for, if they are caught early, they would probably be fairly easily and quickly treated.

The paradigm is that of a chronic disorder where flare-ups are controlled as they occur. However, this picture is a bit too pessimistic. Having been put on the right track, she will function with increasing effectiveness and spontaneity within her limitations in general life situations. The psychological difficulties will be responses to stress situations rather than being part of her daily life style as they are now.

Once again the question of treating the core difficulty, the obsessive processes, must be raised. Without such treatment Marion's therapy cannot be considered to be completed. That I have not carefully weighed potential methods of intervening in this area with Marion is based on three points. First, as I have previously indicated, I do not know how to conduct such interventions. Nor do I believe that effective techniques for such interventions have been developed by *any* therapeutic modality. The chance of success is slim. Second is the recognition that any intervention, from aspirin to psychotherapy, carries with it the danger of unforeseen side effects. Hence psychotherapeutic interventions should be limited to those which have a reasonable chance of success and/or are essential. Third is that I do not believe that such intervention, desirable as it may be, is absolutely essential for Marion. With the anticipated therapeutic outcome, she can lead a fulfilling life within her limitations.

Therefore direct intervention to modify the core disorder, the obsessive processes, is not considered. Such intervention is not absolutely necessary for Marion and, in the current state of the art, the possibility of harm outweighs the chance of success. Of course, while working with Marion or in the post-therapy period, it may become obvious that such intervention is essential. In that case, the risks must be taken and attempts at intervention made.

BIBLIOGRAPHY

AMERICAN PSYCHIATRIC ASSOCIATION. 1968. *Diagnostic and Statistical Manual of Mental Disorders* (DSM II). Washington, D.C.: American Psychiatric Association.
BAN, T. 1964. *Conditioning and Psychiatry.* Chicago: Aldine.
FENSTERHEIM, H. 1971. *Help Without Psychoanalysis.* New York: Stein and Day.

FENSTERHEIM, H. 1972a. The initial interview. In Lazarus, A. A. (Ed.), *Clinical Behavior Therapy*. New York: Brunner/Mazel.

FENSTERHEIM, H. 1972b. Behavior therapy: Assertive training in groups. In Sager, C. J., and Kaplan, H. S. (Eds.), *Progress in Group and Family Therapy*. New York: Brunner/Mazel.

FENSTERHEIM, H. 1972c. Assertive training in marital problems: Case report. In Rubin, R. D., Fensterheim, H., Henderson, J. D., and Ullman, L. P. (Eds.), *Advances in Behavior Therapy*. New York: Academic Press.

KANFER, F. H., and PHILLIPS, J. S. 1970. *Learning Foundations of Behavior Therapy*. New York: John Wiley & Sons.

MARQUIS, J. N. 1972. An expedient model for behavior therapy. In Lazarus, A. A. (Ed.), *Clinical Behavior Therapy*. New York: Brunner/Mazel.

MATHER, M. D. 1970. Obsessions and compulsions. In C. G. Costello (Ed.), *Symptoms of Psychopathology: A Handbook*. New York: John Wiley & Sons.

NORMAND, W. C., FENSTERHEIM, H., and SCHRENZEL, S. 1967. A systematic approach to brief therapy for patients from a low socioeconomic community. *Community Mental Health Journal*, 3:349-354.

SALTER, A. 1949. *Conditioned Reflex Therapy*. New York: Farrar, Straus.

SLATER, E. and COWIE, V. 1971. *The Genetics of Mental Disorders*. London: Oxford University Press.

SMALL, L. 1972. The uncommon importance of psychodiagnosis. *Professional Psychology*, 3:111-119.

SOLYOM, L., ZAMANZADEH, D., LEDWIDGE, B., and KENNY, F. 1971. Aversion relief treatment of obsessive neurosis. In Rubin, R. D., Fensterheim, H., Lazarus, A. A., and Franks, C. M. (Eds.), *Advances in Behavior Therapy*. New York: Academic Press.

WALTON, D., and MATHER, M. D. 1964. The application of learning principles to the treatment of obsessive-compulsive states in the acute and chronic phases of illness. In H. J. Eysenck (Ed.), *Experiments in Behavior Therapy*. London: Pergamon.

WOLPE, J. 1970. Foreword. In Stuart, R. B., *Trick or Treatment: How and When Psychotherapy Fails*. Champaign, Ill.: Research Press.

WOLPE, J., and LAZARUS, A. A. 1966. *Behavior Therapy Techniques*. London: Pergamon.

5

Gestalt Approach
The Case of Marion

MICHAEL KRIEGSFELD, Ph.D.

As an advocate of the gestalt approach, I am responding to the description of the case and request for the treatment approach according to three areas of concern:

1) the structure of the task,
2) the model,
3) my fantasy.

THE STRUCTURE OF THE TASK

I reviewed the material on the same weekend that *The New York Times* (Nov. 25, 1973) had an elegant insert which meant to convey the perfect vacation. A 16-page brochure attracted my interest with its title

THE PERFECT VACATION—IT LIES WITHIN

Your vacation should be as unique as your personality. You are an individual . . . with your own likes and dislikes. So ideally, you should end up with a unique vacation experience that's a reflection of your own inner reality. Don't take someone else's vacation. . . . We've developed, with a team of psychologists, a questionnaire to help you search inside yourself for the key . . . that's right for you. If you're willing to take fifteen or twenty minutes to complete the questionnaire, we'll determine a vacation profile that will tell us a lot about you and the vacation that's right for you. . . . We'll compare your profile to the thousands of vacation experiences we offer, experiences that best fulfill what makes you happy. Based on our findings, we'll send you a letter with our suggestions for your vacation. . . . Everything we've learned about vacations since we started helping people plan theirs, we've fed into our computer's memory bank. It remembers what's available everywhere we fly.

It took me some time shuffling back and forth through the sixteen pages and the many questions before I realized there was a huge gap between their come on and eventual outcome of any vacation plan for myself. I gleaned that this particular airline flew only to warm weather climates and all the programs are designed for warm weather activities. I could wind up sailing, swimming, golfing, or snorkling. As I looked across the room to my skis standing in the corner with their edges sharpened, I recalled the pleasure and excitement of Alpine skiing, listened to the oom-pa band music, felt the wind and the sun on the long meditative ride up the mountain on the chair lift, I knew they could not meet my needs. The nature of the inquiry, the format of the questionnaire, the structure of their programs and services were not related to Alpine skiing.

The analogy here is that the description of the case and the request for describing the treatment approach could hardly lead to a gestalt growth experience as it stands.

THE MODEL

The model suggests a historical-diagnostic approach. Marion who is seen as an obsessive-compulsive by the interviewer, characterized by control, restraint, and caution, with a need to follow a routine, is interviewed in an obsessive-compulsive manner characterized by control, restraint, and caution in a routine of history taking. Out of a process of interpersonal encounter, a thing-like case study is assembled. The implication is that hidden there, waiting to be discovered, is a diagnostic formulation which will lead to a treatment program. At some future date this will be followed by an assignment to a therapist who will carry out the program. Marion's caution and timidity are met with caution and timidity as she is placed back on the waiting list shelf to wait for the psychotherapy thing to be done to her. She worries continuously about her ability to have a satisfactory involvement and feels doomed to repeat the same pattern for her entire life. The interviewer appears to add to and repeat the unsatisfying involvement.

Her heaviness and lack of enthusiasm are met with a heavy and unenthusiastic interview. She is distant from her sister and experienced her mother as careful and critical. In the interview she is distanced by the interviewer who plods along, assembling material for the case history, without any clue as to the nature of the feelings and interpersonal transactions between them. The interviewer is also careful and critical in describing her and consistently erases her qualities: she is "fairly attractive," and then he adds the qualifying "but"; she is "neat and casual *although* it seems that she could be more attractive"; she should look older.

MY FANTASY

Marion comes with her head, teeth not quite hidden behind her best company manners smile. Like a gift-wrapped doll, she is cloaked and stiffly rolls across the floor. Her wind-up mechanism slows her down in front of me as she waits to be greeted, seated, and questioned. I begin wondering what my passing grade will be as she examines the room first, the furnishings next, and finally me. The examination is *Top Secret—For Eyes Only!*

"What are you aware of?" she ignores. "How do you feel?" she avoids. "What are you expecting of me?" she deals with by an innocent, "Didn't they let you read the record? Didn't the interviewer let you know about the problem?"

Soon into the beginning phase of our work in regular group sessions, Marion experiences her skill and satisfaction in the child's game Simple Simon. When Simple Simon says do this, do it, for that is the rule. When Simple Simon doesn't say to do it, don't do it. Sometimes you miss what Simple Simon says, and you begin to do that, forgetting you shouldn't do that unless Simple Simon said to do that. Faster and faster, tighter and tighter, win and achieve to please Simple Simon and then to become Simple Simon. Confusion reigns. Should I do that? or what?

Only losers have feelings—all bad—like shame, contempt, chagrin, disgust, humiliation, embarrassment. Only losers know that their body is to blame. "It just accidently happened that the arm moved." Gradually, in our work the body possession of a symptom becomes awareness of being responsive and responsible.

I become aware of my relaxed poise, my balanced posture, my direct gaze, solid grounding of my feet, my leaning forward towards Marion. Now I am tensing, I am shifting, I share how I am feeling, what I am observing, and noticing that I am avoiding the content of the intellectualizations. I m staying with the emotional and physical communication.

I am pleased with her surprise and recognition of herself and me. I am relaxing. I am excited in our encounter, enjoying the games, becoming playful, annoyed, firm, sarcastic, biting. I share her sadness as she begins to dissolve. I am sweating, my eyes glisten and are moist, I am interested, waiting, I am pressuring, I am ignoring her and tension builds as she asserts her desire to participate in the group session. At times she calls for individual appointments.

Marion teaches others and myself according to her imaginary lesson plan what therapy ought to be like and how the patient should behave. I encourage her to shuttle back and forth as patient and her own therapist, with dialogue in acting out her introjects and projections.

Now instead of being taught, we free ourselves to truly learn through sharing the experiences with her. Marion discovers how much she has swallowed undigested. She becomes aware of her own responsibility for her stomachaches and her need to continue asking for better medicine to swallow. Again and again her unfinished business leads her to ask for *why* feedings. A constant request for a big HELPING of *why this* and *why that* shifts the Simple Simon game of *tell me* to *feed me*.

I tense myself and become aware of entangling myself in *do I have enough? do I give enough? am I satisfying enough?* I share my impatience and my impotence. In the presence of such greed, who could have enough? I won't swallow her manipulations—I don't need to give myself cramps. She is taken aback as I comment that she will cause me to lose face by blotching and blemishing my good reputation. I encourage her to do this openly and directly, taking responsibility for this important part of her personality. I invite her to turn the retroflections outwards in experiments at being critical of others in the group.

She becomes aware of her body posture and tensions as she goes around to different individuals in the group to assert her newly discovered strength. She is caught in existential crisis in deciding whether to be critical of others or herself, make demands on others or only on herself, suffer rejection of herself or reject others. We see the development of her bodily malfunctions, notice the blotches and reddening of her face, and hear her stomach groan and gurgle noisily as she experiments with swallowing and throwing up her old leftover introjects. Marion is growing in her ability to be responsible and in her awareness. She is beginning to discover what she is doing inside and how she is making this happen.

Marion cautiously grades me O.K. and begins equivocating obsessively with catastrophic expectations about the future. She worries endlessly as she avoids the here and now, quibbling and chewing over the process and experience. She and I are torturing ourselves with predictions of future iffiness.

What will happen if she does this on her next date? Her next weekend? What if she goes too far? What if she doesn't go at all? What if they out there don't believe in this stuff in here?

Marion is scaring herself with anticipated fears of loss of control. I make myself crazy with controlling myself from asking Marion to experiment in losing control of herself and to control me and others. Control your control and soon we are into the nursery school game of Show and Tell. We lose our control as we play our own version Know and Yell. If you know what will happen, if you know why it will happen, then you won't lose control and yell. Marilyn knows that she may soon begin to yell.

She discovers she won't wait and increases her group sessions to two a week: one before the future, with plenty of time to make lists of activities and things to do, and the other after, to review her loss of control. Her aloneness shifts to being with others. Sometimes now she can improvise and become playful. Coy and slavelike in devotion to preparations for her weekends, she accumulates and hoards long lists of places to go, people to see, activities to do. Alternatives and contingencies are her signal of how IT out there will fail.

Nothing works out right at first, no matter how attentive she tries to be to instructions she can manipulate out of others.

My experiments are designed to call attention to her feelings and attitudes, sensations, and non-verbal expressiveness. Much of the time she stiffens herself, rigidly attempting to know what is right or what is logical. There are endless questions wanting to know the meaning of what others are doing. She knows that knowing is important and yet she doesn't know. She is confused and confusing in experiments designed to discover how she avoids her own wantingness, emptiness, dissatisfaction, and yearning. This leads to painful and poignant feelings cordoned off long ago. Marion in the here and now is able to sense what is on the outside of the wall she has erected, becomes aware of the process of walling off herself and others, and gradually persists in staying with her desires.

Now she is "helping" others by explaining, justifying, and giving little suggestions. In this way, she can school and teach others in the model of the right relationship designed to get, without actually asking directly. A most significant tidal flood of emotion begins with a few drops of minor irritations; a trickle of whines of unfairness and injustice, a steady stream of complaints about rudeness and cruelty, a torrent of abusiveness and biting remarks, and Marion is on her way to experiencing her hostility and masked sadism as her method of grinding others and myself down.

Gradually, through playing the various split parts and inventing dialogue between them, she touches her longing and dependency. She recognizes the obsequious, ingratiating submissiveness as prelude to expressing her dependency and reaction to her needs. Deference is her mask of inner rebellion and resentment. Unexpressed fears of adequacy and capacity to function in her own interest haunt and worry her. Her judgmental dismissal of selfishness begins changing as she establishes self boundaries of self-interest that are real and satisfying.

In shuttling back and forth in her dialogues, she frees herself, not by alienating the intellectual from the emotional, but by learning the art of integration. Through negotiation, collaboration, and painful staying in the process, she identifies with the polarities and gradually centers her living space. No longer does she need to detach herself and isolate her feelings which lead to turmoil, but instead, she begins to practice getting in touch with her real self. Her intellect is now in the service of her emotions, and her emotions are available in blend with her assertiveness. Impulses can be friends and fun, instead of enemies and disaster. Therapy is no longer just a battleground to bury the feared and attacking monsters, but a living garden of growing treasures. Even her garbage of leftovers can be useful fertilizer for new growth of flowers, foliage and nourishing vegetables. And in the bare places she can seed her impulses and desires, and tend to them with concern and self love. Aggressive weeding and bug control are natural and organic to her process, and she develops in her skill to do this without destroying or injuring herself or others.

One major tool in self gardening of gestalts is the use of dreams. At first her dreams are unrecalled and dreaming is sparse. I ask her to play-act the various parts of the recurring nightmare and fill in with fantasy. She becomes her menacing head without her body. Throughout our work together— which has now gone two years—she begins to fill in with fantasy. She loosens her control as she becomes now a dog and later a wolf on all fours, racing around the wilderness looking for herself as victim. She is very believable as the angry threatening snarler with bared teeth, and wonders what her students and principal in her school would think if they could see her. What would her mother and father think? She plays the various parts and experiences her various splits. Gradually, she is centering between the polarities of over control and under control: her head trips and her body needs, her need to be superior and her sense of being inferior, her wish to devote herself to others and the need to be attended to, nagging and being nagged, femininity and masculinity, privacy and relatedness. The head of her nightmare is fleshed out with a body and gradually other characters and dimensions are dreamed. Lupus dentata, her aggressive biting teeth with which she frightens herself, become lupus cantata—her fullbodied singing and expressiveness. Eventually, she dreams lupus sonata, a coherent self with structure and form and completeness to be appreciated for herself.

We have worked long and hard on identification with the parts and organizing the wholes. She assumes response-ability in working through her own integration, and with new vitality decides to leave.

Unlike the children's fairy tales which end with fixed position of happiness, we know there is no ending. There is self discovery and self acceptance as the basis for continuous growth. In a letter to me, Marion reflects and reviews our work:

> The most important thing I learned about myself was that I complained and complained. It got so bad hearing myself that way so full of shit. Actually once I got in touch with this, I couldn't stand hearing everyone else in the group over and over again. Your lack of attention while I elaborated on shit or intellectual jazz I'm sure helped me awaken.
>
> Another critical area was learning how I couldn't separate myself from my sister's agony and that I allowed her to poison me, to destroy any happiness I could feel. Learning this was most difficult since I still have qualms about letting her fend for herself totally in view of her problems. But I've learned to accept her whining in-

cessantly and her long intellectual discourses and that I can go on with my own life and enjoyment. This was a major breakthrough for me. Another lightning bolt was learning how much comfort I found in concentrating on the negatives and how much I lived in the past. Being afraid to take a chance.

Being afraid to show my *feelings*, afraid of the new, sticking with the old, playing safe and secure.

Anticipating—and always the worst self-fulfilling prophesy of doom. Learning that I was judging myself as my mother had done to me; you should be this way you should be that way . . . learning to treat men like schmoes like she did.

Finding out how strong I was when I dwelt on the negative—how I won't say I'm happy—how I defend against enjoyment, hiding my femininity, ignoring myself. Copping out when I won't make a decision.

One of my grim enlightenments—learning how I sought death. Taking circuitous routes instead of direct ones which get you what you want. Being unable to express feelings—especially anger on the job and elsewhere. Putting on acts of confidence—afraid to let people know I'm afraid.

Not being able to acknowledge a man's attention and interest for fear that he would know my needs and desires.

Not being able to operate between the extremes of apathy or total dissolving myself.

Always judging instead of enjoying—suffering over the past and fearing the future—unable to give myself a vacation. Wondering what's my next move instead of enjoying the moment.

Looking for the easy way out and not being honest with myself.

I think that most of what I learned came through the work with dreams. I can't say it's hogwash. I manufactured them and every part was the real me waiting to be discovered and accepted. Another way that I got to me was through the group experience. Saying things alone in a closet is not like proclaiming them in public. Experiencing the others and how they did the same trips of not feeling and not expressing themselves.

The firmness of your approach—the directness—the caring for the real me not the phony mask—right to the heart.

The playing of roles—the empty chair shtick.

Being afraid to talk openly in the group, feeling anxious, learning how I disturb myself further by not talking.

There are still things I'm shaky about—and will probably be back for a booster—until then love to the group and you

Marion

And so my fantasy for this moment closes and I wonder what I might have written at another time. In the groups, when one person stops working and another wants to volunteer, they will ask, "Are you through?" and in the words of Marion, I would answer, "No, not finished. I'm resting until next time."

6

Psychoanalytic Approach
The Case of Marion

LEON SALZMAN, M.D.

In the brief interview which is presented for discussion, there are sufficient data to categorize this patient as an obsessive-compulsive personality. The overall impression is that of an anxious, frightened, and discontented young lady whose need to maintain control over herself and others has produced a wide series of symptoms which keep her largely dissatisfied with her living. These obsessive tendencies, which are manifest both in her appearance and in her behavior, revolve about her fears of losing control, which she experiences as catastrophic and therefore demands a variety of safeguards.

Characteristic of the obsessive-compulsive maneuvers are the tendency to be cautious and restrained. This results in an indecisive and procrastinating tendency. Consequently she is always uneasy and unwilling to let herself go, so that she feels heavy and lacks enthusiasm. She insists upon an ordered world in order to have some measure of guarantee of her place in it. Her description of a recent event in which she was afraid that she might lose control while driving, which followed an earlier experience when she was extremely fearful on a blind date, indicates that the need for certainty and assurance

71

in her living produces feelings of threat and danger which get visualized in terms of some ultimate disaster like death. One gets the impression of a neat, tidy and well organized individual who attempts to run her life tightly and without spontaneity and enthusiasm. This inevitably results in considerable dissatisfaction, especially in her relationships with men. In this area her expectations of super performance of others as well as for herself makes it impossible to be content with a man who is never good enough for her. Here her demands for super performance from the men must leave her constantly frustrated.

Her description of herself as one who says, "I always have to be in complete control and I think I am just unable to have any fun," conveys the essence of her problem in that the need to control is what prevents her from being interesting and spontaneous. Her sexual activity must be equally restrained and the problem of having orgasm during intercourse is characteristic of such an individual who cannot relinquish control—a stage which is necessary for the development and production of orgasm in the female.

Her early history as presented in the case report does not give us sufficient data to understand the origin or development of this personality characteristic. However, her dominating and controlling mother must have had some influence and must have overpowered the easygoing father of whom the mother was very critical. The family atmosphere was probably one in which the mother was the strong, dominating figure who insisted on exceptional performances in all areas from her children as well as her husband. Nothing was ever good enough, clean enough, or sufficiently satisfactory to result in unqualified approval. The focus was on performance, not affection of which the less compulsive father may have been the major source. Probably his warmth and playful relationship with his children may have protected her from a more severe personality disorganization.

The obsessive-compulsive technique attempts through some fantasy or realistic device to maintain an illusion of having control over one's functioning. This is done through the elaborate device of avoiding commitments and decisions and never exposing oneself to the possibility of failure, thus avoiding the awareness of imperfection, fallibility, and humanness. Her fear of making a mistake is manifested in her need to keep lists to plan her daily activities and to carefully deliberate about any decisions so that it takes her hours to "buy a single skirt."

This need to be infallible and to avoid errors often requires verbal and magical rituals which are efforts at controlling one's universe. The variety of techniques which are designed to produce such fantasy control, however, results in increasing indecision, restriction of freedom, loss of energy, and a failure to succeed in enterprises because of an unwillingness to take risks and to allow enough spontaneity to enter one's living. This is precisely what has happened to Marion, who conveys the impression of caution, timidity, and indecisiveness. The overriding need to achieve some security and certainty requires that she abandon any spontaneity which involves uncertainties of outcome.

It is very important for the patient to understand the role of her obsessional patterns and her obsessional behavior, not because this makes for ultimate change but because it is the background if any change is to occur. The essential task in the therapy of the obsessive-compulsive disorders, or in dealing with the obsessional dynamisms in other personality disorders, is that of conveying insight and initiating learning and change without getting caught in the "obsessional tug-of-war." This pattern characterizes obsessional behavior and results in hostile and antagonistic exchanges with the therapist, as it does with others.

As with all neurotic difficulties, the therapeutic work lies in the identification, clarification, and, finally, alteration of the defensive patterns which maintain the neurosis. Such progress becomes possible when the patient's self-esteem or ego strength becomes sufficiently strengthened to withstand the major assaults against his defenses. While the problems that brought about the obsessional defenses are comparatively easy to uncover, the defensive structure which develops around these issues is most difficult to unravel. For example, Marion's need to give devotion and to "wait on men" does not imply a committed or affectionate relationship, but is most likely a reaction formation, which is a rationalized excuse for saying how hard she tries to become involved. It covers up and distracts from her more overriding tendency to put men at a distance and to alienate them in the long run.

It is paradoxical that in the attempts to clarify an obsessional's life the issues become more complicated and confused. Ordinarily, increasing one's knowledge of a particular problem helps to focus on the relevant components. In dealing with the obsessional, however, new issues and qualifications of the old ones tend to broaden the inquiry. It often appears as though the patient were deliberately confusing the situation by introducing new issues when there is real danger of clarifying something. This would undoubtedly occur as we attempt to explore her relationship with men and women and note her tendency to seek out "weak" men whom she could control but not respect. This dilemma would produce a barrage of self-righteous or indignant protestations which will need to be met firmly and clearly.

The additional factors which are introduced relate to acknowledging responsibility or failure in some activity. Before the patient is ready to accept an observation about some matter in which she played a responsible role, she will try to involve every possibility outside herself. Therefore, it looks as if she does this purposefully since these new factors often lead the investigation into a cul-de-sac from which no fruitful return is possible.

Treatment may be long lasting if one hopes to deal with the extensive personality structure. However, some of the symptoms can be alleviated fairly quickly and, in regard to this particular patient, the possibility of loosening her up by helping her abandon some of her absolutes and some of her guarantees in her living may add new dimension rather quickly. Consequently, my expectation would be that the treatment might last several years. Generally, the program for frequency depends upon the need. I have generally found it most useful to begin treatment with such patients at two times a week and then determine whether more time is necessary. Frequently, the two-times-a-week schedule turns out to be extremely useful since too frequent visits tend to have an effect opposite to what one hopes for in the therapeutic process. Increased dependency, the ritualization of the treatment process, and failure to allow the patient to make her own decisions because of the frequency of visits interfere with the ultimate resolution of this disorder. Therefore, a balance between seeing the patient often enough without excessive visits has to be arrived at. Too often in the past the severity of the disorder automatically was viewed as requiring greater frequency of visits. This often had the effect of stabilizing the illness and preventing any change. The routine four-hour-a-week schedule in the classical psychoanalytic therapeutic program was often counter-productive and inimical to the process of change. It was the unclear and unsophisticated application of the rigidities of classical psychoanalytic therapy that accounts for the enormous difficulties in treating this disorder.

It is clear that themes that become most significant in the

therapeutic process of this condition relate to the patient's needs to guarantee her living and to avoid all risks in her functioning. These themes will manifest themselves in every aspect of her living and will demand that she become a perfectionist with its inevitable consequences. The elements of the individual's need to know everything and so be in control, along with the righteousness that comes with the individual's requirements that she always be correct and virtuous, will become an issue in treatment with regard to her attitude towards others. This matter will become very relevant in her difficulties with her boy friends and her sexual interest in general. Each theme that is introduced into the therapy has to be viewed in terms of the role it plays in maintaining the obsessional structure of preventing the individual from going out of control.

The ultimate goal in therapy is to effect a change in the patient's living, not merely to induce insight. Insight is only the prelude to change; it provides the tools for the alteration in one's patterns of living. But the therapist must also assist the patient in utilizing his new understandings. This demands an approach which is less rigid and less tied-up in traditional methodology. The therapist must feel free to be of active assistance in the process. Obsessional patterns which are so heavily involved with ritualistic forms of behavior cannot be resolved by therapeutic measures which are just as overloaded with ritual. The therapist must be flexible enough to try novel approaches and techniques.

While it is generally agreed that the sex of the therapist is not a significant factor in the therapy of obsessionals, the age, experience, and background are quite relevant—and at times very significant. One factor is crucial: the therapist must not be too obsessional himself, or he will inevitably get caught in a *folie-à-deux* which can prolong therapy indefinitely—if it manages to survive at all. This factor is undoubtedly one of the major issues that prolong therapy in these disorders, as does any tendency to be passive and thereby to encourage the patient's indecisiveness. In this instance, the sex of the therapist seems immaterial since Marion has difficulties at all levels with males as well as females. Presumably her warmer relationship with a less compulsive father may allow for an earlier positive transference with a male therapist. But her disappointments, guilt, and feeling of unworthiness will ultimately involve transference problems whatever the sex of the therapist.

A therapist who cannot get unlocked from the patient's struggles to control because he himself must always be in control either traps his patient into passive compliance and endless analysis or drives him away early by stirring up a great deal of hostility. Under such circumstances, the patient and therapist may get into an obsessive bind in which the needs of each one may be satisfied at the high cost of permanent invalidism of the patient.

The process of change for the obsessional is viewed as a potential source of danger which may leave her vulnerable and uncertain; therefore she is reluctant to put new insights into action. It is not surprising that most of the obsessional's early attempts to move into new situations and relationships will be inclined to falter or fail. Since she has little confidence in her capacity to fulfill her extravagant expectations, she enters every new involvement with some apprehension and uneasiness. Thus her involvements are tentative and uncertain, a situation which prejudices the outcome in advance. She may abandon her efforts too early because she cannot see the project as being successful. If she continues the effort and completes it, she may feel that the situation did not yield so rich a reward as she expected from her new patterns of behavior. The new way of operating initially has more anxiety than the old, familiar way. Therefore, the therapist must be prepared for complaints and grievances about these experiments, which never come off to the full satisfaction of the patient.

The position the therapist must take in these early efforts is to convey the notion that there are no guarantees in living and that every new experience contains some risks—and may even turn out badly. While the therapist is trying to focus on the possible rewards and positive results of new adventures, he must avoid minimizing the risks or giving false guarantees of success. At times the therapist must make it clear that some risks must be taken and new behavior patterns must be tested for therapy to proceed. Obsessional ruminations and speculations produce no changes in outlook or in living; thus a patient must be actively encouraged and assisted in new ventures.

As the patient improves she must be able—through her growing confidence in the therapist and an expanding trust in her own capabilities—to accept the risks and consequences of her new behavioral patterns. She must be able to face the possibility of her worst fears being realized—that she might feel humiliated or look weak and impotent in her new ways of functioning. She must be willing to abandon complete control of a project and allow a situation to develop on its own, often with no certainty of the outcome. Giving up control does not mean becoming apathetic or withdrawing. It means a more realistic acceptance of the world as it is, as a place where one must accept uncertainties in living. The resolution of an obsessional disorder should produce a more mature, more decisive and accepting, and less driven human being—not an emotionless, placid philosopher. The process can be assisted most dramatically by a warm and interested therapist who can inspire in his patient an intellectual grasp of the neurotic issues as well as of the real issues and encourage acknowledgment of feelings in a direct and open way.

Ultimately, Marion will need to become increasingly involved and committed at the risk of being hurt before she can truly accept limitations in herself and others.

Treatment, while difficult, is very often successful. It results in a freer, less restricted, and less rigid individual who is no longer tied to "shoulds"—absolute and impossible demands. A capacity to accept the limitations of one's powers and to recognize the impossibility of overcoming certain existential uncertainties tends to enhance and stimulate activity in the areas of attainable goals. It is not wrong to strive for perfection or to attempt to encompass all that is knowable. It is not arrogant to defy and attempt to overcome the forces of nature, both inside and outside the individual. The danger and the disease rest on the absolute need to do so and the inability to compromise once we have discovered that the goal is impossible.

The unwillingness to do one's best because it is never perfect (and therefore not good enough) is a disease, while the recognition that one can do only that which one is capable of may stimulate the individual toward heroic efforts to fulfill all his capacities and potentialities. An unwillingness to enter the race because there is no guarantee of winning does not develop a champion but an obsessional neurotic. Only taking the risk of losing permits one to win. Only the readiness for defeat and failure allows an individual to perform in a manner which may ultimately prove successful. This is the difference between functioning at one's best and being driven to a kind of "perfection" which makes the individual avoid encounters and contests. Life is a series of risks, uncertainties, and gambles. There are no guarantees and no predictable consequences of our behavior. In the face of a consistency in regard to the universe's major laws, we confront numerous possibilities in regard to its minor principles. To function effectively and productively, we must be satisfied with being able to do the best we can—provided we exert the effort to do just that.

The obsessional demand for guarantees does not indicate a higher virtue or a more dedicated conviction; rather it shows an unwillingness to face life with all its possibilities. The existential dilemma which has confused our generation deals precisely with this matter. To be happy, one must risk unhappiness; to live fully, one must risk death and accept its ultimate decision.

7

Critical Comparison
The Case of Marion

HENRY GRAYSON, Ph.D.,
CLEMENS A. LOEW, Ph.D.,
and GLORIA HEIMAN LOEW, Ph.D.

We study the three therapists' approaches to working with Marion in order to look for essential ingredients, as well as differences in their theory and technique. However, even at first glance what stands out most glaringly is the extreme difference in the writing style of the three therapists. Further, the style of writing seems consistent with the therapy approach of the person writing.

On two ends of the continuum are Fensterheim with his behavioral approach and Kriegsfeld with his gestalt approach. Fensterheim's chapter is extremely well organized and systematic. So is the therapy he describes. Kriegsfeld's chapter is loose and associative—like free flowing fantasy. Much of his therapy is that way as well. Salzman, strangely—or unstrangely as the case may be—appears to be somewhere in the middle. All feel they will have reasonable success in their work with Marion.

Unanswered is the question: "What really makes for the

81

changes?" It is not clear whether the changes occur because of the method or technique, or whether they occur because of the congruency of the method with the personality of the therapist.

While it is certainly clear that we are reading about three different approaches to therapy, it is sometimes even more apparent that we are reading about three different men. Perhaps the therapeutic approach and the person are truly inseparable. We can hypothesize that each therapist was drawn to a style of therapy fitting his personality and thought style.

The one central thread running through all three approaches is the emphasis on risk taking in expressing, asserting and acting in new ways. All see Marion as rigid and constrained with a need to loosen. Fensterheim would have her engage in homework or try out different actions in the assertive training group. Salzman feels she would need to "be actively encouraged and assisted in new ventures." Kriegsfeld would encourage the new actions in the group setting.

All three approaches are similar, also, by what they omit. None gives consideration to biochemical causes of behavior such as nutritional or blood sugar imbalances. Either these are not considered important by the therapists, or else they may be ancillary to their understanding and treatment approaches. No importance is given to the place of constitutional temperament (except a mere mention by Fensterheim), nor to effects of early patterning. All do assume previous learning which will be dealt with in conscious behavioral ways. Fensterheim does consider a physical examination important and pharmacology is considered.

All the therapists imply that they give some attention to history, but differ in their formulations and in the use of these formulations. Diagnosis is of utmost importance for Fensterheim, for his whole treatment plan is directly related to his diagnosis. Thus, the traditional medical model of diagnosis and treatment are most akin to his behavioral approach. In order to obtain the closest definition of the problems and make a differential diagnosis, Fensterheim uses a number of tests and scales, as well as interviews. This approach is in direct contrast to the gestalt approach, where Kriegsfeld has no concern at all for diagnosis. In fact, his orientation would be anti-diagnostic, seeing the diagnostic interview as further perpetuation of Marion's problems. But while he has no concern for diagnosis as a basis for his treatment plan, he does have an implicit dynamic understanding of the patient's experience which echoes throughout. It takes little sophistication on the part of the reader to see the implications of his "Simple Simon Says" analogy.

In Salzman, diagnosis is also important, but one gets the impression that it is not nearly so important for him to be exact in his diagnosis as it is for Fensterheim. More important to Salzman is developing a dynamic understanding of the patient. Etiology is considered an important ingredient in developing this understanding, for the insight from this dynamic understanding will be shared with the patient as an essential part of his therapeutic method.

The role of the therapist will be quite different in each instance. Fensterheim sees himself as an "advanced thesis advisor." *Teacher* would be the other most appropriate word to describe his role function. The personality of the therapist does not appear to be of importance in that it was not mentioned in any way. One might conjecture, however, that to be an effective advisor and teacher, certain personality characteristics making possible a senior collaborative relationship would be necessary. In any case, the personality of the therapist is probably considered to be of least importance in the behavior therapy approach. Whether or not it is in fact of importance is a separate issue to be investigated.

Salzman sees his role as one who interprets dynamics to the

patient, who identifies defenses, clarifies, and encourages action. Contrary to what one would expect from a traditional psychoanalyst, little attention is given to transference. Instead of waiting for the transference to build and then making a precise interpretation at the right time, Salzman deals with interpreting themes presented in the light of his dynamic understanding. In contrast to Fensterheim, Salzman considers the personality of the therapist crucial: "the therapist must not be too obsessional himself, or . . ." He must also "be flexible enough to try novel approaches and techniques." This implies that one further role the therapist plays is that of a model, which will inspire and challenge the patient to be flexible also. And further, he thinks that Marion could be best helped by a "warm and interested therapist."

Kriegsfeld also gives importance to the personality of the therapist, but in a different way from Salzman. Here it is important to provide a new interpersonal involvement for Marion. He needs to be able to give attention to his own feelings and show them with her. One major role the gestaltist plays is that of a director. He asks her to play different parts of herself, different parts of her dreams, much like a form of psychodrama; but the patient plays all the parts—even of inanimate objects in dreams.

Insight seems to play the biggest role in the analytic therapy of Salzman. He stresses that insight alone does not bring changes, but that it does provide "tools for the alteration in one's patterns of living." The only attention to insight given by Fensterheim is to state that he would take occasional times for the patient to discuss with him insights which might emerge. He apparently would not see them as a central part of behavioral technique. The same is apparently true for Kriegsfeld's gestalt. He does not make interpretations or provide insights. However, insight seems to be a result of communication between the split parts of one's self.

None of the three therapists stresses a topological model in unconscious, preconscious and conscious, though an emphasis on the role of unconsciousness is implicit in varying degrees in each. It seems most clearly implicit, strangely enough, in Kriegsfeld's gestalt therapy. The body language, the split parts, and the introjects all imply unconscious determinates. With Salzman, the UCS is more apparent in his understanding of the defenses and the defensive structure of Marion.

In Fensterheim, the role of a concept of an unconscious dimension is most apparent in his frequent use of psychological tests and scales. This use presupposes, in the authors' view, that the tests will reveal some information which the patient is not able to report consciously.

From the different approaches and the different personalities carrying them out, one could expect that Marion would experience each therapist quite differently. She would probably respect her advisor-teacher behaviorist, would feel comfortable around him, and consider him as an ally in her efforts to change. The relationship would not be long lasting (about 10 months) and Marion probably would not involve herself deeply emotionally with Dr. Fensterheim. He would, no doubt, be experienced as a friendly consultant, to whom she could return for further consultation when necessary. His systematic approach would be comforting to her, and the quickly observable progress would be rewarding and kindle faith in herself and her advisor-teacher.

The involvement with analyst Salzman would by its nature be a more involved one. The duration would be about two times a week for several years. Marion would probably see him as warm and interested, though sometimes threatening when he would confront her defenses. He, too, would be an ally, but also one who is not known personally to her. His flexibility would both frighten and inspire her in her attempt to become more spontaneous.

It would seem that Kriegsfeld would be most frightening to her at first, because he immediately is unsupportive to her defensive obsessional patterns. He would gradually become a trusted teacher, friend, human being, and play director to her. Since he would share more of his human feelings and other reactions with her, she would be frightened—then intrigued. She would probably soon begin to experience him as someone she wishes to model her expressions after. While Kriegsfeld does not specify the estimated length of his therapy with Marion, it would probably be somewhere in between the brief 10 months of Fensterheim and the several years of Salzman—e.g., two to three years. Here the behavior therapy would be the least expensive, gestalt next, with psychoanalysis being the most expensive by far.

Is there a difference in the expected outcome by the different therapists? Fensterheim is most pessimistic—but quickly points out that it is realism. It certainly seems that he would expect as much symptomatic change as any of the therapists. The difference lies in the longevity. He would expect Marion's symptoms to re-emerge each time there is a stressful situation for her. Kriegsfeld would not proclaim a cure either, but would see a growth process as having started. Salzman, would apparently expect an internal structural change, which, when successful, would not bring the person back for more. Perhaps all are saying that it takes a lot of time and a lot of work for lasting changes to occur in an obsessive-compulsive character type in a deeply integrated way, whether in large or small doses.

Part III
SCHIZOID PERSONALITY
THE CASE OF ALLEN

Allen is stocky, of medium height, and dresses totally in black except for a white shirt. His black suit, black tie, black shoes and socks, and black eyeglasses give the impression of a serious, odd, and very tense young man. He arrived 15 minutes early for the interview and paced back and forth in the waiting room until his session began.

During the interview he spoke about his difficulties in an uninvolved and impersonal manner. He is obviously very bright but limited in the scope of his abilities. Allen indicated that he is 22 years old and is studying ancient history on a masters level. He is an only child and lives at home with his mother and father.

Allen complained that he feels hopeless and cut off, that he worries excessively, and that his parents have been pushing him to make friends. He himself does not think socializing is very important. However, he plans to attend an out-of-town university to study for his doctorate and for this reason feels worried about his difficulty in making friends. He finds books and writing more rewarding and important than socializing. "If you want to know the truth, people generally bore me," he said.

One specific and seemingly isolated problem for the past 10 years is that he gets very anxious when mother goes out of the house. He also panics when she is late. When asked how long it takes before he panics, he said, "Fifteen minutes." He also insists that his mother be home when he returns from school. Mother accuses him of being very demanding, and Allen admits it, but he says that he can't help it. This problem seems inconsistent with the general unrelated and interpersonally detached life which he described.

During his studies he has developed specialized interest in particular aspects of ancient history. He seemed quite advanced relative to his academic standing. Although Allen scored very high on all college and graduate entrance exams, his grades were below his ability. Allen attributed this to his procrastination and his perfectionistic attitude. The interest in historical events developed late in high school. At that time he also began the hobby of collecting maps for guided tours of old and ancient cities. For example, he had in his collection a tourist's guide to Paris in the 1880's. At night, while trying to go to sleep, he would sometimes fantasize going by himself on a selected tour of a city in the past. These trips fascinated him.

Allen sees himself as puritanical and introverted. "I never really had any friends. . . . I prefer to discuss political and social issues. . . ." He has no interest in girls. He says, "I deliberately do things that are different. I project an odd image . . . but I think it's an advantage really. . . . I want to maintain my own individuality. . . ." He feels more comfortable by himself. As an example of his introversion, he indicated that he is uncomfortable eating with his parents and that he prefers to eat alone.

In describing mother, he says he likes her and that most people do. She is emotional, excitable, and overly solicitous. He is particularly bothered because she is unreliable. She also worries about him a great deal and identifies with his troubles. She has always "counted" his academic accomplishments; he felt pushed by her, but seldom encouraged. He did not feel close to her.

He sees his father as generous. However, he becomes easily frustrated, screams, and uses "nasty" language when angry. He is touchy, but less excitable than mother. Like mother he is never satisfied with anything. Allen could talk to his father, but it was clear that he spoke *at* his father rather than *to* his father.

For fun, Allen reads, takes long walks, and looks for interesting architecture. He prefers a quiet uneventful life. Prior to his seeking treatment on this occasion, he had a dream in which he was lost in a bus or subway. He also remembered another dream he had several weeks ago: There was an atomic war. He was alone on a beautiful island in the Caribbean. Bombs were going off all over. People, seen in the distance, were scared and confused. However, his primary concern in the dream was that he should get home. He was afraid that he might not.

8

Behavior Therapy Approach
The Case of Allen

LEO J. REYNA, Ph.D.

*What Aspects of the Patient Would You Expect
to Focus On? In What Order?*

The first step would be to define the objectives or goals of
therapy by requesting Allen to describe and identify what
behaviors and emotional reactions he wants to strengthen
and those which he seeks to weaken or eliminate. Statements
like "feeling hopeless and cut-off," "worry excessively," "very
demanding," "procrastinating," "perfectionistic," "puritanical," and "introverted" would be examined for the purpose
of delineating their behavioral referents, the settings and
situations for these behaviors, and the consequences of these
behaviors.

Allen's own priorities would play the major part in *what*
behaviors and emotional reactions are selected for change.
The *order* in which the behaviors are changed would in part
depend on Allen's priorities and in part depend on the joint
review by the therapist and Allen as to which of the priority
behaviors (indicated by Allen) are most likely to respond to
change immediately. The basis for the latter consideration
would be that reinforcement for immediate change will effect
the whole change enterprise, including establishing the thera-

91

pist as a positive reinforcer and reinforcing the client for engaging in behaviors for producing change.

The therapist would expect that Allen would rank "making friends" considerably higher in priority than the elimination of his uneasiness and irritable behavior in respect to instances when he doesn't find his mother at home or she is late returning home. At first glance, a behavior therapist might begin by reducing the panic behaviors, since these have so consistently responded to behavioral techniques. However, in Allen's case, the therapist would be well advised to stay with Allen's priorities, since modification of panic behaviors could jeopardize continuation in therapy for increasing his social behavior repertoire. It is evident that, after 10 years of these panic behaviors, neither Allen nor his parents sought treatment. Both Allen and his parents did seek to expand Allen's interpersonal contacts. It is conceivable that if Allen learned to be comfortable when returning home in the absence of his mother, this would strengthen "loner" behaviors and put off indefinitely Allen's interest in making friends. In other words, if Allen, in going off to graduate school, could go to classes and return to his living quarters without experiencing stress, he could go through graduate school securing the bulk of his positive reinforcements from academic behaviors and continue to escape and avoid contact with other people.

Special attention would be given to establishing explicitly and frankly why Allen is seeking treatment, particularly the whole issue of whether he is visiting the therapist because of pressure from his parents versus the extent to which he himself feels that it is appropriate. Furthermore, in exploring this issue, the therapist would assist Allen in making explicit the immediate and long-term consequences of behaviors presently in his repertoire, as well as those for behaviors absent from his repertoire.

A major goal of therapy, from the descriptive material provided to each therapist, would be to increase the frequency
and quality (i.e., behaviors mutually reinforcing to Allen and
to others) of interpersonal contacts. In this respect, the behaviors (and accompanying feelings) constituting "making
friends" would be examined in detail with Allen, since this
is an area of concern for both his parents and himself. In the
devil's advocate format, the therapist would challenge Allen
as to why he should view making friends as necessary. If his
response is "because my parents want me to," the therapist
would challenge the validity of the parents' position. The
therapist would continue to develop this line of exploration
until Allen would unequivocally assert that, aside from his
parents' preference, he could fully identify the positive consequences for increasing his interpersonal contacts and the aversive consequences of his present social behavior deficits. In
the course of this analysis, the therapist, if Allen did not do
so, would examine, for example, what Allen wanted to do
after earning the Ph.D. degree, pointing out that unless he
had an independent income he would have to earn his living,
and that a frequency of interpersonal behaviors greater than
that which he presently emits would be necessary, as well as
desirable.

Once "having friends" has been clearly established as a goal
of therapy, the therapist would begin by asking Allen how he
would arrive at a determination, at some future date, that he
was making friends or that he had friends. The therapist
would explain that there must be some objective criteria for
establishing whether progress in achieving the goals of therapy was being made. If Allen encounters some difficulty in
identifying the behaviors that constitute "making friends" or
"having friends," the therapist would ask Allen to review his
own life and cite any instances, past or present, of "friends"
and "making friends" of his own. If Allen indicated having

acquaintances only, rather than friends, the therapist would ask Allen to discriminate the behaviors (his own and others') that distinguish acquaintances from friends. The therapist would also ask Allen to identify some individual or individuals whom he knows and does not dislike, and who, in Allen's judgment, have friends and make friends. In the course of this discussion, the therapist would help Allen develop the distinction between interpersonal contacts and "having friends." The outcome of this discourse would establish that the more immediate behavioral objective of therapy would be to increase the frequency and quality of interpersonal behaviors (social skills) which are prerequisite behaviors for "having friends." The therapist's next concern would be with delineating with Allen the situational and behavioral elements of social skills.

As always in the pursuit of this kind of analysis, the therapist would request Allen to provide a list of the behavioral components of social skills; whatever necessary, Allen would be asked to cite the specific behaviors of a model whom he regards as socially skillful. (The therapist constantly makes apparent in this way that "problems" are made up of behaviors [and their associated feelings], that these behaviors are under stimulus control, and that these behaviors are maintained by their consequences.) In due course, Allen, with various prompts and cues from the therapist when needed, will come up with a list containing some of the following behavioral components of social skills:

—nodding to and greeting people whom you have met before;

—knowing the names of people to whom you have been introduced or whose names are generally well known to your associates;

—using the names of people when addressing them;

—saying something nice when you admire or are pleased with something that others are wearing, are doing, or have done or said;

—responding to questions by others in a way that "tells" them something about yourself;

—holding an extended conversation (beyond the two or three minutes required to exchange greetings and status of the weather);

—listening to (and recalling) what concerns and interests others;

—smiling and other facial expressions appropriate to the occasion;

—accepting invitations to join others for a meal, movies, a play, a rap session, etc.;

—reducing frequency of avoiding situations that your peers are likely to gather for;

—being able to emit the above behaviors with males and females.

(It should be noted that the frequencies and the consequences of the above can readily be measured and recorded by Allen with practice.)

Initial priority would be towards increasing the frequency of these behaviors, where appropriate, with parents, and subsequently with males and then females. Allen would then be asked, once he has made some male friends (i e , one or more males with whom he can engage in extended conversations, and from time to time eat with and join them in various other activities) , "what other activities (besides eating, etc.) is a friend likely to invite you to join him in or at least inqure about your interest in?" In this way, the area of interacting with females is introduced—as an inevitable outcome of making young adult male friends. Although some time would be spent on Allen's past and present interpersonal behaviors with girls, the therapeutic program would not explicitly seek to alter his current repertoire in this area, but rather move first in those situations (male friends) in which he felt less uncomfortable (i.e., those with a lower frequency of escape and avoidance of people behaviors).

The Treatment Program

Assuming that Allen will be leaving for graduate school in six to nine months, I would view the therapeutic program as proceeding simultaneously along several lines: individual sessions with Allen once a week, family sessions with Allen and both parents once a week, and group sessions with Allen plus five or six other young adults balanced for male-female composition. Family sessions would begin after five or six individual sessions, and group sessions after a similar number of family sessions. The order of the last two formats might be reversed, depending on which is least aversive for Allen.

If expense is a consideration, only two or three nonconsecutive family sessions would be held in place of individual sessions. If only one session per week was financially possible, five to six bi-weekly group sessions would be substituted for individual sessions. Under these circumstances, the main purpose of these group sessions would be to allow simultaneous observation by the therapist and Allen of Allen's interpersonal behaviors.

The Objectives and Content of Individual Sessions

Each individual session (45-50 minutes) is divided into three parts. During part one, Allen would be expected to report on progress made on the previous behavioral tasks assigned ("homework"). Allen has been requested to keep a diary containing the daily frequency for each behavior currently being changed. The therapist would praise Allen for any evidence of progress, and examine with Allen the basis for lack of progress, if any. In those instances where Allen has been unable to make any change, other behaviors may be substituted which Allen feels he could emit, and/or the therapist would examine with Allen what the particular circumstances might be that prevented the behaviors. Where appropriate, the therapist would model behaviors, and then request Allen to change roles and rehearse the behaviors in the consulting room.

In his daily log, Allen has also been requested to identify any new instances of emotional distress, their attendant behaviors, and the consequences of these behaviors. These new instances are categorized within the existing framework of behaviors to be changed, or are separately categorized (e.g., Allen reports that he sometimes wonders whether he is a homosexual).

The second part of the session is devoted to how wanted behaviors can be further increased in frequency, including what might be the most amenable environments and settings for performing the desired behavior. (Throughout these sessions the rationale made explicit to Allen is that by emitting wanted and expected behaviors Allen, at the minimum, will less likely be subjected to the aversive consequences of his behavioral deficits, and that, optimally, the new behaviors will lead to positive reactions from his social environment— other people.) If under the most favorable circumstances Allen insists that he cannot (because of strong conditioned emotional reflexes—respondents) emit a particular approximation of the target behavior, the procedure of systematic desensitization would be employed to attenuate these disruptive respondents.

In part three of the session, a clear statement of the intersession "homework" is drawn up and recorded by Allen in his notebook. Special attention during this portion of the session is given to examining the possible settings that would be suitable for meeting people and would provide appropriate and supportive consequences for the new behaviors. Accordingly, Allen would be encouraged to attend academic and community events such as lectures and meetings dealing with areas of his strongest interest (ancient history, architecture, archaeology.) Initially, the behavioral requirements in these instances would be minimal, consisting of attending social gatherings which he previously avoided. In the beginning, arriving at the very start of these meetings and leaving immediately on their conclusion would fulfill the initial behavioral objective. Subsequently, arriving a few minutes before the start of the meeting and/or leaving a few minutes following the meeting would be planned. Allen would also be encouraged to get a part-time job (and/or volunteer work) so that he might not only pay a nominal portion (e.g., $5.00 per session) of the cost of therapy, but, more importantly, increase the opportunity for discovering and correcting social skills behaviors. To further increase opportunities for interpersonal contacts, his abilities in respect to athletic skills would be explored and, where feasible, some regular participation would be encouraged (e.g., joining a nature club for walking and hiking excursions). At a later stage, Allen would be encouraged to enroll for dance lessons at the local "Y," or to take private social dancing lessons, prior to a "Y-type" group format.

The relationship of the therapist to Allen would at various points be described as teacher and model. In addition, the therapist functions in a neutral role, but only in respect to not providing positive reinforcement for unwanted behaviors and statements, nor making critical, judgmental comments about these behaviors and statements.

The importance of the therapist changes during the course of therapy. In the early stages, the therapist's skill in proceeding at a rate that is tolerable to Allen is critical. How readily Allen is able to feel comfortable with the therapist will importantly influence subsequent phases during which behavioral analyses and programs of change are increasingly shifted to Allen. Ideally, in the last phases of therapy, the therapist becomes a consultant to Allen's proposals for behavior change. The ability of the therapist, however, to function as a consultant is importantly determined at an earlier stage when approximations of consultant behaviors by the therapist have proved to be reinforcing to Allen.

The Objectives and Content of Family Therapy Sessions

A major objective of these sessions is to *briefly* clarify for Allen and his parents the nature of the interactions, past and present, that have established and maintained the behaviors which Allen and his parents are now interested in changing. Apart from Allen's problems, these sessions would also address themselves to enhancing the quality of interrelationships among the three family members, but here also the emphasis would be on ultimately optimizing Allen's behavior repertoire. The inefficient dependency behaviors that each member of the family has acquired and reinforced in each other would constitute an important focus of these sessions.

These discussions and explorations would proceed in a context of "no fault" responsibility, explicating how the process of mutual interreinforcement established and maintained the current unwanted interactions. Since eating with people is a common setting for social contact, the family would be encouraged to strengthen this behavior. More appropriate ways of reinforcing each other would be delineated.

In general, these sessions would provide an opportunity and a forum for members of the family to talk to each other and plan alterations in the family setting and behaviors in a rational and constructive context with the guidance of the therapist. The quality of the marriage would not be an explicit focus of these sessions. Main attention would be on making each member of the family less aversive to each other and having them more frequently reinforce each other for wanted behaviors.

The Objectives and Content of Group Therapy Sessions

These sessions would be viewed as a controlled environment in which Allen could strengthen some of his social skills behavior. The group would be composed of five or six additional members, ranging in age from 18 to 30, and nearly equally divided in sex. The general format for the conduct of the group, held over a two-hour period, would include each member briefly (10 minutes each) describing the behaviors that he or she is working on and reporting progress and difficulties encountered. Following this, the therapist would then invite suggestions by the members of the group as to how other members might proceed to overcome difficulties or how they might accelerate progress already made. These suggestions would be monitored by the therapist. In doing so, the therapist would not adopt a position of directly asserting, "Yes, that's right," or "No, that won't work," but would ask both the proposers and the proposee to develop implications of the suggestion until it became apparent if, and what, alternative courses would appear more feasible.

At a later point, individual members would be asked to "perform" at greater lengths. For example, Allen would be requested to offer descriptions (discriminations) about others' social behaviors, and vice versa.

What Changes Would You Expect as a Result of Successful Treatment?

The behavior changes that would be expected in Allen as a result of successful treatment have already been referred to in the previous discussion on goals of therapy described under "behavioral components of social skills." Furthermore, it would be expected that these behavioral changes be emitted by Allen with one or more other individuals with whom he regularly associates (seeks them out and responds to their invitations) and rewardingly interacts (with associated feelings of pleasure and comfort). In addition, in respect to people with whom he does not regularly associate, he should be able to emit, as a minimum, the social behaviors one would expect under the label of common courtesy, e.g., initiates and returns greetings accompanied by appropriate facial and bodily movements (smiling, looking into the face of the person, etc.), responds to and asks questions, listens and attends to speakers when a member of a small group, etc. Along with these behaviors, there would be associated changes in other behaviors and reactions, for example, reduced frequencies in statements like "people generally bore me," and in emotional reactions (feelings) of discomfort in the presence of other people.

How Long Would Treatment Last, and How Is the Decision for Termination Determined?

The decision for termination would be entertained and made when the above minimal behavioral changes have occurred. Since Allen is planning to leave town to attend graduate school, the length of treatment and the decision for termination are both influenced by this aspect. On the assumption that Allen will obtain his master's degree in June or August, treatment would last for the six to nine months remaining prior to his leaving for graduate school. Considering Allen's long history of social skills deficit, Allen could profit from further treatment; but the therapist would advise Allen to wait and seek further treatment if and when new goals (motivation) for therapy emerge. If this should occur, the therapist would expect it to happen in connection with Allen's wanting to go beyond just a "friendly" relationship with a female, and being concerned about sexual behaviors and about seeking a "closer" relationship. If Allen meets the "right" girl and his life circumstances (school or job, housing, commuting, financial status, etc.) are not overly aversive, he is not likely to seek further treatment. I would expect, however, that the probability of his both meeting the "right" girl and having a favorable set of life circumstances would be low.

What is Your Explanation and Formulation of the Development of This Problem?

The explanation of the *development* of Allen's main problem, i.e., the lack of prerequisite social skills for making friends and fear of separation (from familiar and reinforcing stimuli), would not be a focus of primary concern during therapy. Of major concern, rather, would be the identification of his current behavior repertoire and the variables currently controlling it. Examination of historical data would vary according to how readily current variables controlling Allen's behavior repertoire could be identified. In this respect, his low frequency of social interaction would be viewed as being established in the first instance through negative reinforcement, i.e., escape and avoidance behaviors maintained through the termination of aversive events (contact with other people). Furthermore, many years of escape and avoidance of other people have prevented opoortunities for the reinforcement (positive) of pro-social behaviors. While not necessarily relevant to the program of therapy, the question can be asked as to how other people became aversive events to Allen? Speculation on this issue must certainly include the data Allen has provided that his mother is "overly solicitous," "worries about him a great deal," and that he is "pushed by her." Furthermore, his father is "never satisfied with anything." These statements (which could be further corroborated in family therapy sessions) would suggest a family environment in which Allen was urged and most powerfully reinforced for nonsocial behaviors (learning to speak the language, to walk, to manipulate objects, and learning academic subjects), while providing few opportunities (indeed, often preventing or warning against situations) in which Allen would interact with his peers. This state of affairs creates social behavior deficitis.

Nevertheless, from time to time Allen is confronted by social situations for which he has no behavioral skills (repertoire). As a consequence, he may be punished by peers and reprimanded by other adults (e.g., teachers). Other people now become aversive events, and their aversiveness is likely to be augumented by parental action (protective and solicitous) that further reduces occasions for social contact for Allen. For example, the aversiveness of other people is not likely to be diminished by parental statements like, "What did those nasty boys do to you," "Never mind about that terrible teacher," "Don't let those people bother you; the important thin gis to concentrate on doing your school work well."

In short, an early history of an environment which does not provide explicit reinforcement opportunities for "making friends" results in behavior deficits which from time to time result in punishment by other people, including isolation, removal of attention, even ridicule and physical blows. While the ensuing avoidance and escape behaviors (from other people) prevent subsequent opportunities for the development of social skills, Allen finds his own behavior aversive and escapes from his own behavior when, in response to renewed contemporary pressure to socialize, we note an increased frequency in verbal statements like, "I deliberately do things that are different," and "If you want to know the truth, people generally bore me."

It is likely that Allen's panic when his mother is not around and his insistence that she be at home when he returns from school constitute a threat of loss of a positive reinforcer, i.e., over the years Allen has been counseled and comforted, possibly on a daily basis, by his mother when he returned from school and reported episodes of ridicule, rejection, teasing, etc. by classmates, school staff, neighborhood children and adults. Furthermore, Allen's "demanding behavior" with respect to his mother need not be viewed as "inconsistent" with "the generally unrelated and interpersonally detached life which he describes," since the latter (nondemanding) behaviors are emitted in the presence of other people who have not reinforced demanding behavior (indeed, they very likely punished it), and towards whom "generally unrelated and interpersonally detached life" behaviors are escape and avoidance repertoires.

More on Explanation and Formulation of the Development of Allen's Problem

Some additional behaviors that are likely to have a similar developmental history include "procrastinating" and "perfectionistic" behaviors. These behaviors would also be viewed as escape and avoidance behaviors established by the critical, "pushing," and "never satisfied" parental reactions to Allen's performing behaviors. These particular behaviors—compulsive attending to details and/or the postonement of tasks—are likely to prove even more disadvantageous for Allen in doctoral work where greater monitoring of individual efforts by an authority figure usually prevails.

As for Allen's "puritanical" behaviors, the therapist as always would request Allen to identify the behaviors that have led to this self-description. If Allen, for example, reports that he does not engage in masturbatory behavior or does so accompanied by strong aversive feelings, regards sexual organs and sexual acts as dirty, and feels that intercourse should be reserved for marriage, and even then only for purposes of reproduction, then these statements would, in the first instance, be regarded as having been molded and reinforced by his parents, and probably more so by his mother. These behaviors and emotional reactions have not undergone modification because of lack of social contact with peers and a low frequency of other social contacts. Reading of sex literature that might alter these reactions has very likely been avoided, partly because of a history of punishment of this behavior.

Allen says, "I deliberately do things that are different. I project an odd image . . . but I think it's an advantage really . . . I want to maintain my own individuality . . ." Again, these remarks would be viewed as statements made by Allen to escape the aversiveness of his own behavior deficitis. Finding that he does things (differently) for which he has been ridiculed or criticized, he escapes from this aversive state of affairs by praising himself (self reinforcement) for his accomplishments by declaring, "I deliberately do things that are different," etc. Sometime during the course of therapy, a behavioral analysis leading to the distinguishing features of individuality and oddity behaviors would take place between Allen and the therapist.

We are also told that "Allen . . . dresses totally in black except for a white shirt," and that ". . . (he) give(s) the impression of a serious, odd, and very tense young man." when he arrived for the interview. Here, because of his lack of social, face-to-face verbal skills, social reinforcement through that channel has been absent; but it is clear that his manner of dress does evoke social attention, and may also be reinforced by evoking negative comments from his parents, towards whom he may not be able to emit hostile *verbal* statements.

Are the Explanation and Formulation of the Problem Important for Treatment?

For the therapist, the major importance of the above explanation of Allen's social behavior repertoire lies in his constant vigilance and concern for the appearance of fine-grain behavior deficits and their remedy. Accordingly, Allen would be expected, because of the strong emotional respondents that accompany escape and unsuccessful avoidance behaviors, to initially be at a loss not only as to *what* to talk about in holding a conversation but also in respect to the act of talking itself. Thus, the *rate* and *timing* of his verbal and nonverbal behaviors, as well as the *form* of their delivery, are likely to require modification.

Is it Important for the Patient to Have this Knowledge? How Much and at What Point in Therapy?

The therapist's speculations in respect to the development of Allen's behaviors would certainly be made explicit to Allen. However, the therapist would identify the explanation as speculative—a "good guess" that can nevertheless serve as a frame of reference to emphasize how conditioning and reinforcement variables could have led to his current emotional reactions and operant behaviors, or to their absence. The therapist would explain to Allen that with a greater expenditure of time many more of the details and subtleties of the development of his problem behaviors could with more certainty be delineated, but that the technology of change need not depend on this time-consuming process. The therapist would present to Allen his brief formulation of the development of his problem behaviors fairly early in the treatment program (after three to five sessions), and on a continuing basis briefly throughout treatment when new behaviors (problematic) appear and/or progress in changing behaviors has come to a temporary halt. Furthermore, Allen would increasingly be called upon to offer his analysis of his own behaviors. To assist him in this latter enterprise, the therapist would refer Allen to various textbooks and reprints from journal articles.

9

Gestalt Approach
The Case of Allen

MIRIAM POLSTER, Ph.D.

In the gestalt view, a person grows through contacting what he finds novel and fascinating, either within himself or in the people and events that populate his environment. Selectively, based on the awareness of his own needs, he is free either to assimilate or to reject these experiences of novelty and otherness and to change thereby. Should he assimilate something new, he takes it in as relevant—applicable or useful to him in some way. If he rejects a new experience, he is deciding that it does not apply to him and that he either cannot or will not consider it relevant to him as he presently experiences himself. Either way, growth is inevitable whether it is through adopting a new attitude, a new behavior, a new way of doing a familiar and routine action, or whether it comes from discovering in himself a new strength to resist and avoid an experience he appraises as noxious or undesirable.

Ideally, contact is the end result of unprejudiced awareness. It is not forced, as when a person is consciously "studying," for example, but rather comes from the arousal which is the natural consequence of an unimpeded awareness of something-of-interest. Something interests him—something he becomes newly aware of about himself—a new skill, increased sexual feelings, anger at someone he used to think was infallible. Or perhaps it is something in his environment that draws him—contradictions between what people say and what they do, new shapeliness in girls he went to school with for years. So he learns, not effortfully, but gracefully and easily accumulating knowledge because he is drawn to it by its freshness and he is excited at the perception of uniqueness and change. From this native attraction he takes in new information which alters his perception of himself, of the people about him, and of his world. Gradually, softly, he is changed by this fluid process, this slow explosion into maturity.

Allen is a young man afraid of change; so he remains a young man afraid to make contact. He wants to live in a world which he long ago outgrew, the world of the bright, pre-pubertal schoolboy whose momma waits for him when he comes home from class. He does not want to perceive anything which might excite him to behave differently from his accustomed patterns. Since his world is an illusion, Allen is impelled to maintain the fiction by remaining unaware of changes in himself and those around him. The avoidance of contact in this manner is what we in gestalt therapy call *confluence*. Confluence is the attempt to remain out of contact through the perception of *no* change, *no* difference, *no* excitement. So Allen perceives other people as "boring," uninteresting, not worthwhile, and settles instead for the predictable "excitement" of architectural walks and visits to imaginary historical sites. He does not want to perceive discriminately anything that might disturb his carefully nurtured lack of focus. He does not wish to see anything that might require attention, scrutiny, manipulation, enjoyment, intimacy, because these are contactful actions and might draw from him responses that he is afraid to try. Allen's need to remain in confluence with the world-as-it-used-to-be has diminished his responsiveness to the world-as-it-is.

At best, confluence is an uneasy and unstable state, constantly threatening to come apart at the seams. For Allen, confluence has become a pervasive screen through which he must filter *all* of his present experiences. This means that he cannot question the authority of his parents, he cannot recognize changes in himself, he cannot permit other people to become fascinating. Allen is locked into unity with his past and he cannot question or amend the past on the basis of his experience in the present. He makes no differentiation between himself and authoritative sources—that is, he is confluent with them—by wiping out his own individuality.

Obviously, what Allen has achieved is a makeshift arrangement. His friendless, sexless existence relies on things remaining as they were. His imminent departure for graduate school involves a change in his style of living that even he cannot blot out. He is impelled to look for help. I would expect Allen to have some rather modest goals for his therapy. He is not interested in radical change. He might want to feel less uncomfortable, for example, when talking to other people and he might also want to be able to make one or two friends with whom he could go to lectures or talk over some aspects of his graduate studies.

But Allen is afraid of people. He does not say this, he says rather that he finds them "boring" and that reading is more rewarding for him than socializing. That *some* people are boring is, sadly, true. But that Allen finds *all* people boring suggests to me that he is interrupting himself from becoming interested in or attracted by some lively stimulating person—that Allen does not want to make contact. Allen may be uneasy when around people because he suspects that he might *all too readily* find someone fascinating and he is afraid of the consequences of such an interaction. But what this avoidance does is not only to keep Allen out of contact with some other person's potentiality for being interesting but also, even more

importantly, to keep him out of contact with his own feelings
—in this case, fright, which he misreads and calls boredom.
It is his unawareness of himself that we would begin to work
with here. Allen does not discriminate between his evaluations
and opinions, on the one hand, and his feelings on the other.
The awareness of his own internal state which could help to
orient Allen in making this discrimination has been numbed
for so long that it has become chronically unavailable to him.
The trouble with setting up a pattern of avoidance of contact
is, of course, that it becomes habitual and continues its inter-
ference from a covert, but no less potent, position.

So I might ask Allen to talk to me about some of the people
he knows and how he finds them boring. I would not be
surprised to find that Allen has not observed anyone very
closely—too risky—and so he would not be able to describe
them with much clarity or detail. I would observe Allen as he
describes these people and try to alert him to any signs of
feeling that might surface. So, he talks about a professor whose
dull material and droning voice bore him and I notice a concurrent tightening in his jaw, or clenching of his fist, or a
scowl. I would draw this behavior to his attention and ask him
to intensify and exaggerate this gesture as he continues. As
this developed, I would expect to find some arousal of feeling
and I would ask Allen what he feels as he scowlingly talks
about Professor Jones. He says he feels "annoyed and disgusted." This is already different from feeling bored.

I ask Allen to imagine Professor Jones sitting in the vacant
chair in my office and to tell *him* what he finds annoying and
disgusting about him. "Well, Professor, you mumble . . . and
you don't look at people . . . and even when I raise my hand
to make a comment or to ask you something, since you don't
look up anyhow, you don't even see me and I either have to
cough or interrupt or something or you'll go right on like
nothing happened. And I'm disgusted with the way you have

your course organized. There is no logical order in what you're presenting and I sometimes have the feeling that you just pick up your notes and your lecture that day depends on what you've happened to pick up!" When I ask Allen now what he is feeling, he is clearer: 'I really am *mad!* I'd like to shake that old goat and tell him that he has no right to teach, that he's only there because he has tenure and they *can't* fire him!"

I would point out to Allen that what started out as boredom with Professor Jones turned out to be a much juicier feeling and that although Allen's *judgment* was that Professor Jones is boring, his *feeling* about Professor Jones is anger. With Professor Jones still in the vacant chair, we would then move back into Allen's expressing his anger directly by shouting or gesticulating. With this we would have completed a unit of workthrough from awareness of body sensation and gesture to arousal and awareness of feeling and finally to the expression of feeling.

Another possibility exists concerning Allen's opinion that other people are boring. It could be that Allen is afraid that *he* is the one who is boring and projects this unwelcome suspicion onto other people instead of looking at his own dullness. He says, "I project an odd image . . . but I think it's an advantage really . . ." I question whether Allen settles for being regarded as odd and a loner because he doesn't know how to be anything else and is afraid to try.

One of my goals in my work with Allen would be to help him discover how his awareness can be a fertile and mobilizing influence. If he can be more aware of himself and what goes on around him, he stands a better chance of becoming both interested and interesting. So I might work with Allen by asking what he is aware of as he sits with me in my office. Is he aware of the physical surroundings, does he sense something about himself, does he hear noises outside the room, is he aware of me or do random images and thoughts play hide and seek in his mind? I have no prejudice about any of these possibilities being more worthwhile than any other. My purposes here would be served by any of them. First, I want simply to arouse Allen's awareness, to get his motor running. I want him to sharpen up his ability to see, to hear, to sense, and to welcome these as valuable and rewarding activities. Secondly, I want to familiarize Allen with the buildup of excitement that results from increased awareness and to give him practice in becoming comfortable with it.

If he focuses, let us say, on my office, the way it is decorated, the objects in it, what books I have, and so on, I would ask him to tell me what he can deduce about me from these artifacts. It would be like his visits to ancient cities, but here his skill in imaginatively reconstructing historical cities would be used to understand something in the present and to connect him with a very important part of that present scene— me! This puts to use what might by some other therapies be dismissed as merely resistant behavior. Allen's preoccupation with historical events serves him mostly for deflective purposes; that is, it keeps him from full engagement with events that are occurring in his immediate psychological and geographical neighborhood. But Allen is an intelligent young man, and his resistance is not merely a deadening influence to be removed and discarded. In his deflective movement away from the present into an overriding interest in the past, Allen has acquired skills that could be useful to him in many interactions. There is a very important component of creativity at the core of his resistant behavior. It is this creative part that I want to maintain and to teach Allen how to redirect so that the same keen insight that he applies to understanding ancient cultures can be used to understand contemporaries. So I do not ask Allen to abandon these activities but I try to bring them right into our present interaction.

If Allen becomes aware of something about himself, I would ask him to attend to it quietly for a moment and to observe what happens as he does this. Here again, my basic goal is to restore to Allen a healthy respect for his own experience as a source of information and orientation. Right now he appears to believe that most valuable information comes from outside himself, either from his parents or from other scholarly and reliable authorities. He needs to be reintroduced to the palpable reality of his own senses as another way of knowing. After a moment of attending to his own sensations, then, Allen may say that he feels nervous. I ask how he knows this. He says, "Well, my heart is pounding harder than usual, my breathing is very quick and not very deep and my hands are sweating slightly." I direct him then to try to speak with each of the parts of his nervousness, perhaps to ask each of them what they are nervous about and what they fear might happen here.

Before he does this, I would explain to him what I thought might be gained by this technique. I feel very strongly that right from the beginning Allen needs to know what I have in mind when I ask him to do something. He has to know that he can question me about doing something and that he can refuse to do it if he finds it too threatening or too painful. Furthermore, his refusal to do something need not stop us; we would work then with his objection to the suggested behavior and probably find an entry into the ways he keeps himself from doing something that he may know intellectually might be in his best interest. I am not interested in Allen's docilely obeying my suggestions. First of all, I want him as an ally, not a subservient. Secondly, I am not interested in perpetuating his tendency to swallow whole—to introject—what other people tell him. Allen doesn't need more of this, rather he needs some experience in questioning and possibly even casting out some of the alien standards and values that he has introjected. So I would explain to him how I have found that very often these seemingly superficial bodily signs of nervousness or anxiety have something to add to his experience if he can give them a voice. Each of them can contribute its own perspective to the vague state that he labels anxiety and, by making the experience more specific, can make his anxiety more understandable.

So Allen inquires of his heart what it fears will happen and what it is beating so wildly about and his heart replies, "I'm afraid she won't like me if she really gets to know me," or his breathing might say, "I'm afraid to say anything, I don't know what will come out and I'm afraid to say anything that will sound dumb." Or his sweaty palms: "If she could touch me she would find me unpleasant and she wouldn't like being close to me . . . and besides I don't want to get close enough to touch her either!"

I ask Allen to continue to speak for one of these parts of himself and try again to zero in on the specific fears, what's his objection to saying something dumb in my presence, what might I do? "Well," he says, "I'm afraid you might laugh at me or dismiss me as somebody too stupid to work with." I ask, "What then, after I laugh?" And he says, "It would hurt me, and I would probably get very quiet and not know what to say." "What could we do then, you and I?" I ask. "Well, you might tell me that people very often feel awkward and foolish and that as I get more comfortable with you I'll be able to talk more smoothly and won't worry so much about what I'm saying . . . and I probably won't worry so much about what you're thinking, either!" At which point he and I would probably laugh. He has worked through his "catastrophic expectation" and found that he will come out of it alive. The antidote to his expectation of disaster if he says something dumb is the knowledge that there is always a next moment, and a next. He will not drop off the end of the earth because he says something he thinks is dumb; we will go on. And what he thinks is a dumb remark may turn out to be the opening to coming closer to me, and finding me not such a scary bitch, after all, surely an important step.

What if he speaks to his heart, or his breath, or his hands and they come up with no response, they remain mute? I can ask him simply to have each one of them, in turn, say something like. "I don't want to tell you anything," or some similar phrase that could highlight the fact that there is information there but some part of him is unwilling to give it. This makes him take ownership of his own unwillingness to respond, which would otherwise remain an alienated and disowned part of himself. When Allen can recognize that it is okay for him to say no, he has less need to play dumb or to go blank as a disguised way of avoiding something he doesn't want to do. Highlighting his recalcitrance and making him articulate it is the first step in his knowing that he can say "no" to someone else as well. Until Allen knows that he can refuse another person's request or demand, he will, *of necessity*, limit the way he relates to them. He is compelled to say "no" to the relationship *in toto* because he doesn't know that he could say "no" selectively.

If his awareness of the moment in my office deals with something outside the room, I would ask him to close his eyes and go on a fantasy trip outside. I expect that, in this fantasy, we would find some clue to what he seeks to avoid or what he feels is lacking in the present experience. He may go home in his fantasy, perhaps into his own room. Here we could work with what it is like for him to come into a new situation and start fresh, with no background material and no familiar supports and resources. He may recognize that he needs to explain himself more, and his fantasy trip to his room could be one way to tell me what he wants me to know about him, what he finds essential to his well being. We could move into his estimating what he might find familiar and supportive in his present environment.

Suppose in his fantasy trip home he visualizes a scene with his father and mother. I ask him to bring them, in fantasy, to my office and to imagine what they might say if they were with us. I might ask him to speak to them about his reaction to being in my office, to tell them what he may be reluctant to tell me. He speaks for his parents and in doing this he verbalizes some of their apprehension—and his own—over his adequacy at making friends and their worry about what kind of a future he will have after they are gone.

I suspect that a good part of Allen's insistence on staying at the immature age level he has chosen may be a way of denying the eventual death of his parents, something he both wants and dreads. The rich mix of love/hate/anger that he is sitting on and which limits his own humanity may begin to surface here. So I ask him to carry on a dialogue with his parents (he can play their parts or I could) and reply to their statements from his own viewpoint, perhaps asking them why they hadn't helped him learn how to make friends when he was younger, reminding them how their repeated and vocal doubts about his ability to make friends color every interaction he has and make him stiff and self-conscious just when he wants most to be able to be relaxed. He may begin to voice some of his more assertive needs and tell his parents in this imaginary dialogue that if they didn't help him learn when he was younger he's going to have to do this on his own from now on and not depend on them.

Perhaps his fantasy trip outside the room, instead of taking him home, takes him on one of his visits to a city in the past, like his bedtime fantasies. Here I ask him to take *me* along as an imaginary companion and to comment on what we see and to tell me what is noteworthy and exciting about it. I expect that there would be very little excitement in Allen's manner and I work here on his ability to communicate some of his pleasure in this ancient city by using colorful and descriptive language, or by voice or gesture. Using what he. had been saying, I direct him then to try different ways of talking to me about our tour of this city. I might ask him to talk to me as if he were a native of the city and I a foreign visitor, or as if he were a professional tour guide, or a parent taking a child sightseeing. I might ask him to talk like a circus barker, or a conspirator planning something that he did not want to be overheard. We would work on bringing animation into his tone and manner and excitement into his language.

We could also work with his breathing. Breathing is a basic support system and enhances the ability to permit excitement and to accommodate to the increased mobilization of energy that results. In an individual whose tolerance of excitement is limited, we find that in order to restrict the feared experience of excitement he constricts his breathing and this converts the intolerable excitement into anxiety. So in order for Allen to learn how to tolerate a buildup in excitement he has to learn how to allow an expansion in his breathing and how to experience this expansion as supportive rather than threatening. Allen is afraid of his own capacity to expand, to grow beyond his accustomed limits. He associates expansion more with its explosive and dramatic consequences and needs to learn the steady expansion-and-contraction rhythm of breathing.

In working this way with Allen's breathing, we begin to make inroads into one of his characteristic ways of limiting himself. Possibly he breathes only shallowly much of the time and never really experiences what it is like to have a vital source of energy within himself that he can *himself* replenish whenever he needs to—by breathing. Perhaps he stiffens up against feeling empty and never fully expels the stale air he has previously inhaled but not fully used up. So I direct Allen to use up all the air he has inhaled by just making some sound to utilize the air and fully empty himself before he takes another breath. When he does this he will experience a *surge* to breathing which is a powerful movement, almost like surfacing after a dive, and will sense firsthand how assertive the support system of his body can be if he does not interfere with it. We would work further with the rhythm of his breath, on whether Allen stays longer on the moment after he has inhaled or whether he pauses more after the exhale. I expect that Allen stays longer after exhale, a behavior that often goes along with feelings of inadequacy and insecurity, and I would direct him to try to lengthen his pause on the other pole as well, more to experience a sense of fullness and energy.

From this we could progress into how he integrates his breathing into the production of his voice. Does he exhale, for example, before he begins to speak—a common occurrence —and then his voice comes out unsupported, with none of the breath it requires for vibrancy and timbre? Or does he use his breath in short phrases, almost like little gasps, with no staying power to sustain him so that his voice dwindles off before he has actually finished what he wanted to say? When he continues to talk to me about these ancient cities, I would direct him to focus on the end of the sentence and make sure that it does not fade away, or to use his breath to add inflection to his otherwise monotonous delivery. I would ask him to speak breathlessly or perhaps to singsong or to speak with the accent of the country we are visiting in this fantasy trip.

All of these activities would be devoted to enabling Allen to discover ways of allowing his own excitement to build and to enter into his own expressiveness. He needs to be able to ride this excitement into making contact with me now—and with other people later. We might even further expand his fantasies to include meeting the inhabitants of these cities and talking to them about what it was like to live in those times. Allen could fantasy telling them of "future" developments and try to surprise and delight them, again to emphasize the fascination some people might feel with his own era.

In these early stages of our work together I would want Allen to know that I am available as an ally, companion, supporter, and dispassionate observer in his efforts at exploring and becoming aware of himself. He has to become willing to do risky things in my presence instead of settling for the safe but static routines he has grown used to. Allen is fascinated by facts, but he is worried about people. So, one risk he would have to take would be to recognize that he might want to be interesting. I pointed out how his estimate of other people as "boring" might be the other side of a concern about his own boringness. He has to learn how to be interesting, and how to deal with his own delight when someone finds him interesting. Naturally, we start with his ability to be interesting with me. So I might ask him to tell me stories about surprising or humorous things he has unearthed in his historical studies, strange facts about people and events which pique his curiosity and about which he might have some speculations. We could fantasize about certain periods in history when we might have liked to live and about which of the personages of that time we might have chosen as companions. I might ask him to play some historical character whom he finds intriguing and imagine him on a visit to my office. How might an Etruscan shepherd talk to me? Or Seneca? Or Nero? I might ask Allen to make up a course in history which could be taught by outstanding teachers of that period. I might spend some time asking him to place me in an historical time and setting and explain why he has chosen that particular period and place. He could do this with his parents, too, looking at them freshly and with a more mature perspective.

Another risk that Allen might take would be to fantasize eating dinner with his parents instead of by himself and investigate what about that makes him uncomfortable. Does the scene around the family table become an arena where mother and father pick on him and from which he feels he can't escape? Or do they express their chronic worries so that he feels oppressed and lifeless? We enact just such an occasion, with me playing one of the parents and Allen playing himself. After a while we shift parts, with Allen playing mother or father and me playing Allen. I might show a nimbleness in changing the subject to something I would like to talk about or a stubborn refusal to allow them to pick on me that would surprise Allen. We might then shift roles again, and allow Allen to try out his own inventiveness. Allen has settled for controlling himself, keeping himself muzzled, because he doesn't experience much likelihood of success in controlling others. When a person does to himself what he would like to do to someone else, we call this *retroflection*. The effect to undo the retroflective cycle is to look for the appropriate "other"—that other individual *from* whom we might want some response that instead we provide for ourselves, as in self-pity or self-praise, or *towards* whom we might want to behave in a way that we now behave towards ourselves, as in self-accusation or self-love. We could keep practicing until Allen feels fairly comfortable at directing the conversation where he wants it and is able, perhaps, to control and silence his parents occasionally.

We could make up a fantasy dinner party, with people Allen might like to talk to as he was eating. What people would he like to invite to dinner? How would I be as a dinner companion? I could ask Allen to bring some food along and schedule our appointment at mealtime so that we eat together. What does he become aware of then? I would not be surprised to find that Allen is embarrassed about any behavior he might consider "animalistic," such as eating. He describes himself as "puritanical." When we eat together he may become uneasily aware of how much noise he makes while eating or he may feel that he looks funny or disgusting as he chews his food. I direct him, instead of trying to minimize these actions, to exaggerate them, to chew harder, to make more noise, to smack his lips when something tastes good and to bite more energetically into something solid or crusty. I may give him a homework assignment to do between our sessions; he is to choose his food for these qualities once or twice before our next meeting. He could have a lamb chop and eat it directly from the bone instead of cutting it with knife and fork. Or a hard piece of cheese, which he is to chew completely into liquid form before he swallows it. I expect this would be hard for him because he would like to do to his food what he does with the rest of his experience—swallow it down as quickly, effortlessly and with as little attention as he can. I want to interrupt this routine and encourage Allen to discover that eating and biting and chewing can be fun and that he is losing something when he merely gulps things down.

This activity may lead to working with what other things Allen finds disgusting, so that he avoids contact with them by quickly taking them in and then putting them out of his mind. This is characteristic of Allen's style. His life has become a chronic deflection, an attempt to water down or minimize any experience which might possibly become exciting. Deflection is the commitment to keep oneself off-target, never quite in focus, of saying the trite, conventionally established formula. Allen uses up a great deal of his energy in activities which will have exactly *no* impact because they are concerned with topics and people that are immutable, fixed, embedded in the past. When confronted with the present, where anything just *might* happen, Allen withdraws, becomes colorless, bored, and prefers to be studiously alone. In working with Allen's disgust, I am seeking to awaken live, vigorous feelings, feelings with surge and power.

There are two important directions that I see in working with Allen's disgust. First, there is the opportunity for Allen to explore healthy disgust: disgust as what he may have swallowed or taken in from people as he was growing up but which may no longer be serving his needs at all. On the contrary, keeping down this unwanted crud from the past may be siphoning-off a lot of otherwise productive energy. Disgust at an outmoded value or belief is the preamble to vomiting it back up and is the beginning step in bringing back Allen's own gulped-down protest, which I suspect he swallowed at the same time. So we go back to the family dinner table fantasy with Allen speaking for his parents and discover there that Allen has introjected more there than the food; he has taken in his mother's concern about him and has accepted without question that he is vaguely unsatisfactory and disappointing, a source of trouble, worry, and not much pleasure. On this basic theme Allen has gone on to embroider his own suspicions that he is probably a pain in the neck to other people as well and so he feels pretty hopeless about himself.

But in the imaginary dialogue with his mother at the dinner table, I hear a small voice of protest, some refusal to accept meekly such a bleak self-portrait; we have the beginning of a polar struggle between Allen's introjected negative self-evaluation and his growing sense of protest. I ask him to play both parts of the polarity, the devaluator and the small voice that feels he may not be that bad. At the beginning, most of the vigor would probably be on the negative side as Allen speaks more energetically, with better language and stronger voice and gesture. This is Allen's topdog, the dominant faction in the conflict, the part of himself with which he is most consciously identified. His expression of self-worth, on the other hand, might have little spirit, sound rather cowed and submissive. I bring this to Allen's attention, pointing out that this side, his underdog, doesn't come off very assertive, and that he appears to be doing a rather ineffectual job of standing up for himself. I ask Allen how he might bolster up this part of the polar struggle, and he says, "Well, maybe if I stood up and walked around while I was talking, I always think better when I walk." So I tell him to do this and to add anything he can by way of support when he plays the underdog. I may even suggest that he use his breath more fully when he speaks, or that he point accusingly at the chair where he sits when he speaks for the critical "topdog." As the topdog answers with the force he has had from the beginning, the underdog also speaks with increasing passion and energy, and we finally arrive at the point where both factions within Allen have equal vigor and recognize that they must work *jointly* towards a new alignment of forces where each of them has a voice but where neither is the controlling tyrant. Allen needs to retain some ability to criticize himself, to evaluate his own efforts—this is one way in which retroflection serves a useful function—but this must be tempered by his own equally accurate sense of what he can do well and has accomplished successfully.

Allen's need to deal with feelings of disgust may also be a deflection from some of his anxiety about his own sexuality. He makes no mention of sexual feelings and says that he has no interest in girls. Again, I recall that he calls himself "puritanical." His intolerance of his own sexuality is really another aspect of his general reluctance to tolerate a buildup in feelings of his own excitement. His unwillingness to deal with his own arousability deprives him of the chance to learn how to move with his own excitement, to use it as a mobilizing and orienting force which can connect him with others, instead of isolating him.

Let us suppose that our earlier work with awareness had extended Allen enough so that he could permit and recognize some buildup in sexual sensations. I might be interested in discovering what would occur at bedtime, perhaps, if Allen were not to engage in his customary historical tours and instead merely pay attention to what he is thinking or feeling before falling asleep. So I give him this direction as a homework assignment, something related to our therapy that he can do outside of our regularly scheduled sessions. I expect that these sensations would still reflect Allen's tendency to deflect from powerful sensation, to diminish his experience. So these sensations would be both mild and innocuous, limited to non-erogenous body parts. In working here with Allen, I would shuttle back and forth between intensifying his awareness of his own physical sensations as he remembers what he felt like at bedtime and also mobilizing and teaching him how to make good use of what support is available to him. First of all, as he permits his sensations to grow, he can breathe regularly and nourishingly. This simple function is the most basic support that Allen can provide for himself. In breathing well, he is accommodating himself to the full growth of sensation. In doing this, Allen may become aware that he is feeling anxious and scared. Breathing allows him finally to know this and permit it, instead of numbing himself against it as he has habitually done previously. My presence in this action is important; Allen is raiding enemy territory, unexplored and unclaimed areas of his own experience, and he needs to know that I provide some additional support by staying close to his experience, by moving slowly into scanning what is taking place within him, and by responding sensitively to his tempo, respecting his need to slow down at frightening times and his ability to move faster when he can. I can let him know that what, at this moment, *he* finds only scary, *I* can find exciting. It does not scare me and perhaps need not scare him, either.

Whatever sensations Allen becomes aware of, then, we work with his learning how to make room for them, either by allowing them to grow in intensity or scope. A shivering or tingling in the small of his back might grow until he feels he is trembling deeply and from this awareness he might move into the thought that he would like to hold and be held by someone.

"Whom would you like to be holding you?" I ask, and then direct him to fantasize this, thereby moving the increased sensation into contact, albeit a fantasized one, of a less disguised erotic nature than Allen has so far permitted himself. Or, the growth of the sensation could turn out to take the form of including more and more of his body, so that what started out as a tingle in his back moves into a tingle or shivering all over. Or it might flit around, appearing now in one part of his body, now in another; his hands start to tingle, or his cheeks or his chest.

I ask him to speak for these vibrating parts of himself and have them talk of how they feel, what they want to do, and even to have them dialogue with each other. Perhaps the tingling hands say, "I would like to touch you, cheeks, or you, chest, but I feel that it's wrong to touch myself except when I'm drying myself after a bath, or cutting my nails, or something like that!" Allen might speak for his cheeks or chest and talk of their wish to be touched softly and their regret that foreign prohibitions prevent Allen even from providing some of this affectionate care for himself. This is the beginning of Allen's eventual movement into expressing and seeking satisfaction for his own sexuality. First he can recognize what he feels sexually, then he can learn how to make room for these sensations and not numb himself. Finally he can learn that these sensations move towards expression and need not be stifled and disowned. If we start with Allen's giving himself permission to stroke his own cheeks or to rest his hands gently against his own trembling chest, we can move on to acknowledgment that perhaps there are other parts of his body that want contact also.

When we reach this point, Allen might be ready to invent bedtime fantasies that could enhance his sexuality and lead to his learning to masturbate satisfyingly. There is very little information given about Allen's sexual activity, but it sounds

sparse. Before he can express himself sexually with anyone
else, he has to be able to be comfortable with his sexual feelings. It may well be that Allen has to know how to make love
to himself as a way of getting ready to be able to make love
to someone else. Certainly, he must get beyond the pre-pubertal, sexless role he appears to be stuck with at the moment
and which is so anachronistic for his 22 years. We could work
with some of the sexual fantasies that Allen invents, intensifying his experience of them. What does he conjure up to
arouse himself, is he active or passive in these fantasies, does
he vary his fantasies or do they become routine and mechanical? I would work towards Allen wanting intimacy, not just
proximity. So I would ask him to pay attention to details of
his fantasy, to notice or to imagine things about his love-part-
ner that he finds particularly appealing, to try to add another
sense, imagining perhaps what this person might smell like or
what her voice might sound like or what she would be like
when she walked, anything that would add dimension to his
fantasy. I would move on from this fantasied interaction and
ask Allen to pay attention to the people he meets outside of
therapy and see whom he finds appealing and what it is he
finds attractive about these people. I would explore with him
what he imagines he might be like if he, too, possessed these
desirable qualities. How would his life be different if he could
smile radiantly or talk easily or make jokes or play the guitar
or be sensitive to the feelings of other people or dance well . . .?
As Allen explores the possibility of being like these people,
he is beginning to explore ways in which he might be easily
social and friendly and he may even begin to acknowledge that
he might want to be like them instead of wanting to maintain
what he calls, "my own individuality."

Allen is also rich in dream activity and this would be a
vital part of our work together. We would begin with the two
dreams he has already reported and there would undoubtedly

be more dreams as our work progressed. Since our basic method would be similar with subsequent dreams, a detailed description of the dream workthrough with the two given in the history will serve as illustration.

In the gestalt approach to dreamwork, we take each part of the dream as a possible statement by the dreamer about himself or as a way of his trying to make contact with some important aspect of his existence. We do not view the dream as a disguised message, but rather as a creative effort where the dreamer is giving us as rich a picture of himself as he can. So I would ask Allen to enact each part of the dream, to play the bus or the subway. There would be important differences between these two vehicles, by the way; some of the most obvious are that a subway runs on tracks while maintaining its connection to an external source of power while the bus at least has an independent and self-contained engine. I suspect this metaphor would reflect Allen's sense of his own ability to function autonomously.

Allen begins by saying, "I am a subway. I travel underground and only a rumble every now and then gives anything away on the surface that I am moving around down here. People up there on the street don't even know how active and busy I am. I just follow my tracks around from one part of the city to another, doing what I'm supposed to do, carrying people around to places that they want to go, with no argument or deviation from my fixed route . . ." We start to investigate how closely this assumed role of the subway fits his actual existence; in what way does the life he is leading conform to his portrayal of the subway? Suppose he says that he doesn't like people to pay too much attention to him, he doesn't like them to know what's going on down inside. "What's your objection to having somebody know how you feel?" I might ask. He might answer that it has been his experience that "If someone knows what you are thinking or feeling, they will holler at

you or get mad and you will wind up feeling lost and alone."
I point out to him that when he says "you" it sounds like he
really means himself, "me." When he says yes, that *was* what
he meant, I suggest that he play Allen-lost-and-alone-on-the-
subway, really dramatizing his feeling of being trapped on this
vehicle, moving forward to he-knows-not-where. Here is our
opportunity to work with his feelings of fright at moving
ahead, not knowing what lies in store, into an uncertain future and feeling unsupported and tenuous about this movement. He does not even experience the movement as his own,
he is not walking, after all, but rather being carried along as
a passenger on a vehicle that propels him towards some unknown destination. We begin a dialogue between Allen-as-
subway and Allen-as-passenger, articulating his subterranean
desire to move on, to keep going (to go away to school, perhaps to grow up?) and the power that this force has. Allen-as-
passenger, on the other hand, is afraid of the unpredictable.
Allen can also play the unknown destination, the strange subway stop, vague, shadowy and far away from home. As he
enacts each of these dream parts, he is pushing out his accustomed sense of self, his contact-boundaries, those self-imposed
limits of experience which he deems acceptable primarily because they are familiar and impose no demands for new behavior. But Allen may be saying in his dream that he is ready
to explore moving beyond these comfortable but rigid boundaries. These limits are Allen's personal Maginot Line, dug in,
deeply entrenched, but hopelessly outmoded and actually dys-
functional.

The second dream that Allen reports is even more rich in
detail and in possibilities for workthrough. Again I begin by
asking Allen to play various parts of his dream. He chooses to
start with the ominous upheaval which serves as a threatening
background for the entire dream, the atomic war. Allen speaks
as the atomic war: "I'm really a powerful and threatening

force in Allen's life. I make great changes for him, I disrupt his peaceful routine and I really shake him up. I'm the product of tremendous scientific progress but I also have a destructive capacity that most people can only guess at . . . nobody can really comprehend the damage that I can cause. I drop my bombs, first one here and then one there!"

I ask Allen what he feels and he replies that he feels scared and helpless. This sounds more like a bombing victim rather than the powerful bomb itself, and I point this out to Allen. He agrees, observing that he does feel like a victim in some ways. I direct him to play the victim, then, to cower in his chair, perhaps, to hunch down as if he were under attack. I ask him how he feels doing this and he says it reminds him of how he used to hide as a child when someone was trying to get him to do something he didn't want to do. "What is it right now that you don't feel like doing?" I ask. He may answer, after thinking this over for a moment, "Well, you know, I'm really not all that excited about going away to graduate school. I mean, I'm going to have to leave my family and I've got my things all arranged the way I like them now and I'm not sure what it will be like at graduate school." I ask him to fantasize his arrival at school, what he thinks might happen, what he might do? Bit by bit he imagines what he might encounter at school and I bring him into touch with the possibilities for his own action by asking him to imagine what he could do under the various conditions he is apprehensive about. He can see that much of what will happen to him at graduate school will continue to be under his own control, and that he is not merely the impotent victim who cannot act in his own behalf. He has choice and judgment, both of which he has used before and both of which can serve him well now, too.

Perhaps Allen next chooses to play one of the atomic bombs that are dropping all around in the dream. Sooner or later I might even suggest that he do this by way of bringing him

closer to acknowledging the explosiveness in himself and helping him move past being afraid of it into coming into contact
with some of his own useful and restorative energy. I direct
him to play a personal bomb, some explosive or loaded possibility in his own life. Softly he says, "I'm Allen's anger . . .
I'm angry at my mother for never leaving me alone, for worrying about me, for making such a big deal about my problems that I don't even want to talk them over with her. She's
always pushing me, nagging at me, picking on me, hovering
over me . . . she's suffocating me! What's more . . . I'm mad at
my father, too. He gets just as upset as she does and I wind up
with nobody to talk to . . . nobody stays calm enough to help
me talk out my troubles and so I just have to bottle them up
over and over and over again until I feel like I'm going to
explode!"

At this point I would want to know what physical sensations
Allen is aware of. I would expect that he might be holding
his breath, clenching his fists and, in general, doing everything
he could to water down and control his own angry feelings.
If Allen were himself not aware of these manifestations, I
would point them out to him and direct him to attend to them
more closely. What might happen, I would ask, if he were to
breathe more fully and to use this breath to express—in
sound, not necessarily in words—his feelings towards his parents? Could he roar, growl, scream, whine? Could he bring his
clenched fists into this expression in some way, by pounding
the arms of the chair, perhaps, or shaking his fists as he makes
the vocal noise? His anger, as he keeps it impacted in him,
requires so much energy to keep it under control that it is no
wonder that he has none left over to use for making contact
with other people. He is afraid to express his anger against his
own parents but until he can do so now—and probably many
more times in future therapy sessions—even in fantasy, he cannot risk contact with anyone else for fear that the rage he is

holding back will interfere in this new relationship. So he *will* not find anyone arousing since arousal is the very emotion he dares not permit. People *must* appear boring to him until he has completed the workthrough of his anger against his parents.

Our work with him playing the bombs would, I suspect, begin to uncover the hidden side of his close attachment to his home and his parents; that there *are* times when he wishes he could make them disappear, almost like a bomb wiping them out. Behind every expressed fear there is always the unexpressed wish that the feared event would occur. Behind Allen's fear that he might never be able to get back home, that he would get lost, is the wish that he could get lost—that he could leave home and never find his way back. At the moment he sees this as a highly charged possibility, but in less dramatic form this is a move towards independence. Perls often defined growing up as the progression from environmental support to self-support. By envisioning this as a damaging and explosive process, Allen immobilizes himself from moving in this direction. So Allen might explore, in fantasy, what it could be like never to have to come home again, never to report to and depend on his parents. What might he be like if he were to determine his own life style, how might he want to live, and how might he achieve this without wiping his parents out?

Perhaps next Allen would move on and play the beautiful island: "I am a lush, peaceful haven in the middle of a warm sea. I have green trees and fragrant flowers and fruits on me. People come to me looking for rest and peace and I warm them with my sun." Once again I would ask Allen how *he* is like the tropical island, if there is anything that applies to his own experience of himself. He might reply, "Well, I'm smart, I know a lot of things that I could tell people and keep them amused and delighted. I don't make a lot of demands on most people, I'm easy to be with because I leave people alone. I like things to be peaceful and serene." I might remind him that in his dream this island was under attack and ask how he wars against these beautiful qualities in himself, how he keeps them under attack. We can also explore how he is an island, separate and isolated from the others, and how he maintains this condition. What are the advantages of being an island? The sense of self-determination, perhaps, not having to accommodate himself to anyone else, a sense of one's own limits and not worrying about excessive ambitions or needs beyond these narrow limits. We could move then into some of the disadvantages of being an island, feeling small, maybe, and inadequate to tolerate very much action, people or traffic, populated sparsely and then only with a small and largely transient population, a lovely place to visit, possibly, but not really home.

This is how Allen would work through the dream, playing each part of it, playing also the people in the dream, seen in the distance, scared and confused. Allen could engage in a dialogue between individuals that he might be able to fantasize visually and himself. How would he address them? Would he ask some for help? Would he comfort some, argue with some, form a friendly alliance with still others? All of these are avenues whereby Allen can meet himself and come to better terms with those alienated pieces of himself.

The work with Allen—assuming that his therapy would not be interrupted by his leaving to go to graduate school—would extend over a considerable length of time, two or three years. Ideally, we should meet during Allen's early period of adjustment at graduate school to deal with the specific difficulties as he encounters them. He needs the opportunity to try out the new patterns of behavior while he still has the support of the therapeutic relationship with me. Throughout the course of our work together, the emphasis would be on present experience, bringing Allen's narrative about his outside experiences to life right in the therapy session in some of the ways that I have described. In this way we could focus repeatedly on how Allen keeps himself from engaging fully in his current interactions. When Allen is able to meet contemporary situations with some sense of his own choice of action, when he can experience being with people whom he actively chooses for friends, instead of remaining bogged down in his love/hate relationship with his parents, when he no longer finds all people boring and could manage and enjoy some of his own animation and excitement, then I would begin to consider that Allen was ready to terminate therapy.

In writing this, I have been uneasily aware that it has been like speculating about what might have happened if Lincoln had never been elected president. There are so many directions that therapy *can* take that speculations about what one *might* do are valuable primarily as statements about the essence of the therapeutic methodology. I have tried here to convey some of the basic principles of gestalt therapy and some sense of the scope of therapeutic possibilities that these principles permit and encourage in both practitioner and patient.

10

Psychoanalytic Approach
The Case of Allen

PAUL STARK, Ph.D.

The case offered here is a bare outline, enough to raise many questions, scarcely sufficient to answer any. Perhaps a good way to begin would be for me to share the thoughts, questions and hypotheses that occur to me as I read the material. It would be helpful to move back and forth between the case presentation and my comments as you read them.

Allen dresses totally in black except for a white shirt—what can this mean? He wants to be seen, but so do people who wear reds and purples, flowing hair and bare feet. Black—sad, serious, depressed . . . menacing? The "blackshirts," the gangster . . . dark glasses that prevent eye-contact . . . a wall to contain him, to shut out the intruder. The Priest, the Minister, the Rabbi also wear black. Has this person renounced pleasure? He paces nervously . . . the wall shakes.

He presents himself for help, but speaks of himself in an impersonal manner. He studies ancient history. He wants to know himself, but he dare not get too close. An only child— is the family too close for comfort?

He feels helpless and cut off. This is understandable because he lives behind a wall. Nevertheless, he is agitated and not resigned or apathetic. This is a good sign and indicates that he is still struggling. This paragraph reveals the intensity of his ambivalence, his active struggle with his fear. His parents want him to socialize. His own wish is partially denied. Nevertheless, he chooses an out-of-town university and in this way indicates his desire for outward movement. What about the parents who push him to make friends? Do they really want this . . . if so, how can we understand his isolation? We know the mother of the phobic child is ambivalent about separation and communicates double binding messages which tie the child to her. Is this the case here? He says, "Do you want to know the truth?" Of course, I want to know the truth. When you ask me that, I get ready for the lie. . . . "People generally bore me." This translates freely into "people are intensely interesting to me, but contact with them raises such anxiety and fear in me that I must turn away. I describe the exhaustion caused by this constant conflict as boredom."

He panics when mother is out of sight. Panic, the impulse to flee in face of danger, is the obverse of attack. Does this mean that when mother is not present the latent hatred for her threatens to erupt and he fears for her life? The interviewer does not elaborate on the nature of the panic. I would like to know what he consciously fears. Mother may also stand as a barrier between him and self-destruction. Would he harm himself without her presence? When asked how long it takes before he panics, he says, "Fifteen minutes." There goes 15 minutes again. He arrived 15 minutes early for the interview and paced back and forth in the waiting room before the session began. Does this mean that when he is 15 minutes early, I am 15 minutes late? And is this a clue to the nature and intensity of the initial transference? Mother accuses him of being very demanding, yet she acquiesces. Is she saying, "I do this because you need me to. If not for you, I would be free. I wish you would not cling to me." The reverse may well be true. Allen protects his mother's phobic lifestyle. Unfortunately, we know practically nothing about her. I would like to hear specific dialogue around this issue. The interviewer says that this problem seems inconsistent with the patient's general unrelated and detached lifestyle. It is an article of my faith that nothing is unrelated. Imagine a person grasping a source of live current. The compulsive muscular contraction binds him to the source of his pain and paralysis. Allen's panic in relationship to his mother can be compared to this situation. He tries not to notice, but he will remain paralyzed until the current connecting them is cut.

During his studies, he has developed specialized interests in particular aspects of ancient history. I wish I knew what particular aspects. Does this represent a beginning delusion? Or alternatively, is this evidence of his ability to sublimate and use constructively his pathological situation? This would be very important to know. Could it be that the interviewer did not ask? If so, what was happening in this interview? Was the interviewer intimidated by this formidable patient? Was he antagonized or bored . . . did the patient's double messages vis-à-vis interpersonal contact create anxiety and withdrawal in the interviewer? Was there a subtle sadism in the patient's manner, an anal-retentive withdrawal which led the interviewer to withdraw in turn? Certainly, I feel teased at this point.

Procrastination and perfectionistic attitudes—anal character traits predominate. He is interested in particular (peculiar?) aspects of (his) ancient history and he wants a guided tour. This is a good sign. He knows he must discover his ancient history, old experiences cut off by repression waiting to be recalled, recognized and made known to his present self. At the same time, these imaginary trips bind the anxiety generated by his sexual curiosity. His fascination with these tours protects him from looking at nearer and closer things. What were the sleeping arrangements in this boy's home? How free or secret were sexuality and bodily display? And what are his masturbation fantasies? Has masturbation been totally suppressed? He calls himself puritanical, the black is a clerical black. He also says he is introverted—yes, but not introspective. He really does not examine himself, he externalizes. He must remain isolated to maintain his sense of self. The wall holds him together as much as it shuts others out.

He has no interest in girls. That, of course, is to be expected with so much repression of affect and impulse. He has little energy to contact others and heterosexual involvement would be particularly dangerous, threatening an eruption of feelings, inviting merging and dissolution of his ego. He is uncomfortable eating with his parents and prefers to eat alone. When we eat, we destroy. The cannibalistic anxieties of early infancy persist. Do sexual tensions and oedipal anxieties also interfere with eating? Does he have particular food preferences or aversions. Is he a vegetarian? Increasingly, we get a picture of a person barely containing impulses which threaten the tenuous stability he has achieved. Outside stimulation as well as internal temptations must be held to a minimum lest his strength be overwhelmed and catastrophe overtake him.

The parents are described. Neither one can be pleased, and Allen carries this insatiable standard within him in the form of his perfectionistic demands. In this context it is understandable that he procrastinates since to procrastinate makes sense in a situation where failure is guaranteed. She "counted" his academic accomplishments (and his bowel movements?) and presumably found them wanting. There is little hard fact here, but we do get a sense of an excitable, demanding, inconsistent (intrusive?) person. She "identifies with his troubles." There is a lack of distance here. If his problems are her problems, who is there to give perspective? And, of course, in a situation like this her troubles are his. To be a separate person requires heroic efforts and we understand and sympathize with the patient's distant demeanor.

Sometimes a father can come to the rescue, be seen as a refuge and a guide, give perspective. But here, unfortunately, is a man who is described as easily frustrated and who screams and uses nasty language when angry. In this context, the father's "generosity" would have to be inquired about. Is this a giving which builds his son's self-esteem or is it indulgence which undercuts the ability to overcome frustrating obstacles?

"He prefers a quiet and uneventful life." In the circumstances, this may show commendable good sense.

Finally, two dreams. The first, "prior to his seeking treatment on this occasion." Does this mean he has had previous treatment? If so, it would be terribly important to learn the history of that treatment: why sought, how the patient evaluates it, why terminated. Both dreams have positive aspects. In the first, he *is* en route, albeit lost. We have already learned that he is looking for a guide. The second dream is richer, but has dangerous elements. The beautiful island of his fantasies is breached by atomic bombs. His disavowed anger escapes containment, and destruction threatens those he loves and hates. His primary concern in the dream is to get home. Why? For safety? To see if his mother lives? He is "afraid" that he might not make it. Perhaps there is unconscious recognition here that the journey he must make is an inner one which will permit him finally his wish to leave home.

Let us ask ourselves, what is a schizoid personality? What are the essential conflicts from which he suffers? In what way could we hope psychoanalytic treatment would alter his unhappy way of living?

To answer this, let us first recapitulate the state of the infant in the first few months of life. He is, of course, totally dependent on his environment for survival and suffers periodically from tensions in the form of hunger, fatigue, the need to urinate, evacuate his bowels, etc. Primary in all of this and the first need which preeminently requires another for its satisfaction is hunger. Hunger which is satisfied at the mother's breast in a good feeding. The infant experiences a state of blissful satiation which is succeeded once again by painful tension (hunger followed by satiation again), etc. These experiences occur at a time when the ego of the infant is a fragile thing, his perceptual ability is limited, and tensions are experienced globally with little capacity for moderation through the anticipation of future satisfaction or the memory of past satisfactions. Further, we know that the infant is incapable of accurately separating external and internal stimulation or even of recognizing in a consistent way different aspects of external presence or things. This is the phase of development where external objects are considered "good" or "bad" depending on whether they satisfy and diminish painful stimuli or on the contrary increase pain and anxiety. The infant hates the bad object and loves the good without awareness that the same object may be involved in both cases.

This splitting of the object (mother's breast) into "good and bad" is paralleled by a similar split within the ego into good, i.e., self-enhancing, or bad, i.e., painful parts. The good experiences coalesce ultimately into the central ego or self with which the individual identifies himself. The bad experiences form the basis for the dissociated, disavowed parts of the self. In the Freudian scheme, these experiences form the core of what later becomes the super-ego. In Fairbarn's conception, these dissociated parts of the self constitute what he calls the anti-libidinal ego. In the course of normal development, the balance of experience is sufficiently positive so that a relatively large part of the self is accessible to awareness and in contact in a positive way with the real world. Where there is a preponderance of negative experiences, the central self is limited and large segments of the self are cut off from this central core. This limits the individual's capacities for adaptation and for the acquisition of successful pleasurable experiences.

The characteristic defenses of this period of development (the first 3 to 6 months of life) are *splitting* and *projection*. By keeping the good and bad objects separate and by projecting bad parts of the self on to the external world, the infant attempts to preserve the good part of himself in contact with the good object. Communication between good and bad parts of the self threatens the extinction of the central ego. If the initial period is sufficiently catastrophic, the infant's capacity to move into the next stage of development (the depressive position) is severely limited. This all important developmental period is characterized by an awareness of whole objects possessing both good and bad qualities. It is at this stage of development (about the sixth month) that the capacity for guilt develops, which is to say, the awareness of being able to injure the good mother who has in a particular instance behaved badly. With this comes remorse and a wish for reparation. If this stage is achieved with relative success, subsequent development proceeds along neurotic lines. Failure to successfuly achieve this position through excessive splitting leads to schizoid, potentially psychotic adaptations.

The schizoid person, then, is one whose early experiences have been so frustrating that there is set up within him a world of harmful, painful objects which are readily projected on to the world around him. He anticipates human interaction as probably painful to him and seeks a way of living which is distant from people. At the same time, schizoid people have an intense hunger for gratification and are driven to get needed satisfaction from others. It is the bane of the schizoid's life that he experiences hunger for others as potentially devouring and destructive. No sooner does he begin to get close to someone than his fear of destroying that person drives him away. He then finds himself alone, frustrated, and once more longing for contact, and the painful oscillation begins again. Because this dilemma has its origins in the oral period, the schizoid feels that intimacy is a matter of swallowing or being swallowed and either solution is terrifying to him. The schizoid tries to solve his dilemma by emptying himself in "objective" pursuits. Allen, of course, manifests many typical schizoid traits. His dress warns people off. He says people "generally bore me." He says intimacy is a threat to his identity, saying, "I never really had any friends . . . I project an odd image . . . but I think it is an advantage really . . . *I want to maintain my own individuality.*" In these statements he reveals his fear that if he gets too close his self-identity will dissolve.

To recapitulate briefly, we would say that Allen suffered excessive frustration in the early oral period of development. As a consequence, he was left with impaired ego resources and with a persistent hunger for object relations, which hunger he perceives as a dangerous threat to those to whom it is directed. He has tried to adapt by maintaining a distant posture and by developing intellectual interests which separate him from people. However, his wish for intimacy is not yet dead and occasionally breaks through his protective wall. Understanding his fundamental dilemma is very important both for the therapist and for the patient.

It will be a long hard task for the patient to acquire this knowledge: to learn its source in early life experience, to see its ramifications in his current life, and to move into other relationships through building a new relationship with the therapist. Certainly, we could expect this to be a matter of years. The first, most difficult task would be establishing a working relationship with the patient. That is a relationship in which there is sufficient trust so that the inevitable fears, demands and hatreds generated in treatment would not lead to precipitous flight, but could be contained and ultimately examined for the light shed on his problems.

How the patient will relate to the therapist depends in large measure on the expectations and distortions generated by his experience of his parents in childhood. His descriptions of them, while they can by no means be taken as accurate, can be extremely useful as a guide to the transferential dispositions he will bring to the therapeutic relationship. The transference is, of course, both the chief barrier to, and the primary vehicle of, change. It is a barrier in that it stands between the patient and the possibility of experiencing the world in a new way. It is the vehicle of change in that understanding it is the avenue to experiences that though repressed continue to determine his behavior. His relationship with the therapist will be compounded out of the transference and whatever he can perceive of the real qualities of the therapist. The therapeutic problem here is that neither parent appears to have offered any consistent model for constructive discourse, so that it will be hard for him to see the therapist as anything but self-involved, exploitative and unreliable. Furthermore, we would expect him to feel that he is not measuring up to the therapist's expectations. This self-effacing attitude would alternate with equally intense perceptions of the therapist as inadequate and altogether unworthy of him.

Allen's agitation while waiting for his initial interview suggests that the first theme in therapy will relate to the therapist's availability and reliability in the face of Allen's urgent needs. The initial transference would be to the preoedipal mother and a delicate balance would have to be maintained between being available when truly needed while not being so available as to threaten the sense of objectivity and distance which Allen also needs. The problem is that the therapist could become in Allen's mind a bad object, which he hates and from whom he would have to run away. Paradoxically,

Allen's relationship to the good object might also be fraught with danger in that the gratification would intensify his hunger for closeness and once again generate fears of swallowing or being swallowed. An additional complication is that the schizoid character also envies and hates the good object for the very good qualities he needs but does not possess. Fearing that his envy will injure its object, he will either try to spoil the relationship or terminate it. My hope is, through listing these various sources of danger, to indicate the fragility of the bond between the patient and therapist in this case. Probably the best stance to take is a relatively "cool" one in which the therapist tries to be helpful in an objective way without appearing overly involved or pressing prematurely for intimacy or positive feeling.

In the matter of frequency of contact, I think three sessions a week would be advisable and I would permit frequent telephone contact at the beginning of therapy. One could expect this stage to proceed for a long time as Allen increasingly allowed himself to experience the full extent of his hunger for the therapist alternating with his intense fear of "destroying or being destroyed." During this period of forming a working relationship, it would be appropriate to support his intellectual interests and his work adjustment without subjecting them to analysis.

Once a relatively firm relationship is established, we might expect him to begin making friends. This would, of course, arouse sexual anxieties and it would be unwise to prematurely encourage heterosexual involvements. Only after his basic conflict was thoroughly understood and some friendships operative would one want to turn attention to work and intellectual pursuits. In the context of more satisfying personal relationships Allen might consider the meaning of his interest in "particular" aspects of ancient history and specifically of the fantasy tours he takes at night. The symbolic meaning of this interest could be explored so he could understand the defensive nature of some of it and begin to attach some of that curiosity to his own ancient (anxious) history. Finally, once he has achieved a stable vocational goal and is able to maintain some friendships, one would want to tackle the problems of intimacy. One would do this with the hope that he could achieve ultimately a satisfactory heterosexual adaptation.

The above is a general plan of action. We know, however, that therapy does not ordinarily unfold according to the book. Sexual anxieties will press strongly at the beginning of treatment, vocational decisions may not wait on complete understanding. The deepest oral yearnings and fears may surface only after many years. In short, we would be surprised if in the course of treatment we were not surprised by unexpected developments and new knowledge.

The primary danger in treatment, as I have indicated, would be Allen's impulse to run when he sees his therapist as being either all good or all bad. To counter this, it might be a very good idea for him to be in concurrent group therapy with another therapist. This would provide him with a therapeutic haven if he should have to run from too close a relationship with the individual therapist. In a group he could also try out new ways of relating while having his individual therapist as a "good object" when that was needed. Ultimately, one would hope he would graduate to a sole relationship to the therapeutic group and finally achieve a successful adaptation without therapy. The journey is a difficult one. He will need all the skill and good will that his therapist can muster. He will need, as well, good fortune in the myriad accidental influences that will help to either impede or sustain him on his way.

11

Critical Comparison
The Case of Allen

CLEMENS A. LOEW, Ph.D.,
GLORIA HEIMAN LOEW, Ph.D.,
and HENRY GRAYSON, Ph.D.

If Allen were to seek help from Dr. Stark (the analyst), Dr. Polster (the Gestaltist) or Dr. Reyna (the behavior therapist), one of the expectations he would encounter would be that all three therapists would require him to *talk* with them. Also, all therapists would function with the hope that the experience with them would lead to change in Allen's thinking, feeling, or behaving. The *kind* of things he would be talking about, the *kind* of experience he would have, and the duration of treatment might, of course, differ. Whether the theoretical orientation or its related techniques alone accounts for the difference, or whether it is the personality of the therapists is difficult to determine for certain. Nevertheless, all three therapists assume implicitly that if behavior has been learned then it can also be unlearned, and that therapy is a situation in which such unlearning and learning can take place.

An interesting question to consider is, "Which of the three therapists would Allen choose if he had a chance to shop?" That is, if *he* were able to "interview" each therapist for one session, which of them would he decide to stay with? And on what basis would that choice be made? Would it be because of the sex of the therapist? Would it be based on the understanding he experienced? Would it be because of the promise of cure he sensed? And would the choice be benefical or deleterious to his growth and development?

One way to imagine what Allen may experience is to compare what the major focus is in the therapists' thoughts and feelings during the early contacts with him. We see that Stark's foremost concern is with *understanding* Allen's psychodynamics. His first thoughts are in response to Allen's appearance and the *meaning* it suggests to him. "Allen dresses in black—what does it mean? He wants to be seen as menacing and sad . . . dark glasses are a wall to contain him." From the beginning and continuing throughout the treatment, Stark focuses his thinking on Allen's dilemmas. The personality is always seen in terms of dynamic opposites or conflicts. Stark writes for example, "He presents himself for help, but speaks in an impersonal manner; 'people bore me' translates freely into people are intensely interesting to me . . ." Allen's panic when mother is out of sight is seen as an impulse to flee which is the obverse of attack.

In his thinking Stark shows a great deal of sympathy and understanding of Allen. The boredom is seen as a natural exhaustion caused by his conflict about intimacy and protection from an intrusive and inconsistent mother. "To be a separate person requires heroic effort and we sympathize with the patient's distant demeanor." We imagine that if Stark would communicate this attitude, Allen would experience a profound sense of respect for his struggles. However, Stark does not indicate the extent to which he would *share* any of his thoughts with Allen, or how he would communicate this understanding.

One of the sharp distinctions in Gestalt therapy is that in

the beginning Polster is thinking of what to *do* with Allen. Her thoughts are involved with how to generate feeling in him, how to "get his motor running." The focus is on *action* rather than understanding. Polster directs and guides Allen toward specific behavior in the session, and "alerts him to any signs of feelings that might surface." She asks him to talk of people he knows, she asks him to intensify and exaggerate gestures expressed non-verbally (e.g., clenched fist), to express feelings to an imagined professor in the empty chair, etc. Thus, Polster wants to increase awareness of body sensations and feelings and to give him practice in becoming comfortable with them.

In describing Allen's difficulties Polster uses the concept of confluence—the attempt to avoid contact with himself and the world through "the perception of *no* change and *no* excitement." Like Stark, she also assumes the presence of certain feelings underlying manifest behavior. Thus, she assumes that beneath boredom there is much anger. She utilizes specific techniques to evoke this feeling. Polster sees Allen's unusual behavior not only as resistance but as a positive aspect of him, as does Stark. The archaeological trips are viewed as creative components to be nourished. While Polster accepts creativity at face value, Stark looks to underlying meanings. This highlights differences in philosophy and technique. Stark needs to uncover and to peel the onion. Polster is less interested in exploring and more in encouraging a particular ability (e.g., creativity).

We imagine Allen would experience Polster as warm and actively interested in working with him. He would also perceive a direct and immediate encouragement to feel and to make contact. Such an experience in which Allen would feel intimacy and immediate contact would be welcomed by Polster, but be viewed by Stark as undesirable and even detrimental (at least in the early stages).

In marked contrast to the Gestaltist and analyst, Reyna's immediate and foremost concern is to establish objective goals. Detailing specific and troublesome behaviors, selecting priorities, and concretizing a list of social skills are critical from the beginning. More than the other two, Reyna continually focuses on developing and maintaining motivation for treatment. He asks Allen to be explicit about reasons for treatment, challenges his goals, and asks Allen what he wants to change. Also unique to Reyna is that he educates Allen about human behavior. For example, he teaches that "problems are made up of specific behaviors, that these are under stimulus control. . . ."

Basically, Reyna's approach is cognitive and task-oriented. Although feelings are considered as accompanying behavior, they are usually discussed parenthetically. Conceptualization of Allen is in terms of the skills he possesses (or lacks) to bring about positive reinforcement. For example, Allen has few behaviors which constitute "making friends." Conceptualization of the development of his problems is not a primary concern, except in terms of presence or absence of reinforcements. In contrast to the elaborate concerns with fantasies, dreams and dilemmas of the Gestaltist and analyst, there is little attention to the internal mediating process. Allen's stated objectives are taken at almost complete face value—there is no search for latent motives or metaphors. Of the three therapists, Reyna's treatment techniques are most distinctly tied to the objectives set by Allen.

We imagine Allen would be most comfortable with Reyna. His treatment would be highly structured, motivation would be kept at high levels, and he would receive immediate rewards. Reyna, initially, would be seen as the "teacher" and "model" and Allen as the respected student. This academic role is comfortable and very familiar to Allen. While Stark expects Allen to eventually develop negative feelings (transference) , Reyna anticipates becoming a "consultant." Like Polster, Reyna plans to be perceived as neutral or positive and not use himself as a target for negative attitudes from Allen. Also, his concern is with the here and now.

In terms of the relationship with the therapist, Stark wants to become an ally, which he sees as difficult with Allen. His approach is continuous and slow. Trust is crucial because Allen will be expected to weather the storms of the transference. Allen would become frightened because he would experience himself *as if* he was indeed the little child with the mother, or perhaps father, during treatment. Thus, Stark would be the object of hatred and struggles. However, Stark is very sensitive to Allen's immediate needs for reliability and availability. But even here, Stark's behavior is constantly dictated by seeing Allen in terms of the past. So, for example, Stark is cautious about availability so as not to arouse the fear of being swallowed. Note that Stark is the only therapist who *prepares* Allen for his treatment (analysis) . In this preparatory stage, Allen is supported in his intellectual pursuits and permitted frequent telephone calls. The actual "analysis" and problems of intimacy and sexuality would begin only after this initial stage is satisfied.

Polster, on the other hand, develops the relationship by focusing on the here and now and tries to quickly connect Allen with her. Thus, she asks him what *he* deduces about *her* from the artifacts in the office. She wants to engage him in the present. The relationship is intended to be positive throughout treatment. The stress on the here and now and the immediate generation of feelings may either scare Allen or fascinate him. At any rate, he would experience a liking and warmth from Polster. She would share her thoughts and feelings with him: they laugh together, she asks him to be her companion in fantasy, etc.

Most significantly, Polster, like Reyna, explains her technique and informs Allen of their purpose. Both feel that Allen would benefit from such knowledge. Stark is not specific, but it is doubtful that he would tell Allen about what and why he is doing. Such revelations would probably interfere with the transference.

In comparing the conditions for change, the relationship with the therapist appears to be one of the primary vehicles of change for Stark. The nature of the relationship becomes the model and analogue in which Allen works out his infantile conflicts. This then generates "healthier" relationships outside the treatment situation. Secondly, Allen will change only if he understands how his unconscious affects his current mode of adaptation. Stark suggests that Allen come three times a week, and duration of treatment we assume would be three to five years. Group therapy is also suggested.

For Polster, a good therapeutic relationship is important but not critical in providing change. Of primary importance is contact with feelings and "unprejudiced awareness." Allen will be helped if he can increase his responsiveness: be excited, creative, and intimate with someone. Distinctive in her work is the focus on the body and its sensation of feelings. Like Stark, she sees the past as influencing the present and seeks to unlock Allen from it. However, there is little or no attempt to make connections between past and present, as with Stark. Therapy would last about two to three years, with no more than three times per week.

The conditions for change for Reyna are that Allen be motivated, directly involved in establishing a therapy program, and accept the therapist as teacher and consultant. While there is some role playing and rehearsing within the office, the bulk of change is expected to occur outside the office. This is a unique feature for Reyna and it requires Allen to keep a daily log of the progress of the assignments. Thus, Allen's ability to perform homework is the key to his change. In keeping with Reyna's attention to the environment, he is the only therapist who involves Allen's parents in treatment. Allen would have one individual, one group, and one family session each week. Reyna assumes he has only six to mine months time before Allen goes to graduate school. Additional treatment would be recommended only when new goals emerge.

From the therapist's viewpoint, it seems that Stark would have the most personal difficulties to deal with in treating Allen. Allen would be most intimately involved with Stark. Stark, as an analyst, would himself be the target of expressions of infantile feelings ranging from love to hate to rage. Such feelings expressed as attacks, demands, and dependency would be directed at Stark. Perhaps that is why analysts are encouraged to get a 5000-hour checkup. Polster, on the other hand, asks Allen to yell at an imaginary figure in an empty chair, but not at herself. Her approach is to continually maintain a positive relationship, to show Allen that she is not a "scary bitch." Reyna would probably have the least personal difficulties to cope with. Allen would not be expected to become intimately involved or to work with feelings. The nature of this relationship (student-teacher) is relatively more objective.

In sum, the analyst and Gestaltist are most similar in theory and in practice. They are both concerned with past influences on current behavior, with the unconscious, with mediating process and feelings. Reyna, the behaviorist, appears most different, but shows more similarity to Polster than to Stark. Both Reyna and Polster are explicit in defining the treatment to Allen; both are unconcerned with the diagnosis of "schizoid" personality. The diagnosis has little or no implicit meaning to them, but it does for Stark.

Part IV

FRIGIDITY
THE CASE OF JUNE

June, a sales representative for an airline company, had been married for three years. She is an attractive, shapely, 23-year-old woman who seemed seductive in her behavior. As she appeared for the initial interview, she was neatly dressed and presented a very poised demeanor. As the interview progressed however, anxiety became apparent, as manifested by her shaking hands, trembling voice, blushing face, and excessive smoking. She spoke with much control and restraint as she related her reasons for seeking psychotherapy.

> I have a problem with my husband. I have not enjoyed sex since we got married. It was pretty good before, but now I can't stand for him to touch me. It's just getting unbearable! If he touches my breasts, I get cold shivers and my body tightens up all over. Sometimes I feel like screaming when he touches me! We do still have sex sometimes, but I don't enjoy it at all. In fact, it repulses me. I feel I have to go along with it sometimes, or he will wonder what is wrong with me. I don't think he is aware that if we had no sex relations, I'd be quite happy.

June's husband, a 27-year-old stockbroker, was described as domineering and dominating. He has outbursts of rage when he feels frustrated by her. At times, she has feared that he would injure her. She feels that she would be defenseless, since "he is a very big man" (actually he is 6'4" tall and weighs over 200 pounds).

June also reported that she had trouble sleeping. The only way she could manage to go to sleep was to "conjure up a fantasy I used to have a lot when I was younger." This fantasy appeared at the age of 13 and is as follows:

> I am on a pier and a pirate ship sails in and docks. The pirates rush over to me and grab me and tie me down on a table and do all sorts of things to me. When I masturbate with this fantasy, then I can go to sleep. This is also the only way I can have an orgasm. I've never had an orgasm while making love with a man.

June's job was presented as another area of difficulty for her. She reported that she goes in late, calls in "sick" frequently, or takes extra long lunches. This time is often spent going to "trashy" movies, reading "trashy" novels, or watching soap operas on TV. "I know I'm asking for it at work, but I can't seem to do anything about it."

June described herself as being very close to her father as a young girl. With her mother's encouragement, she played in bed with him on Saturday and Sunday mornings until she began menses—then refused to get into bed with him again. Thereafter, her relationship with her father was primarily one of arguing and fighting. She portrayed her father as "an intelligent man who has suffered from never completing a formal education . . . a domineering person . . . incapable of holding a conversation with someone unless he lectures. It was disillusioning to me to find after I grew up that he was talking about nothing." June's father was a factory worker.

She perceived her mother as a martyr, but one who always saw the patient as a perfect little angel who could do no wrong —even after she broke a shampoo bottle over her own head at age nine. "She is just a mother," she said in response to a question about her mother. "She had to work all her life as a cleaning woman and resents it. She also resents my father for being a mechanic in a factory."

At age 17 the patient had her first affair with a 38-year-old man which resulted in a pregnancy. June told her mother, who then aided her in getting an abortion without the father's knowledge. This was never discussed again. Two months after the abortion, she had sex with another man, eight years older, again without contraceptive precaution. She said that sex was enjoyable, but that she did not have an orgasm.

June was also worried about her drinking. "I often get drunk at parties or after a fight with my husband. I often get so drunk that I don't remember what went on." In addition, she sometimes had suicidal ruminations after marital fights; occasionally she threatened suicide openly.

She has no close friends, but she and her husband socialize frequently with other couples. In this context she generally feels inferior and inadequate, thinking that she has nothing of value to contribute.

12

Behavior Therapy Approach
The Case of June

ARNOLD A. LAZARUS, Ph.D.

There is a widespread, but erroneous, belief that a behavioral approach treats symptoms and ignores basic interpersonal and intrapersonal processes. While it is true that certain individual behavior therapists may engage in little more than the treatment of presenting complaints, there is nothing even within the strict confines of social learning theory to preclude the adoption of a more sophisticated framework for problem identification, thus broadening and extending the range of behavioral techniques.

Many cases of sexual apathy and revulsion may require no more than sex counseling and perhaps a course of relaxation training and desensitization. In the case of June's seemingly interrelated anxiety, aggression, insecurity, and their ramifications, much more seems to be indicated. Although the case material was very scanty, it nevertheless brought to mind a large number of interrelated questions:

1. What is the intent of her seductive behavior?
2. Is there something about "being married" that inhibits her sexual pleasures? If so, what? Responsibilities? Restraints? Implicit or explicit demands? The attainment of a goal? Fear of pregnancy?

157

3. If she is simultaneously repelled by and afraid of her husband, what keeps them together? Why, in fact, did they get married?

4. Why was she attracted to a domineering and dominating man? What bearing does this have upon her relationship with her domineering father?

5. Did the husband have outbursts of rage before they married? If so, did these outbursts have any effect on her sexual desires and feelings at that time?

6. If the husband's rage reactions were only manifest after marriage, what aspects of his own cognitions and/or his wife's reactions provoked these outbursts?

7. In what ways, other than sex, has she been frustrating him? What sorts of demands does he place upon her?

8. Why do they have no children?

9. Is guilt a prominent feature with her in general, or more specifically sex-related?

10. Is there a component of enjoyment being allowed only when she is coerced into the act as opposed to willingly submitting to, or initiating sex?

11. Is her disinterest in her work directly connected with her present job? Is she working because she wants to or because she feels that she has to? How does this color additional attitudes towards her husband?

12. Is she invested with seduction fantasies concerning her father? Apart from being domineering, in what ways is her husband similar to her father?

13. To what extent is she emulating her martyr-like mother?

14. How crucial is the anger that she aims at herself and at her husband, if not at men in general? Is her major manipulative ploy a passive-aggressive stance? How does this relate to her own negative self-evaluation?

15. What other intrapunitive and extrapunitive devices does she employ?

16. Is her drinking a psychic anesthetic? How does it fit into her general manipulative tactics?

17. Are her negative attitudes toward her parents tinged with shame, and if so, how does this affect her self-concept?

18. What is her marriage relationship like in other (non-sexual) areas? How much basic communication is there? How freely do they each share their genuine feelings?

19. Is June an only child?

20. Why is June seeking therapy at this particular time?

GENESIS AND DESCRIPTION OF THE PROBLEM

Raised by a domineering father and a somewhat passive but resentful mother, June's patterns of imitation and identification were probably ambiguous from the start. Her childhood encounters seem to have resulted in a conformist "little angel" pattern in which her anger was sometimes deflected onto herself; "she broke a shampoo bottle over her head at age nine." (Does the inclusion of this fact in the brief clinical history imply that self-destructive behaviors were a characteristic feature?) At puberty and adolescence, when she began to challenge her father's supreme authority, their relationship soon altered from being "very close" to "primarily one of arguing and fighting." (To insist that the change in attitude and behavior between father and daughter was necessarily sex-related is an *a priori* assumption not evident in the initial case material.) When she is 23, we see clear evidence that she is an anxious woman, and we can readily infer that she has learned to conceal her anger except perhaps in numerous subtle (passive-aggressive) gestures, the brunt of which is fully experienced during and after bouts of excessive drinking.

She appears to lack the capacity to form any type of meaningful relationship. No mention is made of any long-standing or close relationship, and one may gain the impression of a semi-social-isolate whose dissident parents and childhood peers failed to provide her with clear-cut goals in any sustained direction. The problem seems to boil down to that of an anxious, angry, and yet emotionally impoverished young woman with limited capacity to invest anything of consequence in her day-to-day interactions. Work appears to be little more than another outlet for her aggressive (and potentially self-destructive) manipulations. There seems to be a basic lack of identity and purpose. She is neither a doting daughter nor a doting wife; she seems to lack a clear-cut role as a working girl, a homemaker, a potential mother, or simply as a human being. Her "frigidity" appears to be one facet of her inability to feel enduringly positive toward anyone or anything. Possible guilt feelings and misconceptions arising from an inadequate sexual education are also likely features.

June's problems appear largely attributable to the fact that her home seems to have provided so few opportunities for her to acquire prosocial, self-confident, goal-directed aims and purposes. She would seem to regard both her parents as "losers" and would not deliberately seek to model herself on either one. The absence of any significant traumata during her childhood and adolescence would lead one to conceptualize her problems under the rubric of *response deficits*. In other words, her overall problems do not appear to be the result of violent upheavals which contaminated neutral events with neurotic anxiety, but seem to stem from real or imagined deficiencies in her own repertoire of emotional and interpersonal skills. One of the principal goals of treatment, then, would be to equip her with (by training her in) a significant range of effective behaviors.

INITIAL TREATMENT PLANS

The manner in which I understand, explain, and formulate the development of a patient's problem is important, although not crucial, for the treatment. Therapy, as I practice it, is largely a matter of teaching people adaptive responses and rational attitudes in their present day-to-day living. Obviously, if I feel that someone's problems stem from specific misconceptions, I will aim to alter these cognitive errors. If my history-taking unearths certain anxiety-generating experiences, these will alert me to likely areas of hypersensitivity in the client and enable me to select and apply several anti-anxiety procedures. In June's case, for instance, had she dated her "frigidity" to her abortion at age 17, it would have been necessary to explore her attitudes and experiences at that time with a view perhaps to desensitizing her to painful memories and associations. Since June's sexual revulsion is post-marital, despite the fact that she has never been orgasmic heterosexually, I would be inclined to focus most of my attention upon her marriage dyad and to search for the interplay between the anxious and aggressive maneuvers with her husband. The fact that many of these reactions on her part may stem from the father-daughter relationship need not necessarily be emphasized in therapy. In zeroing in on her salient problem areas and in devising and selecting seemingly appropriate corrective measures, I would need answers to each of the questions raised at the beginning of this paper. Many of these questions could only be answered over time, as I got to know her a little better, and as I had the opportunity to double-check my impressions and her responses. Other questions and issues would doubtless emerge from this material, and would, in turn, influence the course of treatment.

An important decision would need to be made almost immediately. Would it be better to see June and her husband in couples therapy than to treat her or them individually? Would it be advisable to schedule one couples meeting and one individual session with each of them per week? I may discuss these alternatives with June during the initial interview, and would certainly ask to see her husband at least once before our third or fourth meeting. If June or her husband were opposed to a mutual treatment process, this would form the first line of therapeutic inquiry. If not, the decision to see them jointly and/or individually would depend upon their own feelings in the matter and upon the degree of cooperation that they could muster. When destructive tactics undermine the potential benefits of conjoint therapy, I tend to see the spouses separately until they have acquired more constructive patterns of battle and communication.

Other options also present themselves. Would they derive more benefit from a couples group? Perhaps June would profit from a therapy group once a week while also receiving conjoint therapy once weekly. Or perhaps the husband would do well in a group while June received individual therapy. The point to be strongly emphasized is that I have no predetermined therapeutic plans, but try to tailor my treatment to the essential needs of my patients. For instance, a comment from June to the effect that each time her husband touches her breasts she conjures up images of her father's irate countenance may deflect therapy into channels that would call for personal exploration of the father-daughter relationship, and possibly also involve June and her parents in family therapy.

To avoid clouding or complicating the issue, let us assume that, upon interviewing June's husband, it appears that his input accounts for about 25% of their sexual and marital problems. Let us depict this 6'4", 200 pound, twenty-seven-year-old stockbroker as a fairly reasonable man who feels frustrated and perplexed at his wife's apparent lack of ardor, and who inadvertently reinforces her anxiety and anger by rewarding them through attention, counter-aggression, and so forth. Furthermore, it would not be farfetched to assume that he probably lacks the skills and graces of a proficient lover, and that his oral and manual caresses would be enhanced through instruction. The allegation that he is domineering and dominating would need to be independently evaluated; if it is confirmed, he would probably need to learn the advantages of reciprocity over coercion, as well as the essential differences between assertion and aggression. Indeed, the husband may suffer from premature ejaculation and may have led his wife into adopting the patient role. Consequently, I would probably want to work with the husband individually (in addition to possible conjoint sessions) about once every two weeks. When so doing, it would be important to determine whether June may develop paranoid reactions about a possible collusion between husband and therapist. If this were the case, I would prefer to avoid seeing the husband individually. And if June's general antagonism towards men tended to disrupt or impede therapy, two immediate options would present themselves: (1) referral to a female therapist, or (2) treatment of the marriage dyad by a male-female therapy dyad.

Of course, the final therapeutic arrangements will depend more upon the availability of services than upon idealistic conceptions. Thus, I may justifiably feel that a couples group would be more suitable than individual or couples therapy, but if I have no ongoing group at the time, and no access to a trusted colleague conducting a couples group in the area, I will try to extract the most out of the next best therapeutic modality.

FURTHER ASSESSMENT AND THERAPY

Let us assume that the foregoing considerations have led me to see June once a week in individual therapy, once a week in group therapy, and every two weeks in conjoint therapy. My next step would be to determine June's range of fears and hypersensitivities, and the characteristic way in which she copes with these situations. Apart from the usual anamnestic interviews, I would probably administer a Fear Check List, an Assertion Questionnaire, and a detailed Life History Questionnaire.

The most probable dimensions and areas of hypersensitivity would presumably include criticism, rejection, disapproval, and failure. Her characteristic responses to situations involving real or imagined confrontations with these subjectively painful events would most likely entail silent withdrawal, passive-aggressive tactics, drinking, and, when sufficiently intoxicated, overt aggression and suicidal threats. Conspicuously absent in her repertoire would be assertive (as opposed to aggressive) behaviors. There would also be a notable paucity of any consistent rational or inductive reasoning.

Within the first month (4-6 visits) the basic case material will have been gathered, the husband will have been interviewed (assuming a fairly "typical" therapy progression), and June will have attended one or two group therapy sessions. Furthermore, depending upon various points of emphasis that may have been underscored during these sessions, June and her husband may have been asked to read a carefully selected book on sex, marriage, rational living and/or assertive behavior. If June is at all literary and non-resistant to bibliotherapy, a fair amount of reading material will constitute an important therapeutic adjunct. (This aspect of therapy generally consists of having the patient study the relevant books, chapters, and articles, making notes, raising questions, criticisms, objections, and keeping special track of information, ideas, hints, and suggestions that seem especially pertinent to their own problem areas. Patient and therapist examine, evaluate, and discuss all these aspects together. Specific attention is devoted to ways and means of applying these data and insights into action patterns that can alter the difficulties that led the person to seek therapy in the first instance).

THE MAIN FOCUS OF THE INDIVIDUAL SESSIONS

The weekly individual sessions would last an hour and would probably aim to promote more effective ways for June to deal with self-criticism, anger, and hypersensitivities. Depending upon her preferences, techniques such as desensitization, assertion training, role-playing, behavior rehearsal, thought stopping, relaxation training, emotive imagery, and rational-emotive therapy would be introduced. If she seemed averse to these methods and preferred simply to discuss, evaluate, probe, and examine her past experiences and present responses, no effort would be made to coerce her into undergoing more precise behavioral techniques. If, after some half-dozen individual sessions of this interactive evaluation, no headway seemed to be evident, she would be gently coaxed into considering the addition of more specific behavioral tasks and strategies. Whatever the means employed, the goals of these individual sessions would be to decrease self-contempt, to enhance prosocial skills, to diminish hypersensitivity, to increase assertive behavior, and perhaps above all, to alter the self-defeating attitudes and irrational cognitions that may lead to so many of her inappropriate and immature behaviors.

The tenor of these sessions would be didactic, flexible, and genuinely empathic. My role as her therapist would be relatively informal and self-disclosing—unless it was evident that she was more likely to grow and to change within the context of a more formal, traditional doctor-patient relationship. My style would be to teach her to accept utterly frank feedback, and to discriminate between my thoroughly non-judgmental attitude towards her as a human being and my incisive criticisms of her maladaptive behaviors.

In view of her many response deficits, I would estimate that at least 50% of our individual therapy time would be spent role playing significant interpersonal events. In rehearsing her behaviors, we would probably cover the gamut of past and present parent-child interactions, employer-employee relationships, and a range of real or imagined authority figures and significant others, including, of course, husband-wife communications. In each instance, the purpose would be to provide her with useful and appropriate words, gestures, phrases, all as an approximation to the more global skill of expressing one's genuine feelings and learning to relate openly, constructively and appropriately. Since each of these goals involves subjective judgment (what is appropriate? what is open? what is genuine?), a good deal of discussion would follow each and every behavior rehearsal. Listening to playbacks on a tape recorder after each 10-15 minute interaction usually proves a useful way of shaping more veridical behaviors.

The correction of misconceptions and the specific alteration of irrational ideas (faulty self-talk) would also probably form a constant treatment objective from session to session. For example, false romantic ideals, childlike love demands, and perfectionistic standards would be parsed and challenged. If sexual myths were discovered, time would be devoted to dispelling them. Thus, an important educative function of the therapy would be to provide factual information on a variety of issues.

In the individual sessions, several other techniques may be introduced if indications lead me to believe that they would augment the therapy. Thus, hypnotic techniques and a variety of imagery techniques may be employed to enhance self-confidence. For example, it is well-known that some people gain mastery of difficult situations by actively imagining or picturing themselves successfully performing these difficult tasks. If June continued feeling repulsed by sex, she may be relaxed or hypnotized and asked to picture several progressively more intimate sexual scenes with her husband, and enjoined to project herself into erotic and stimulatingly vivid coital encounters.

It must be emphasized that what is being presented is a fairly "typical" case of broad spectrum behavior therapy. If different zones of hypersensitivity were elucidated and other areas of problem interaction and intra-individual concern emerged, they in turn would become the proper focus of therapeutic attention.

THE MAIN FOCUS OF THE GROUP THERAPY

My therapeutic groups usually comprise approximately 10 persons (equal numbers of men and women if possible) who meet once a week for about 1½-2 hours. The climate of the group is supportive and constructively critical. June would find, perhaps for the first time, nine other people who are prepared to respond to her without the usual interpersonal duplicity, hostile games, phoniness, and manipulations. She would find the general candor most unusual (perhaps frightening initially) but the overall atmosphere of openness and togetherness would probably prove contagious, in the most positive sense of the word. The group, of course, would provide a useful means of modeling new and adaptive behaviors, as well as the opportunity to learn through personal rehearsal or vicariously when observing others exchanging and imitating new adaptive behavior patterns.

My treatment groups usually devote considerable attention to issues of friendship: what constitutes true friendship and how one proceeds to develop close friendship. In many of the groups that I have formed since 1956, close and enduring friendships have developed between compatible members. The opportunity to make a friend, or at least a few meaningful acquaintances, would enable June to examine and re- examine her self-worth and obtain a rich source of personal reinforcement hitherto beyond her capacities.

The group would also afford June the opportunity to double check the impressions and points of emphasis derived from individual sessions. Regardless of the therapist's credibility, his views and opinions are still those of one individual as opposed to the consensus or range of alternatives available from nine other people.

Over the years, I have noted that people like June with somewhat self-destructive tendencies often act out by missing and avoiding a number of individual sessions, but rarely miss their group meetings. It would seem that being an integral part of a group—perhaps for the first time—constitutes a potent source of reinforcement that usually transcends the gains derived from hostile and asocial manipulative ploys. To feel wanted and respected by several people in one setting provides a basic source of gratification that is not easily duplicated.

THE MAIN FOCUS OF THE CONJOINT SESSIONS

The initial emphasis would probably center around the viability of the marriage dyad. While the main intent would be towards the achievement of marital harmony, an issue shared or perhaps initially kept to myself would be the question of whether marriage therapy or divorce counseling seemed most appropriate. Assuming that June and her husband were motivated to enhance their relationship, various ways and means of improving communication would be discussed, and immediate feedback would be provided of their destructive marital games and feuding tactics. Ideally, videotape playbacks of their real or simulated arguments and quarrels would provide a useful means of shaping constructive discussions. At least, audio-recordings of arguments—at home and in the consulting room—would provide *in vivo* opportunities for acquiring a new style of personal negotiation.

An important aspect of these fortnightly meetings with June and her husband would be to develop and extend what Masters and Johnson call "the sensate focus." In essence, they would be encouraged to explore a mutual range of non-erogenous tactile stimuli and very gradually to extend their caresses to erotic zones and gratifying sexual intimacy.

The couple would be requested to keep notes of their fights, quarrels, and disagreements, which would be discussed in therapy. In each instance, I would inquire about events leading up to the argument, the substance of the disagreement, and the manner in which it was finally resolved. I would be on the alert for common tactics such as intimidation, power assertion, withdrawal of affection, and unilateral decisions. Each argument would be further assessed in terms of mutual problems that were solved, as opposed to the type of quarrel in which nastiness and spitefulness merely tended to beget more of the same. Here again, in teaching them new ways of dealing with old and familiar differences, role playing and behavior rehearsal would be the most likely techniques of choice.

DURATION AND OUTCOME OF TREATMENT

In line with similar cases successfully treated in the past, I would estimate that June's therapy would need to extend over approximately 30 weeks. She would thus receive 30 hours of individual therapy, 45 hours of group therapy, and 15 hours of conjoint therapy. Of course, unforeseen problems could easily impede therapeutic progress and call for more meetings and different procedures, thus expanding overall treatment time. But rapid gains could just as readily accrue and significant change may be evident in the first three months.

Successful therapy would find June to be far more relaxed, outspoken, more tolerant of her own personal shortcomings and those of others, more direct in all her dealings with others, less inclined to resort to manipulative games, petulant rage, and passive-aggressive tactics. Her marriage would afford opportunities for intimate sharing rather than competitive striving, and gratifying sexual intimacy would be one consequence of closer and more open communication. During the course of therapy, I would anticipate that June would learn how to commit herself to and become involved in day-to-day events. More satisfying vocational outlets would be sought after and probably found. I would expect her drinking to become an occasional social pastime rather than a psychic analgesic or conjugal weapon.

Assuming that her husband had no great investment in dominating or suppressing her, he would probably help to maintain June's changed behaviors, especially since he would have been involved in the process from time to time, would derive direct sexual and personal benefits, and would have learned to appreciate the important distinction between rational assertion and irrational aggression. If the husband's covert agenda made it necessary for him to undermine June's progress, the course of therapy would not flow as smoothly as depicted. In the latter case, more conjoint and individual sessions with the husband would obviously be indicated.

I find that termination of therapy is usually initiated by my patients. "I'd like to see how I make out on my own for a while." "I've been feeling pretty good. Maybe I ought to stop coming every week." In most instances, I tend to feel similarly and may even have encouraged termination inadvertently. On occasion, I may be the one to initiate termination. "I think you're doing fine. Would you like to see how it works out if we see each other every second week now?" Occasionally, there is some crisis around the issue of termination—a resurgence of anxiety, or even explicit statements about dependency—but, in my experience, these are rare. I believe that this is largely due to the fact that, although the goals of therapy may be modified and redefined from time to time, I try to ensure that the patient holds them in constant focus and their attainment signals the logical point of termination.

Again, let it be clearly understood that wherever I have provided precise recommendations, techniques, or estimates, they stem from statistical averages derived from my experience with similar-sounding cases. Obviously, every case is somewhat individual and unique, and treatment interactions cannot be clearly predicted in advance.

13

Gestalt Approach
The Case of June

RAINETTE EDEN FANTZ, Ph.D.

One of my first awarenesses of June as she walks into my office (via a typewritten history, it's true) is that of a woman to whom control is important. By this I do not mean to imply that she is successfully in control; I mean rather that the "mask" of control is one she finds essential to wear. Her initial demeanor is poised. She speaks with control and restraint. But almost immediately her anxiety manifests itself in her shaking hands, trembling voice, blushing face and excessive smoking.

Almost instantly I ask myself, "Why is it important for this young woman to create the illusion of control?" And further, "What is she controlling or restraining?" I would try to share my thought process with June. I would let her know that I am aware of her anxiety since I can observe it in bodily manifestations and that I am also aware of her need (as exhibited by her attempt at poise and her resort to smoking) to keep it in check. My immediate expectation would be that she would crush out her current cigarette in my ash tray and look somewhat harried. Almost universally, people entering therapy regard observations of their behavior as criticisms and consequently curtail the behavior. Since this is not the result I'm aiming for, I share this fact with her and explain that one of the reasons I call attention to certain things she does is to let her know that I observe them and to discover if she is aware of them as well. Not too surprisingly, people are sometimes quite unaware of behavior which strikes others immediately. My intention, as a Gestalt therapist, is to ascertain among other possibilities whether her behavior is intentional or merely habitual, how she brings it about, and whether she chooses to continue it.

I would then return to her attempts to control her manifest anxiety. There are several ways in which this could be approached and if we continued to meet, we would in time explore all of them. To begin with, since the Gestalt therapist tries to work as much as possible in the present and also tries to use the relationship between therapist and client as a vehicle for progress, I would ask her to consider the possibility of my presence as a source of anxiety and as a demand for control. After all, we are the only two people in the room. What might there really be about me that aroused anxiety in her? What might happen if she allowed the anxiety to surface? Could she fantasize my reaction if she really let go? Who was there in her family who might have reacted in that way?

Of course, I have no way of knowing how she would respond to my attempts to know her. On the one hand, she shows a pattern of escapism. She escapes from her job into movies and novels; she escapes from her husband into pretense; she escapes from social confrontation into liquor. She might choose to escape from me into evasion. On the other hand, her difficulties at this point have become extreme enough for her to want help and this, coupled with her ability to fantasize, offers some kind of handle.

If the first line of approach elicits some opening up, I might discover that she's afraid to abandon control because she might then never regain it. This is a very frightening fantasy and certainly one with which I sincerely sympathize. I could convey this and at the same time try to discover whether this has in fact ever occurred. If it has not, and I strongly suspect that it hasn't, I might shift the focus to some of her bodily symptoms. I could ask her to notice the trembling of her hands and, instead of trying to quiet them by smoking cigarette after cigarette, to emphasize the trembling and see what happens. Again I have no idea what would actually happen. But *what* happens is not terribly important since whatever happens can be worked with. Chances are that this early in treatment June would be unable to completely abandon herself to her anxiety. She would be more likely to endure the trembling momentarily and then tighten up against it. It would be important to explore her feelings as the process developed, what she felt about herself, what she felt about me, what images if any came to mind, what sensations she experienced, and what she did to bring them about or stop them. If her hands finally clenched into fists, what would she feel like doing with them? Whom might she hit or stop herself from hitting? Could she picture herself doing this?

I anticipate the clenched fists at some point in therapy, whether they clench initially or not, because June's fantasy of the pirate ship indicates a strong sado-masochistic component. Although the masochism comes through in her choice of a husband (a strong wish-fear that he might harm her) and in her cavalier treatment of her job which dares the gods to do their worst, the sadism is nowhere so overt. Rather, it shows itself in her passive-aggressive attitude toward her husband, going along with his wishes for intercourse, but allowing him no real pleasure. In cutting herself off from her aggression, June cuts herself off from any real sense of power. All that remains for her is to turn the aggression against herself and silently suffer—as did her mother in the martyr role.

Very well then, I anticipate the clenched fists. I would ask June to picture herself beating at someone with them and to try to get with the feeling that accompanies this. Now I don't know whom she would beat at—there are several likely candidates. There is her father whom she resents because he betrayed her when he turned out to be "empty." There is her mother whom she probably resents for being "just a mother" and a martyr to boot. And finally there is her husband whom she resents because she is afraid of him and thinks of herself as defenseless—a myth.

To get her to beat at any one of them in fantasy would be a fine beginning, particularly if she could verbalize feelings along with the action. If she could go one step further and act out their response to her aggression, we would really be on the way to understanding some of her anxiety-control dilemma.

If, however, this particular exploration appears unproductive, we could return again to her physical manifestations and look at them from the point of view of polarities. Poise and anxiety are in a sense polar traits. When we find them existing in an individual at virtually the same time, chances are good that neither of them is well-integrated. In other words, neither trait is an integral part of June which she can fully accept as part of herself. I could tell her that her attempts at poise suggest to me that she is unwilling to accept her anxiety as belonging to her or at least unwilling to share it with someone else. My supposition is that she feels anxiety is bad or that others would think it is. I might ask her to try to play out the opposing traits in herself by creating a dialogue between her poised self and her anxious self, one side in effect speaking to the other. If she chooses to do this, she makes at least the implicit statement of ownership which can be the beginning of unmasking—not only for me but for herself. If she chooses not to create the dialogue, I would try to find out what she finds objectionable in the process. Again, it doesn't matter essentially which alternative she picks, although both she and I might find the creative act more involving, since either direction would permit some kind of discovery. *The important thing for me is to stay as close as possible to what is happening in the room at the time.*

Now it's quite possible that we might spend an entire session dealing with the elements of anxiety and control in the manner suggested above and disregard content completely. But once we do look at content it becomes clear that underlying it are the same elements—anxiety and control—once more providing a conflict.

In her relationship with her husband, June experiences fear and revulsion. When he makes love to her she gets "cold shivers" and "tightens up all over." Sometimes she feels like screaming when he touches her. In spite of these very strong expressions of emotion, June apparently does not scream, nor even curtail sex completely. Instead, she *controls* her feelings and expressions of anxiety out of fear of her husband's rage. My fantasy of June is that she lies rigid in her husband's arms. I would tell her this, and I would expect that she would acknowledge the rigidity. In Gestalt Therapy we consider bodily rigidity to be a defense against some kind of movement, in essence a muscular phenomenon. A motoric impulse or need that has been met with punishment is suppressed by contracting antagonistic muscles and the body goes into a clinch. I would tell her this too. I would expect June to think, "Well, all right, there's where I am, what can I possibly do about it?" My answer would be, "several things."

One possibility would be to assume that when the body goes into a clinch the personality divides itself into two parts, the part that wants to express an action and the part that wants to extinguish it. Now June has already admitted to wanting to shiver and wanting to scream. I would ask her to play out in dialogue the part of herself that wants to shiver against the part that wishes to suppress this. I anticipate an immediate denial of any part *wanting* to shiver. I would not be able to accept this, and I would tell her why not. The shivering which to June at this point may be only an expression of disgust is to me an expression of excitement. Part of my reason for thinking this is based on theory—when the body begins to react against its repressive self, tremendous excitement is felt, followed by fear and a return to the clinch—but part of it is based on my association to her pirate fantasy. In the fantasy the pirates grab her and tie her down on a table and "do all sorts of things" to her. Essentially, in a much lower key, this is precisely what her husband does when she doesn't consciously want sex. The pirate fantasy, when accompanied by masturbation, culminates in orgasm. The reality, when accompanied by tightening up, results in nothing.

If at this point June becomes able to accept the possibility of wanting to shiver or, to put it another way, to be excited, I would have her continue with the previous dialogue and try to discover the reasons for her fear of excitement. Once again I have a hypothesis, namely that the fear is associated with masturbation, particularly with the punishment that might follow discovery by her parents and the guilt that she may feel because of the sadistic nature of the concomitant fantasy. I might relate this notion to her at some later time, but not at the time of the experiment since I would want what emerges from it to belong to June rather than to me. If the experiment is fruitful, if for example June does discover in her dialogue between the part of her that wants to shiver and the part of her that wants to suppress the excitement that she is afraid of discovery and punishment, we could then examine the current reality—namely that she is no longer a child without rights or power of her own and that excitement (of a sexual nature) might be greeted with delight and enjoyment, rather than disapproval and punishment. To make this even more believable, June could act out two further scenes, one of her mother or father responding to her excitement in masturbation and the other of her husband responding to her excitement in lovemaking.

It's important to realize that the above experiments may be too risky early in the therapy sessions. This would not stop me from suggesting them—after all, they might not be. If, however, I find that they are, it is incumbent upon me to decelerate, lower the risk level. I could do this by suggesting that June try out the dialogues in fantasy and then tell me what happens. If even this is too threatening, we could try to explore the threat. Here I would expect to encounter her own judgmentalism which she perhaps would project out onto me. If I do encounter it, I would work with it.

First I would try to explore her fantasy of my judging of her. What might I condemn and how would I express my condemnation—by withdrawal, by attack, by an air of superiority? Which of these attitudes or other modes of condemnation could she conceive of using herself? Would she argue and fight as she had with her father; would she dismiss the person judged, as she had her mother, "as just a mother" or just a bore or just a factory worker? How would she judge me? In other words, I would attempt, with encouragement and constant feedback of my knowledge of the difficulty involved for her, to get June to experience her own projections as a part of herself. I would ultimately attempt to have her experience these projections as possible introjections, behavior that she has seen in powerful "others" and swallowed whole, so that she can either spit them out as not belonging to her or digest them so that they become integrated and acceptable.

If June is able to work at the high-risk level, if she is able to engage in the dialogues, particularly in the one involving shivering as a possible indication of excitement, I would at some point, when it felt appropriate, suggest that she fantasize being in bed with her husband. Then, if she encounters the tendency to shiver, she could allow herself to go with it and then exaggerate it. If the urge to scream entered into the fantasy, I would ask her to permit it to take over, to start first with small sounds which might gradually swell to grunts and finally to moans and shouting. I would pay great attention to her facial expressions and body movements as she did this so that I could share any information with her and also be alert to any real signs of discomfort or fear. I would also ask about her feelings as we went along so that I could see if they were congruent with her physical and vocal expressions.

I would anticipate a real feeling of relief in June if she could carry this experiment to its culmination. A tremendous amount of tension would have been experienced and released. In addition, June might be able to make the association between what she was experiencing and the experience that might occur with orgasm. This could be extremely exciting. Certainly if either of these things occurred, I would suggest that she allow herself to give vent both to the shivering and vocalizing in bed with her husband.

Now it might very well be that although June could do the above experiment in therapy where she was not presented with any kind of threat, she might as yet be unable or unwilling to try it at home in the lion's den. The timing essentially would be up to her. It is part of our therapeutic task, June's and mine, to enable her to become ready. Again there are several things that we might do.

One of these has to do with the pirate fantasy. I would share with June my notion that her husband in some way brought to mind her pirates. I would ask her if she could see any similarity between them. I would expect that in time she would. Be that as it may, I would suggest that she enact out the fantasy in therapy, first describing herself to me as she would be in each part. The pier, the ship, the pirate, herself, even the table. Needless to say, I would look for all manner of protestations. "It's silly! It's nonsense! I can't." Here I would persist.

I would explain that in fantasies and dreams we have some of our most relevant clues to the person's alienated self as well as to the parts of him that he really claims as his own. If June could bring herself to describe herself as the parts of her fantasy, a fantasy that has been important to her for 10 years, she might begin to have some feelings for formerly unexplored parts of herself.

I don't know how the parts would be sensed by June. I don't know whether a pier would be apperceived as a fixed, solid object that allows for anchoring or a flimsy thing with its legs in sand. I don't know if a pirate ship would be regarded as a black galleon, formidable and foreboding, or as a slim ship, free and floating. I do know that if June could enter into the creative experience of exploring her own conjurations, she could meet a new or long-since forgotten June who is far from the unidimensional creature she has made of herself. A perturbing happening without doubt, but enlivening.

If she could describe herself as the varied parts of the fantasy, if she could in effect *be* these parts, I would then have her enter into dialogue between the different Junes—between the pier and the ship, between the pirates and June, between the table and June. While she is the pirates, I would expect her to come into contact with her own aggression, her drive toward domination, even her need at times to be cruel. I would not expect any of this to be done with ease; I would foresee, instead, embarrassment, pain, tremendous reluctance. But I would hope to let her know, by sharing, the humanness of aggression, domination, cruelty and also the primitiveness of the early repressed emotions which make them so difficult to encounter and recover in adulthood. Further, we would explore the ways in which she could express some of these feelings at a level that could be acceptable to both her and her world.

We would do the same kind of thing with her need to be hurt, her desire for punishment, and her fear of it.

It would be interesting for me at this point to discover when her fantasy appeared in relation to her menses. We know that the fantasy first appeared when she was 13 and we know that she played in bed with her father until that time. I am curious as to the kinds of games they played and I would try to persuade June to re-create them in the therapy milieu. Once more I would ask her to play both parts, that of her father and that of the young June. We would look at her feelings and emotions as she did this and try to recapture some of the fun and excitement that must have been there at the time. I would also have her tell her father in fantasy why she can no longer play in bed with him after the start of her menses.

I have various fantasies about this myself. If her fantasy started before her menses, it's possible that she could have regarded menstruation as a punishment and the actual blood as evidence of some kind of torture. If the fantasies started subsequently, they could have been triggered by the blood, which could also have been seen by June as a sign that would let her father know somehow that she had been masturbating and was, therefore, bad. Of course, none of my formulations may be applicable, and chances are good that I might never relate them to June, but my having them would motivate me to try to find out what actually transpired between June and her father. What was it that transformed playful, possibly loving behavior into arguing and fighting? Does her father represent the pirate in the fantasy; did she choose her husband because she could see him too in that role? Does she ever have her pirate fantasy while he is making love to her? Certainly we could explore this. We could conjecture as to what might happen if she did have the fantasy during intercourse.

We could then return to the actual relationship between June and her husband. She has already described him as domineering and dominating. Were these things true of him before she married him? Chances are good that they were. Did she perhaps choose him *because* he was domineering and dominating? Are these traits that she actually admires or do they give her a chance to play the martyr, the "poor, little me" that her mother played? Or both? If he is really dominating and she tells herself that he can hurt her, does this give her an excuse not to truly exert herself and so escape the consequences of her own decisions? We have some evidence that she doesn't make decisions easily. She does not choose to leave her job nor does she choose to stick with it. She does not choose to work at developing close relationships nor does she choose to do without people. Rather, she allows things to happen to her without actively shaping her own destiny.

She does this with her husband. She is afraid to tell him she would rather not have sex, but she makes sex unsatisfactory so that he might not want it so often. Her excuse is that she feels defenseless. In other words, she ties herself down just as the pirate (herself) tied her down in her fantasy. But let's examine her defenselessness. Could it be a myth? Are there ways in which she could hurt her husband, either physically or psychologically, if she really wished to? I would ask June to consider the possibility of wanting to hurt him. We could examine her frigidity as a tool which she uses to punish her husband for his aggression without appearing to be aggressive herself, thus escaping imagined retribution. She might then fantasize ways in which she could actively hurt him, thus making real contact with him. Karate?

On the other hand, there is the possibility that his domination which she decries is indeed something which excites her. The frigidity then might be a device to prevent contact and so protect her from the excitement which she may regard as dangerous—punishable. To maintain frigidity, one has to maintain confluence, a blurring of figure and ground. In Gestalt

Therapy we postulate that frigidity is a kind of scotoma brought about by a particular conflict that is too painful to deal with; its context is therefore desensitized. We find during exercises on body concentration that sensations of numbness exist, rather than aches and pains. I would ask June to lie down on the floor and notice where her tensions are—slowly. I would ask her to describe to me what she feels in the different parts of her body and also the possible absences of feeling. I would expect that June would experience either a stiffness or rigidity in the small of her back or her groin or, failing that, a numbness, fogginess, nothingness. I could move with either of these possibilities. In the first case, I would have her explore what she is stiffening against. In the second, I would have her concentrate on the numbness until she had a veil to lift or a fog to blow away. In both cases, I would suppose that she was stifling her pelvis and that the initial need or wish was to express some kind of movement with it. If either of these things occurred, I would have her explore the movement that she has been repressing and finally exaggerate it. It would then be important to have her consider doing it in bed with her husband and to link this up with the current developing possibility of his expression of delight rather than anger.

To put it more succinctly, we would try to uncover in whatever ways we can those things that June really wants and needs as opposed to those that she has drifted into, and we would try to build a more effective repertoire of behaviors to satisfy her actual, current needs. In pursuing her anxiety-control dilemma, it becomes clear that June's contact function is distinctly impaired. We are made aware of this in her relationship with her husband; she goes along with him rather than coming in touch with him. We see it in her relationship with her father, where her only awareness of communication is arguing. We catch glimpses of it in her as yet unexplored relationship with her mother, in which she is apparently protected but not really talked to. We observe it in her dearth of close friends.

June's drinking is further evidence for this. As she puts it, "I often get drunk at parties or after a fight with my husband —I often get so drunk that I don't remember what went on." I would be curious as to the reasons for not remembering. Might she wish not to remember? Could she then disclaim any unwanted behavior? What might this behavior be? Could she conjecture what she might do that one part of her might find unacceptable? If she could, we might then have a dialogue between the part of herself that chooses to behave in a certain fashion and that part of herself which tries to suppress that behavior or at least hide it from her aware self. Might the behavior she forgets while drunk at parties be the same kind she forgets after fights with her husband, or might her actions be quite disparate? I would guess that her behavior at parties while drinking might be construed as seductive, even intimate behavior which she would prefer disowning since it's really behavior which leads to contact. I would share my guess with her and ask if her husband had ever remarked on this facet of her activity. I would also share with her my idea that liquor serves as a source of instant gratification, allowing one to act with strangers in a way that shortcuts the "getting to know you" process. This enables one to experience momentarily the pseudo-joys of pseudo-contact without the necessity of establishing step-by-step the disclosures and real sharing that develop into an actual sense of intimacy.

If June can at least intellectually accept my construct, we could try to search out her fears related to disclosure. I have reason to believe that these would be centered around her own sense of inferiority. She has already admitted to feeling inferior and inadequate in a social context; she thinks of herself as having "nothing of value to contribute." If her fears do lie in this area, we could move in several directions. We could determine what important people in her life she also labels inferior. Her father for never completing his education, for being merely a factory worker, for talking about "nothing"? Her mother for being a martyr, for being merely a cleaning woman, for being "just a mother"? Who else? How does she consider herself to be like them? How does she consider herself different? Does she judge herself by the same standards as she judged them? Is it her assumption that others use the same standards to judge her? Would I? How could she check this out?

My aim in making the above inquiry is to delineate June's system of introjects in a slightly different way than we did when we were exploring her fear of disclosing her excitement. The same themes come up in somewhat different context again and again in therapy, in a by and large ascending spiral. One of the things that strikes me as we examine June's possible figures for identification and introjection is that neither of them are endowed by her with any positive traits. This does not mean that they had none, but it does mean that June doesn't focus on them. Consequently, when she takes them in as introjects, she only adds to her own sense of inferiority.

When it becomes time, then, to establish new relationships, June encounters difficulty in going through the contactful things which would build friendships because she is afraid of disclosing her own worthlessness. As a therapist, it behooves me to be aware of how this factor interferes with the therapeutic process and to point this out to June. It also becomes my responsibility, and indeed my pleasure, to let her know when I really like or appreciate something she does or says, or even the way she looks. Part of my function is to call her attention to positive aspects of her being, to make her aware of her current assets and her potential.

We could further focus on her system of values. If she feels *she* has nothing of value to contribute, who does? How is she like those people—in whatever infinitesimal way? What would have value for her? What could I do for her that would be valuable? What could she give me of value? What could she give me this very minute? Could she present me with her presence? How? Would she try?

I think I would share with her my idea that all contact is made through the senses, through the media of sight, sound, smell, touch, and taste. We would try to find out which of these she used most, which least, which, possibly, not at all. We could set up a series of experiments in which certain senses were temporarily abolished—closing her eyes, talking to me with her ears plugged, not talking at all—so that she could experience deprivation and frustration and discover how she compensated, if she did. We could discover what made her most uncomfortable and what she did about it. In so doing, she would be giving me something of value, and I would be sure to tell her so.

I would tell her too that all contact is made with emotion, with anger, pain, delight, or love, and that if she wants this for herself she will have to take the risks affiliated with the kindling of it. After all, she is willing to entertain the notion of suicide; she is willing to consider the extreme of non-being. At least she uses her own possible suicide as a threat to her husband. Of course, suicide, like liquor, provides instant surcease from all troubling situations and also, like liquor, allows for no solution. It is a final, negative way of affecting her environment. Could she consider the opposite of suicide? What would that be for her? Would she fantasize killing her husband instead of herself? Could she fantasize his trying to kill her—and possible ways in which she might stop him? Or could she fantasize actively living, interacting with her environment, shaping it to suit her needs or accepting parts of it as different from her and separate. Our task here would be to get a sense of where her boundaries are—where her father, her mother,

her husband end and where she begins. Our task is to differentiate *June* out from all her surroundings and to discover where her power lies.

What we have been faced with so far is a June who introjects, who swallows, whole, large portions of her environment so that they lie heavy in her and affect her behavior in ways over which she has little conscious control. One of the chief problems of the individual who introjects, certainly one of June's prime difficulties, is the inability to mobilize aggression in a creative way. She is consequently unable to destroy (dis-integrate) portions of her environment, concepts that have been dropped on her, so that the parts can be re-formulated (re-integrated) and new concepts (which belong to her) can be engendered. To enable her to grow in this area would be the cardinal task in therapy.

Gestalt Therapy, in much the same way as other existential therapies, depends for success on the building of a relationship between therapist and patient. This means that I, as therapist, have to share important parts of myself with June. I demand from myself the same sorts of things that I would hope eventually to get from June—honesty, openness, attempts at contact, awareness of her feelings and my own. In many ways I would serve as a model, inasmuch as what I am might enable June to be. In essence, I give permission. I give permission to experience each moment as it occurs and to share the discoveries of that moment. I give permission to be angry, to be sad, to be ridiculous, to be inconsistent, to be funny, to be dull, to be human. And I can give permission only by actually being these things myself. Of course, I also reserve the right to be brilliant and wise and exciting and to hope that she could also find these qualities in herself.

If our therapy is successful, I would expect June to experience herself as a "compleat" human being, a woman aware of her strengths and her weaknesses and able to utilize the former and obtain help or understanding for the latter, particularly from herself. I would expect June to know her own dimensions, her own boundaries, and to be able to make contact with other people with boundaries of their own rather than to merge with another's neurosis. I would expect June to formulate a new value system based on who *she* is and where *she* is and what truly matters to her as an individual instead of being immobilized by outworn concepts that never fit her in the first place. I would expect her to have an effect on her world. Above all, I would wish her to know that she could control her actions if she chose to do so, but to know, too, that control is not always desirable, and to be able to choose, when she wished, to abdicate it in favor of excitement and pleasure.

How long would all this take? I have no idea. It would depend on the depth of her initial resistance, her willingness to involve herself in therapeutic risks, and the satisfactoriness of her relationship with me. It would depend in part on how often we saw each other, which in turn is determined by her need, her ability to pay for therapy, and on the number of hours I have available. Chances are that we would start with one hour a week and experience the impact of that before we tried for more. But like everything else we do in therapy, the spacing of the visits would be affected by the moment-to-moment happenings in the session and the prevalent events in her outside world.

When June's experience of that world begins to approach her inner fantasy life in terms of excitement, vitality and need fulfillment instead of turning it into anxiety, it is time for our therapeutic journey to end. It is time for June to go forward on her own.

14

Psychoanalytic Approach
The Case of June

BENNETT SIMON, M.D.

This essay, in describing the psychoanalytic approach to the treatment of a woman with a frigidity problem, will focus on features that are most characteristic of and, in some instances, unique to the psychoanalytic approach. If certain aspects of psychoanalytic treatment are not elaborated, it is not that they are unimportant, but simply that they are, so to speak, the minimum working requirements for the method. A word about these: a certain measure of trust of the therapist is a prerequisite; an emotional stability and a life situation that allow the patient to come regularly and often enough to sessions and the ability to pay for the treatment are also indispensable; verbal ability, per se, is not as critical as the willingness to accept the idea that talking things over can help; an "ego" that can tolerate the stresses and regressive pull of analytic treatment is also a prerequisite.

Some sort of "working alliance" or "therapeutic alliance" is necessary for the treatment to begin and to proceed, though how much of such an alliance and what kind of alliance are subject to wide variation from patient to patient and from therapist to therapist. While most therapists would agree that the conscious profession of willingness to come and to be helped cannot always be taken at face value, most would also agree that without some clear sense from the patient that this was the case, treatment could hardly get off the ground. Even psychosis, *per se,* or even a measure of psychopathy, *per se,* does not constitute an absolute contra-indication to analytic treatment, but rather might constitue some stringent limitations on how much could be accomplished, or pose special problems of technique.

This list of "background factors" or "prerequisities" for treatment could be expanded, and each item is worthy of intensive discussion. Analysts might differ as to what constitutes the *criterion* for whether or not these are fulfilled or differ on the relative weight they might assign to each item. However, all would agree that this list, or some such list, is crucial. Next we turn briefly to the question of what uniquely defines "psychoanalytic treatment."

By "psychoanalytic treatment" I mean "classical" Freudian psychoanalysis, or psychotherapeutic modifications of analysis that are informed by the principles of analysis and modified with an understanding of what differences the modifications might make. There is room for considerable difference of opinion as to the exact definition of and boundaries of "Classical Freudian Analysis," but perhaps a brief list (in anticipation of the detailed discussion) of what is fundamental to the theory and practice would be clarifying:

1. The importance of the method of free association.
2. The therapist *primarily* interprets, and does not *primarily* advise, counsel, or direct.
3. The evolution of a transference.
4. The transference must be interpreted.
5. The underlying assumption of the importance of unconscious mental process.
6. The corollary assumption of the importance of learning about and understanding the childhood experiences, conflicts, and dilemmas of the patient.

The usefulness of technical features such as the couch, frequency of sessions, the relative anonymity of the therapist, and the relative "abstinence" of the therapist should be judged as to whether they facilitate or impede the use of free association, evolution and integration of the transference, and general progress. (See E. Glover, *Technique of Psychoanalysis* [N.Y., Intl. Univ. Press, 1955] and J. Arlow and C. Brenner "The Psychoanalytic Situation," [in R. E. Litman, Ed., *Psychoanalysis in the Americas*, N.Y., Intl.. Univ. Press, 1966].)

DISCUSSION OF THE CASE

I. What is the "problem"?

Is it frigidity? Obviously we are dealing here with a troubled and disturbed *person*. Her relative lack of sexual pleasure is one among several serious complaints, which include: interpersonal conflicts (not only sexual ones) with her husband; trouble falling asleep; a variety of difficulties with her work; a propensity to get herself into difficulties and, seemingly, to almost enjoy or be excited by the difficulties; troubled relationships with her parents; excessive drinking to relieve unpleasant feelings and anxieties; suicidal rumination; paucity of any deep or close relationships with peers; a feeling of marked inferiority, especially prominent in social situations. She is not free to love and not free to give creative expression to her capacities. An important psychoanalytic assumption is that these symptoms, complaints, and behavior patterns have an organic unity. A further assumption is that these phenomena have a *meaning* (or meanings) and that the meanings are to a greater or lesser extent disguised.

II. The precise description of the problem(s)

It is important that the therapist get as clear and detailed a picture of the complaints as is feasible, both in terms of assessing the overall functioning of the person, i.e., a "clinical" assessment, and from the point of view of estimating the suitability of psychoanalytic treatment. In terms of the "chief complaint" of "frigidity," it is important to have more detailed description than is now presented (i.e., what is learned in the first few interviews.) However, where the psychoanalytic method radically diverges from, say, descriptive psychiatry, or even phenomenological psychiatry, is the notion of how facts, descriptions, and data emerge. They unfold during the course of treatment and, almost always, there are left lacunae, areas of vagueness, etc.

Early in his psychoanalytic writings Freud pointed out that even the full description of symptoms, hysterical or obsessive, could not be elicited by direct questioning alone. To illustrate, consider the masturbation fantasy that is reported by the patient (I will assume that this fantasy was not reported in the very first session, which would be rather unusual). It is likely that such a fantasy might first be reported and perhaps subsequently revised, in the setting of a particular therapeutic interaction, such as the patient teasing or provoking the therapist to some form of attack. The therapist points out to the patient that she seems to be inviting attack, or to be presenting herself as a victim awaiting the attack. In association to this confrontation, the patient then reports the fantasy of rape and assault. It is also common that the patient might report the fantasy, but not at first mention its connection with masturbation. In the course of further interpretative work, such as when the therapist perceives a hint of excitement and pleasure in the patient reporting some disaster in her life, the connection with masturbation would be made by the patient. (Or if consciously known already, she might then have a much more intense affective reaction in relating the fantasy and its association with masturbation).

Another illustration. The description of the patient's frigidity is in some respects incomplete. What about the quality, intensity, and location of orgasm? What about important fluctuations in the intensity of her current sexual loathing for her husband? Are these other, seemingly non-sexual sensations associated with intercourse or masturbation (anal sensations, feelings in the chest, abdomen, mouth, visual experiences, etc.)? Or, consider the much vexed issue of "clitoral" *vs.* "vaginal" orgasm. In one instance of a woman with some frigidity problem, the importance of anal sensations and the pleasure of anal stimulation first became apparent to the patient (and the therapist) in the course of a discussion of an event in her pre-pubertal years. Her mother gave her an enema, and *explained* to the patient what she was doing, why, and told her something of what the inside of the rectum and colon was like. (The patient experienced this as a welcome and wonderful enlightenment, and was tremendously grateful to her otherwise distant mother for the explanation.)

Similarly, though a patient could report early in treatment that clitoral stimulation gave her some sort of diffuse orgasm, but neither vaginal stimulation nor intercourse did, the fact remained as rather lifeless "information." However, one day, as the patient was coming closer to experiencing satisfying an intense vaginal orgasm, she came to the session with two pocketbooks, hers and her little daughter's, explaining that the latch was broken on the little girl's purse and she was taking it to be fixed. In this setting, when the clitoral-vaginal distinction arose in discussion, it was possible to point out that her clitoris was her "little girl purse" and the vagina her "grown-up-lady's purse." The "fact" for the first time became emotionally meaningful to the patient and was integrated into her understanding of her symptom, seeming to lead to further improvement in functioning. (Cf. Glenn, J. and Kaplan, E. H., Types of Orgasm in Women, *J. Amer. Psychoanal. Assoc.*, 16:549-65, 1968.)

A corollary of this point is that, though a great many facts and details about the symptoms are *potentially* of importance, it is, in actuality, only those symptoms that emerge in the cause of therapeutic dialogue that are truly useful to the patient and therapist.

III.   The meaning of the symptom

As stated above, a basic psychoanalytic assumption is that symptoms (or inhibitions) have a meaning and, as a corollary, may "communicate" their meanings to the important people in the person's life. One clue to the "intention" of the symptom is the effect the symptom has on others. In this instance, the sexual inhibition apparently frustrates and enrages the husband. This is hardly conclusive *proof* of the intent, but certainly *suggests* that. The inhibition expresses her *wish* to enrage and frustrate the man. Other possible meanings might be guessed at (again from the impact of the sympton), e.g., a wish to be punished, a wish to prove marriage is a disaster, etc.

What strikes this writer as especially prominent in the case of June is the suggestion of a *pattern* that involves a defense and gratification of several wishes. The history details an excessive, almost overtly sexual closeness with the father (fostered and stimulated by the mother), which took a dramatic turn when the patient reached puberty. It was not enough to now refrain from entering the father's bed, but she had to fight with the father and became disillusioned with him. This sequence appears to be repeated in the relationship with the husband, in the turn from pre-marital sexual ease and pleasure to her marital state marked by aversion to intercourse and provocative arguing.

What is being accomplished with this pattern? In the relationship with the father, the danger of forbidden sexuality is kept at bay by the fighting and undoubtedly a great deal of anger towards both father and mother is expressed. Her fantasy of sexual assault by the pirates reinforces the impression that the fighting itself is a sexual gratification. In technical psychoanalytic terms, there is a defensive regression to an earlier and safer level of psychosexual functioning in the face of real and/or imagined dangers attending more mature sexual gratification. How and why she is repeating this pattern with her husband would be elucidated only in the course of treatment.

One might reasonably conjecture that there is a wish and a need to make men impotent, both for reasons of safety and to express some *resentment* at the (alleged) superiority of men over women (or over what men should do for women). Related, too, is her very low self-esteem, which perhaps alternates with an exaggerated and grandiose picture of herself. The history of her mother's never criticizing her and of her attitudes towards work suggests a sense of once privileged (but now dethroned) royalty. This feeling might have derived from the privileged relationship with the father, while other important potential sources of self-esteem either were not available or were undermined by the parents.

One gets a strong sense of how she at first idealized and then later came to belittle the father. The mother apparently also contributed to whittling down the father to life-size or less. At the same time, the image of the mother *resentfully* working as a cleaning woman is not especially suitable as a focal point around which a growing girl can easily form a high opinion of women and of herself.

One typical and recurrent finding in the analysis of women (with or without frigidity problems) is that complaints against the mother, combined with feelings of marked inferiority, betray an anger that the mother did not, or would not, provide the little girl with a penis (or that the one penis that was available, the father's, was primarily for the use and pleasure of the mother, e.g., to give mother babies, but not to give babies to the little girl). This finding does not mean that "penis envy" is the final, reductive explanation of a particular woman's behavior, but rather that a particular set of fantasies (or fantasied assumptions) underlies her behavior, e.g., that women are penis-less men rather than women, or, an exaggerated notion that the penis makes its owner into a worthy, illustrious, and superior human being. Such fantasies are not the "cause" of the symptoms, but probably the "final common pathway" through which the major causal determinants act to shape symptoms and interpersonal behavior.

The interplay between the anatomical fantasies and the relatively low self-esteem of this patient is, in fact, a rather complex one, involving, among other facts, identification with the low self-esteem of one or both parents and the *defensive* use of the assumption that a woman could or ought to have had a penis. The patient's sexual involvements with men considerably older than herself and without any contraceptive (leading to pregnancy and abortion in one instance) probably represent attempts to gratify several needs. The feeling of entitlement to the love, penis, and procreative power of an older man, combined with some self-punitive needs, found expression in pregnancy, abortion, and the breakup of the relationship.

This brings us to the importance of guilt in the genesis and maintenance of the sexual inhibition, as well as of the other symptoms. The details of what the guilt is about and why it should be handled through symptoms are important, but would await clarification in treatment. Aggression towards the mother, wish to displace her, forbidden sexual wishes towards the father are likely sources of guilt. The details of these are crucial but are not apparent at the outset.

Another recurrent theme in the analysis of women with frigidity problems is that of the need to retain a close, intense attachment to the mother. A mature and satisfying sexual life

may be seen, in fantasy, not just as forbidden, but as dangerous, interfering with a certain kind of pseudo-intimate relationship with, or dependence upon, the mother. Frequently,
the clinging to the mother is intertwined with major defensive
needs in handling aggression towards the mother. Anal fantasies and derivative symptoms are often the expression of
these conflicts.

*IV.   The ways in which the meanings inherent in the
        symptoms may be expressed*

How might these meanings be expressed? Or, to put the
question from another perspective, what are the data emerging in treatment from which one infers the kinds of meanings
discussed above?

Especially important is that at various points in the treatment one would expect to see instances in which the vagina is
equated with (or confused with) another organ of the body.
Mouth and anus would be most common, but the possibilities for representation would include a large list. Perhaps, for
June, as suggested by her problem with drinking and by the
(suggestion of) inhibition in speaking in social settings, one
would guess that the *vagina as mouth* would be particularly
important. Dreams, fantasies, slips of the tongue, jokes, literary illusions, and memories might all point to a fantasy of the
vagina as a mouth that is devouring or tearing with its teeth,
or limitless in its demands. Thus, a patient with orgastic difficulty, soon after discussing her problem, dreamed of a refrigerator, her refrigerator, which was well stocked with food, but
was being robbed by the mother. The vagina may be also represented (as in this dream, too) as a kind of treasure trove,
where secret goods are stored. Fantasies of a special prized
treasure, hidden deep within, that no man can get to no matter how often he enters the cave appear to represent an elabo-
tion of a fantasy of a penis, hidden deep within. To experience

orgasm, for such a woman, may be equivalent to yielding up this treasure or this treasured illusion.

It should be emphasized that, though there are some typical themes, one must listen for the idiosyncratic meanings of the various parts of the genitalia. As a specific example, Freud pointed to cases where the clitoris stood for a child, particularly a younger sibling, and where clitoral masturbation was accompanied by the fantasy of "a child is being beaten." For some women, the hymen represents a prized possession, which could be flaunted, equivalent to a penis. Such women might well consider themselves as still virgin, no matter how often they have had intercourse, and consider withholding orgasm as preserving the hymen, with its prized phallic connotations. Similarly, the vagina as anus might be an important theme— a dirty place, where all the man finds is feces. Pregnancy, the baby inside the uterus and the birth process may be represented in an amazing variety of forms—sleeping beauty within the tower, habits of fecal retention and defecation, claustrophobia, psychogenic vomiting, etc.

Analysis of these fantasy representations of the female (and male) anatomy typically lead back to childhood memories and fantasies, often as recalled in childhood games, fairy tales and detective stories, as well as in memories of explicit sexual play, exploration, or seduction.

In general, memories of childhood (as well as of adolescence and early adulthood) play an important part, not only as a way of understanding the genesis of the various conflicts operant in adult life, but also as expressions, in disguised form, of the ongoing conflicts. Freud called certain memories "screen memories" in the sense that they screen off from view certain even earlier memories which are more painful and need to be hidden or "screened." But, for all practical purposes, any memory might serve as a "screen" or defensive distortion and analyzing the distortion can be most fruitful.

Thus, one patient, initially suffering from a *total* lack of any sensation in her genitals, recalled, painfully, her memory, as a six-year-old girl, of lying awake in the dark, feeling terribly isolated and incredibly lonely. When the therapist pointed out that in fact the patient slept in the same room with her three younger siblings and only a few feet away from where the parents slept (the living room), the patient recalled that the door to the bedroom was always kept open and that she was often quite awake and alert to any sounds or movement from the parents' sleeping area. Further elaboration confirmed the therapist's surmise that the sense of isolation was in part defensive in the setting of tremendous overstimulation and overexposure (in word and deed) to adult sexuality, both on the part of her parents and of other adult relatives who lived nearby. These constructions were consonant with and further illuminated her repetitive behavior as an adult—she could be sexually close to a man, attuned to and responsive to the nuances of his sexual states, but without any arousal or sensations of her own.

Another pathway by which conflicts (and attempted solutions) are expressed is through the day-dreaming life of the patient. In the case of June, there is not only the recurrent masturbation fantasy, but the complaint of all the time spent watching "trashy movies." The analysis of the content of these "trashy movies" might well reveal more of the fantasy life of the patient. Again, these adult fantasies frequently have a history of several metamorphoses, and the elucidation of the earlier stages of the fantasies gives important clues to the vicissitudes of conflict over the course of development. The extent to which this metamorphosis of the fantasy can or needs to be reconstructed is highly variable. As the earlier forms and variants of the "pirate fantasy" would become clarified, the elaboration of the childhood experience and traumata that helped shape the present symptom would emerge.

V.   The importance of understanding the childhood experience of the patient

Strictly speaking, what is important in an analysis is that which elucidates and helps shifts the balance of forces in the current conflict. From this viewpoint, childhood material is one of several areas of the psychic life, any of which may be of special importance at any one point in the treatment, or with any particular patient. Yet, such a bald statement is misleading since, in fact, the re-experiencing, remembering, reconstruction, and finally some sort of revision of personal memories do seem indispensable to successful treatment. It is somehow important that a patient weep once more (or perhaps for the first time) over the doll her father promised, but never gave; or experience something of the mixture of rage, humiliation, and sexual arousal of a 10-year-old girl whose mother habitually scrubbed with a stiff brush her "dirty" genitalia. Perhaps these experiences, or re-experiences, with the adult, observing ego (of patient and therapist) looking on, allow for a more *convincing* demonstration to the patient of the persistence of that childhood view of the world.

Side by side with this "revival" of childhood treatment is the painstaking reconstruction of the repetitive interactions between parent and child, the emotional tone in daily living, the "atmosphere" inhaled (and also exhaled) by the child. In the case of June, the elucidation of the theme that the mother saw her "as a perfect little angel who could do no wrong—even after she broke a shampoo bottle over her own head"—could lead to a richer and more vivid understanding of (what I surmise to be) some of her character traits. These include difficulty in accepting criticism, a pattern of hurting herself in order to demand that others set limits for her, and doing something exhibitionistic or outrageous to provoke a response from those close to her.

*VI.   Which of these various formulations are communicated
to the patient, when and how?*

The answer to this question is that any and all of these formulations (speculations, etc.) are to be shared with the patient in direct, simple and personal language at the time when
it seems clear to the therapist that some particular formulation
is true and that the patient has indicated she is ready to hear
and deal with it. Matters of timing and tact are, of course, important. ("Call a spade a spade, but don't use it as a club,"
protested one patient to her therapist's accurate, but overly
aggressive, interpretation of an unpleasant side of herself.)

However, such statements as these verge on the formulaic,
and even suggest that conscious calculation on the part of the
therapist is the main part of the interpretative process. Such
a view would be quite a distortion of the actualities of the
analytic process. Typically, the therapist knows what and
when to interpret because there has been a kind of interchange, meeting, and "resonance" between therapist and patient. The therapist's formulations arise in the setting of his
impressions about and reactions to the patient, at a conscious,
preconscious, and unconscious level. His formulations also
crystallize over time and are shaped and modified in the context of constant interaction with the patient. The skill of the
therapist probably resides in some mixture of factors: an ability to be in touch with his "intuition," being guided by it, but
not totally ruled by it; focusing his own memories, feelings,
and free associations in such a way that they are directly relevant to the patient's problems; learning from previous experience with other patients and being able to modify what he has
learned according to the particulars of the present situation.

Another corollary of this view of how things actually happen in treatment is that the *sequence* in which material emerges is highly variable from case to case, (though not entirely
unpredictable for any particular patient) .

The process by which this "resonance" between patient and therapist takes place is at best imperfectly understood, but it is some such process that is really at the core of the therapeutic situation.

VII.   *What does the therapist do?*

The unique and characteristic function of the psychoanalytic therapist is to *interpret*. He may do many other things that an outside observer would take note of—question, clarify, remain silent, be helpful or friendly, give advice or direction, etc., but it is the conscious act of *interpretation* that distinguishes analysis from most other verbal dialogues and verbal psychotherapies.

What is an interpretation? It is a formulation that ties together past experience, the transference situation, and the current conflicts of the patient. Rarely does any one interpretation do all of this, or explicitly do all of this. But any particular interpretation of the relationship between childhood experience and the feelings towards the therapist, for example, would likely lead to the *patient* relating the interpretation to current conflicts.

What does an interpretation "look like"? Its form is variable, its effects highly variable, and so forth. But, from the case material supplied, we could offer a hypothetical instance of an interpretation and its sequelae that might emerge in the treatment of June.

Following periods of repeated and prolonged silence by the patient, punctuated by a rather sweeping, negativistic response to everything the therapist has said, the therapist interprets: "Your silence and your negativism are a way of being frigid to me. You have made yourself and your mind as unresponsive to me as your body and your vagina are to your husband. You do this with me because you are afraid of the sexual arousal you feel while lying on my couch."

Such an interpretation serves several functions at once. It ties together seemingly separate compartments of behavior and declares them as one. It addresses itself to a prime *resistance* of the patient to utilizing the interventions of the therapist and declares the resistance as a *defense*. It adds a motive for the defense by indicating that the patient sexualizes the analytic situation and responds *as if* it were an actual sexual situation. It leaves unanswered the question of why the patient needs to be frigid with her husband.

June might become even more sullen after such an interpretation, with visible evidence of an inner struggle between silence and speaking, and even between moving and not moving on the couch. "But you are silent with me," might suddenly burst forth from the patient. Therapist: "And this is your revenge for my silence, just as you felt entitled to revenge yourself on your father for humiliating you by his disdainful silence that day when you were 13 and, etc." Then some weeping—as the patient might say, "You mean you don't *intend* to humiliate me! I'm so ashamed now when I think of how I reacted the other night to my husband, who seemed quite worried and preoccupied about a problem at his work, and I carried on and finally provoked a fight because I couldn't stand to think he was deliberately ignoring me and pushing me aside."

Such an interchange might take place in a few minutes or its components might be spread out over several occasions. It is also possible that the therapist's intervention might have been to point to the evidence of a *struggle* within the patient, that she is attempting to deal with the inner struggle by means of a struggle between herself and the therapist (or her husband). Such an interpretation might then lead to the patient associating to the times of her life when in fact she saw her parents fighting (one with words, and the other with disdainful silence) and felt torn in her loyalties to both of them. These variations in the nature of and the style of the interpretation might be seen within the same treatment situation at different points in the treatment, or might be functions of personal styles of different therapists (and different patients).

VIII.   What does the therapist mean to the patient?

Certainly, from the patient's perspective he may mean many different things. Teacher, model, impartial judge, doctor, helper, etc., might each characterize the way a particular patient consciously thinks of his therapist. Another kind of expectation may flourish, either preconsciously, or else suppressed out of shame, fear, etc. Typical of this kind might be therapist as "mind-reader," therapist as seducer or lover, therapist as "redeemer," or therapist as one-who-will-take-advantage-of-you if you let your guard down. This latter group merges imperceptibly into the *transference* expectations, or perceptions that the patient has of the therapist. The variety of roles into which patients may unconsciously cast the therapist is infinite, though for each patient only a few are prominent, or more accurately, only a few are prominent enough to be amenable to interpretation. The therapist may be male, but as the patient's transference needs demand a mother figure, patient's fantasies of the therapist undergo an appropriate change. What is important is that the analytic process permits both patient and therapist to move beyond simplifications such as "I am a mother, or father, or teacher, to you," and to explore and understand the nuances of, for example, what a *teacher* means to the patient, what a *doctor* means to the patient, what *kind of father* the patient recreates in transference.

We are aware that various features of the therapist's behavior may well have special significance for the patient and that these do not always become explicit in the course of the analysis. The importance of the therapist as a model of steadfastness, of integrity, or of moral flexibility, or of good humor, with whom the patient may identify (or whom she may just imitate) , may not be easily apparent during the analysis. (Often, a third party, who knows both patient and therapist, can more readily detect these identifications.)

IX. *What might one expect in therapy and as a result of therapy?*

There is the story that Freud was once asked, "What is the goal of psychoanalysis? Bigger and better orgasm?" To this he gave his famous summary, "No, to enable the patient to love and to work, *lieben und arbeiten.*"

What one would anticipate in this case is that, in the course of the unfolding of themes and of the analyst's interpretations, there would be a gradual expansion of June's insight into herself, changes in her capacity to relate more comfortably in day-to-day work and living situations, and improvement or remission of the sympton of lack of orgastic response. We would also expect a growing awareness both of her capacity for love and tenderness and of how afraid and inhibited she has been to express these feelings.

Once again, it should be emphasized that these changes take place in a manner that is idiosyncratic to each person, in an array of interweaving themes of a beauty and intricacy that is difficult to reproduce. The changes often appear as surprises and unexpectedly there is remarkable improvement in other areas. Thus, therapeutic work on the theme of her guilt and the masochistic pattern of dealing with unacceptable guilty feelings might well lead to a clarification of her chronic sense of inferiority in social situations. Projected guilt, manifesting itself as a sense of being criticized by others and as a feeling of personal inferiority, might play an important role in creating and perpetuating her social difficulties. Interpretations of the competitive rage that prevents her from forming close friendships with women might be followed by a dramatic improvement in her capacity to enjoy intercourse with her husband.

Particular to this case, one might well anticipate two problems in treatment that would require careful understanding and tactful analysis. One is the tendency to self-defeating, masochistic provocation, which sooner or later must involve the therapist. The therapist must be in touch with his urges to respond with sadistically motivated comments or interventions and use the awareness of these urges as a guideline for interpretation. For the therapist to *act* sadistically would mean a conjoint acting-out of the patient's fantasy and signify a failure to analyze the fantasy.

The second problem is that of keeping clear of the boundary (or lack of boundary) in such a case between "acting-out" and "action," especially constructive action. The involvements with older men, without contraceptive precautions, for instance, strongly suggest that this patient, at various difficult points in the analysis, would act-out her conflicts rather than primarily or exclusively work on them in analysis. For this patient, two plausible forms of acting out would be (a) an extra-marital affair and (b) a pregnancy. Of course, both of these could also be steps in a new resolution of her conflicts. Also experience shows that women with severe frigidity problems are often married to men who themselves have serious sexual difficulties, or else to men who become uninterested or impotent as the wife becomes more aroused and receptive. If, in the intensity of a sexualized transference to the analyst, the patient seeks out an affair with a man and establishes that now, with a man who cares and who is potent, she is orgastic, is this acting-out or a necessary trial action possibly leading to a new and better relationship? The answer is that either or both may be true and, again, careful interpretation rather than prohibition or encouragement is what is most required.

Also in the course of "working through," one might well

see transient new symptoms develop, particularly phobias. A phobia, in this instance, would likely represent a recurrence of a forgotten childhood symptom and analysis would reveal that the phobia represents some of the same conflicts as does the symptom of frigidity, e.g., fears and wishes about bodily contents and bodily penetration, but now projected onto outer space (the street, the elevator, etc.) instead of inner space. The appearance of a "new" symptom is often an index that, in fact, change and growth are taking place.

Among indications that deep and enduring change is taking place are:

   a. Some revision in the patient's initial view of her own history,

   b. Some flexibility in the habitual character style—the obsessive becoming a bit hysterical, and the hysterical a bit obsessive.

   c. A growing capacity for self-analysis and evidence that the patient can use it as a tool when not in analysis (e.g., on summer vacations).

   d. A revised view of the analyst, especially with some perspective on her idealized fantasies about the analyst and his power.

X. Termination

The basic criterion for termination, put in simplest terms, is the shared sense of therapist and patient that they are reaching the limit of what can be accomplished and that a good deal has been accomplished.

The termination phase may revive some old (and seemingly resolved) problems and symptoms. In fact, the revival of a symptom may even be a clue that it is appropriate to talk of termination. One would expect that termination would especially reawaken conflicts involving separation and loss, and this is frequently so. But again, the variety of issues that appear in this setting is astonishing and should not be prematurely reduced to any one formula, such as "separation anxiety."

Termination should also leave the patient with an awareness of what might be particularly troublesome future life situations, as part of the patient's realistic assessment of both her weaknesses and strengths. (With June, for example, she and the therapist could fruitfully consider how she would react to the death of one of her parents).

Finally, a word should be said about "Post termination." The analytic process, under optimal circumstances, continues well after formal treatment has stopped. A good deal of evidence points to the conclusion that the transference relation diminishes in intensity, but can readily be relighted, and that an important part of the capacity for post-analytic self-analysis is tied up with so called "unresolved" transference feelings. Inner dialogues between patient and therapist can be an important tool of continuing self-analysis.

XI.   How long does all of this take, how much does it cost, and how often does it lead to a remission of the problem of frigidity?

Classical analysis is 4-5 sessions per week and typically would run into a number of years. Three to five years would not be unusual. Once or twice weekly psychotherapy would also typically extend over a period of years. At a (modest) estimate of $30 a session, the costs are enormous.

Though many changes take place with treatment, it is fair to ask about specific improvement in the symptom of frigidity. There is great variability in outcome and also as to when in the course of treatment one would see the symptomatic improvement.

At present, to my knowledge there are no published reliable

figures on the efficacy of analysis and psychotherapy for frigidity. The following statements, then, are based on:

A. The author's impression of the literature and oral reports of very experienced analysts.
B. Cases he has himself treated, or supervised, or heard presented in detail by colleagues.

1. In women, where there has *never* been an experience of orgasm referable to anywhere in the genitalia, induced by masturbation or intercourse or even homosexual contact, the likelihood of experiencing full, satisfying, vaginal orgasm is quite small. The likelihood of there being marked improvement in their capacity to enjoy intercourse and to relate more comfortably and more meaningfully with men is considerable.

2. A previous history of satisfying orgasm, which later the patient no longer experienced, is, in general, a better prognostic sign and indication of a fair likelihood that, with treatment, the previous level of enjoyment can be again attained. Here, too, a large measure of general improvement in overall functioning and modifications in ways of relating to men (and to women) can be anticipated as an outcome of treatment.

3. Women for whom there has been a temporary change in a well-established capacity for orgasm, (as is often seen where pre-marital intercourse with the boy friend is highly pleasurable, but with marriage the relationship changes for the worse), might typically experience return of full function early in therapy, with little or no specific interpretative work by the therapist.

4. In a large number of instances, there is, as a result of therapy, marked change in the quality and intensity and location of the orgastic experience. Quite often, women who have not come to therapy seeking help for

a sexual-response problem have discovered in the course of treatment that their previous functioning was less than satisfactory and has, in fact, improved considerably.

It should be added that there are exceptions to all of the above and that clear, systematic data are hard to come by. Conspicuous failures tend to get reported by analysts less often than dramatic therapeutic successes. Nevertheless, it is this writer's impression that were data to be carefully compiled, they would indicate a substantial therapeutic yield as a result of analytic treatment. In addition, such a compilation would aid substantially in improving our ability to pre-select and match up patient with therapist, and patient with therapeutic modality.

15

Critical Comparison
The Case of June

GLORIA HEIMAN LOEW, Ph.D.,
CLEMENS A. LOEW, Ph.D. and
HENRY GRAYSON, Ph.D.

As June walks into the office of any of our three therapists and begins to relay her problem as she sees it, a similar cognitive event is occurring in the minds of all therapists. They are attending to June's appearance, listening, asking some questions, and formulating in their own minds many questions that are not expressed. The focus of these unexpressed questions highlights what is similar and different in each approach.

Simon, the psychoanalyst, sees June as an individual whose childhood experiences, which remain with her in the form of unconscious mental processes, interfere with full and adequate functioning. He sees himself as one who must interpret, or help June make cognitive connections. To do this he must make full use of the transference. He interprets through the transference, tying in this way past to present and present to past.

Simon is asking himself whether June is motivated for treatment, whether she has the emotional resources (ego) to tolerate his method of treatment, and if she is attempting to formulate her problem in terms of the "meaning" of her symp-

toms and behavior. He assumes, as he states, that June's behavior has unity and meaning, but that such meaning is in
good part disguised.

None of our theorists views June's frigidity as her primary
or central problem. For that matter, neither does June as she
freely admits to many other problem areas. Simon, when one
reviews his chapter in bare outline, seems to see June as a girl
who has a very poor self concept and who is caught in the trap
of perpetuating self-defeating behavior in all aspects of her
life. The frigidity itself is seen in symbolic terms, with many
possible meanings, including guilt, penis envy, overattach-
ment to mother, and childhood fantasy and confusion involving the vagina.

However, Simon would not take a direct approach to an-
swering the questions he is entertaining about June. The
reason for this is that he feels data must emerge in a "dynamic
context" to be meaningful. The true understanding of the patient must emerge in the course of treatment or all that will
emerge in answer to questions is the patient's conscious understanding of herself. What Simon does not say is that it takes
considerable intuition, knowledge, and skill to sense and pick
out the proper connections between maladaptive conscious behavior or symptoms and unconscious antecedents. And once
becoming aware of the connections or answers, so to speak,
the therapist must then sense the best time and way to convey
this understanding to the patient. Accordingly, when the patient recognizes and fully accepts the infantile unconscious
motivation for her behavior, she will begin to improve.

Let us compare this to Gestalt therapist Fantz's view of
June and her idea of how she would help her. Fantz sees June
as a person with great polarity of desires and feelings. Large
parts of herself are alienated and unclaimed. Therapy is an
"unmasking" process whereby June begins to take ownership
of all the disparate parts of herself and begins to discard those

parts which are unsatisfying to her. As in all existential therapies, the will of the patient is strongly emphasized. The therapist aids the patient in experiencing herself. The patient is thus freer to make decisions about her life. Fantz tries to work as much as possible in the present and to use the relationship between therapist and client as a vehicle for progress. Change comes about by experiencing the total self in the present.

Let us stop here for a moment and make some comparisons between Fantz and Simon's work. At first glance, we notice that Fantz refers to June as the "client" as contrasted to the "patient." This seems to reflect the existential philosophy of humanness and selfhood and the greater sense of equality that exists in this theoretical approach. There is more discussion of this point at the conclusion of this chapter. The analytic approach, based on a medical model, views June as a patient, implying pathology and less of a one-to-one, informal relationship between June and her doctor.

A further comparative issue is the greater emphasis on the present in Gestalt therapy, with less need to understand the past. Fantz refers to family history and past history only in trying to grasp June's sense of identity so as to understand what interfered with total self acceptance and to understand parts of herself that were poorly developed. However, in both therapies we encounter the emphasis on the use of the relationship between June and her therapist. Simon refers to this as utilizing the transference, but Fantz sees herself primarily as a model and as one who maximizes the client's self actualizing.

The goal in Gestalt therapy is to fully appreciate oneself in the present. Awareness is a goal in itself which is seen as allowing change to occur. But the awareness appears to be much more of a guts level awareness, a body awareness arrived at through physical means. When Fantz asks June to exaggerate her trembling or to explore what she is stiffening against in sex, we have an example of working for awareness by physical means. An analogous but not identical aspect in psychoanalysis is to make the unconscious conscious, to become aware of unresolved conflict from the formative years by free association, for example.

Fantz also formulates many questions as a way of understanding the patient, some of which she immediately shares openly. For example, Fantz initially turns her attention to why June needs her "mask" of control and to what she is trying to control. In bare outline, Fantz appears to view June's problem as follows. June introjects large portions of her environment, thus allowing little conscious control of feelings. She is unable to mobilize aggression in a creative way and is "sado-masochistic" and "passive aggressive." June has difficulty relating to others, is overcontrolled and stifled by inferior feelings and feelings of worthlessness. Her frigidity is seen primarily as a defense against excitement because of guilt and a fear of punishment. And so we see many overlapping conceptualizations of June's personality, behavior, and symptomology in Fantz' and Simon's analyses, while at the same time observing many differences in the approach or techniques of helping the patient. We can't avoid observing that Fantz uses conceptualizations that must have had their origin in psychoanalytic writing—terms such as "sado-masochistic" and "positive-aggressive," or references to the primitiveness of early repressed emotions. It is in this dynamic understanding of the patient's personality that Gestalt therapists owe a debt to analytic theorists.

Now, let us compare Lazarus' conception of June's problems and how his behavioral therapy approach based on social learning theory could be applied. Lazarus sees June as a "semi-social isolate who lacks identity and purpose." She is described as "emotionally impoverished." He views June as anxious and aggressive, but unable to express her aggression appropriately in an assertive, non-manipulative manner. Lazarus feels June's frigidity is only "one facet of her inability to feel enduringly positive toward anyone or anything." He feels guilt and sexual misconceptions might also be contributing factors to her frigidity. Thus we see similarities to both Fantz' and Simon's descriptive understanding of June's personality dynamics.

Lazarus formulates many questions at the beginning of therapy that bear resemblance to those asked by Simon and Fantz. He is interested in family determinants and history as well as present manifestations of conflicts. However, June's personality is explained in terms of response deficits. Lazarus states, "June's problems appear largely attributable to the fact that her home seems to have provided so few opportunities for her to acquire prosocial, self-confident, goal-directed aims and purposes." There is a paucity of learning, the patients is deprived and viewed as a student who must be re-educated. According to this viewpoint, therapy must condition and teach new "rational attitudes," modes of thinking and adaptive behavior. The goal is to eliminate maladaptive behavior by replacing it with learned adaptive responses, "to train the patient in a significant range of effective behaviors." Thus Lazarus' approach is distinguished in both conceptualization of the causative aspect of June's problems and his technique of treatment.

Now that we have reviewed how each theorist conceptualizes his approach and how he views June's personality, let us turn to a comparison of some questions of technique and other areas of interest.

What does each theoretical approach require of the patient because of its own method of treatment? The psychoanalytic approach requires good verbal ability, as well as a relatively strong "ego." Gestalt treatment requires the ability to fantasize and role play. Behavior therapy would seem to stress most the willingness of the patient to cooperate with the therapist and also the ability to role play.

In this use of role playing in both the Gestalt and behavior therapies we see an acting-out of fantasy that is vented only through verbal expression or free association in analysis. It is similar to a comparison between dreaming (a cognitive expression) and sleep walking which includes motoric expression along with the cognitive activity.

The importance of the motoric or body component in Gestalt therapy seems to be a major factor in treatment, that is, the patient is engaged in a physical as well as in a cognitive way. "The patient is encouraged to verbalize feeling along with the action." Most analysts would agree that any good interpretation must be well timed and engage the feelings of the patient, but Fantz in her repetitive role playing, exaggeration of body responses (such as trembling), and loud vocalizing seems to engage the feelings of the patient more dramatically.

Behavior therapy engages feelings in its desensitizing and relaxation training techniques, for example, as well as in role-playing, but in a more circumscribed manner than Gestalt therapy.

Dreams are dealt with quite differently by analyst and Gestaltist. The behaviorist doesn't stress interpretations of dreams at all. The analytic view of dreams as the expression of unconscious wishes neeeds no elaboration. The Gestaltists view dreams as expressing "alienated parts of the self," as well as parts of the patient "that he really claims as his own." All the parts of the dream are enacted by the patient to gain better undestanding and full acceptance. Nevertheless, one has to ask the question how different is the concept "alienated self" from the concept "unconscious."

Further, the Gestaltist would let the interpretations "emerge from the patient," holding back until the proper moment. The behaviorist would be more direct and abrupt in dealing with interpretations, asking the patient to accept "utterly frank feedback" and emphasizing that he is being nonjudgmental and not critical. In fact, what is meant by an interpretation would vary from therapist to therapist. Simon's definition of a good interpretation as linking the past, the present conflict, and the transference bears rereading here.

Lazarus certainly makes the greatest appeal to the conscious ego. He does not speak of resistance, unconscious wishes, or transference. Sessions deal with more effective ways to handle feelings of self criticism, hypersensitivity, and anger. There are questionnaires, checklists, homework to do, books to read, and sexual techniques to explore and practice. Fantz seems to only occasionally make a suggestion that "would carry over to the patient's private life. Simon, it would seem, would not do this at all. Both Simon and Fantz ask few direct questions because answers must come out of the context of the session to be valuable.

Lazarus also extends himself into the patient's private life by actively bringing in family members for treatment. He would work on the communication in the marriage, "the destructive marital games and feuding tactics." He mentions that under certain circumstances he would even bring in June's parents for family therapy. He offers many alternatives to the patients, such as group therapy and conjoint couples therapy. Again, a classical analytic therapist would probably involve himself the least with individuals related to the patient and the Gestalt therapist would fall somewhere in between the other two.

Now let us turn to the experience of therapist and patient. How does each view the other and how does each experience therapy.

Lazarus views the patient as a client and a student. He feels understanding is important but not critical for treatment. In his initial view of June, he seems to have a negative reaction to her, but one feels he will work with her nevertheless. He is very active in his approach and discourages dependency and intense involvement by keeping goals in the forefront. He speaks of "coaxing" the patient to try recommended techniques. Nevertheless, he is sensitive to keeping the anxiety level of the patients low and tries to enlist the patient's cooperation in all that he does. As he does it, he attempts to be didactic, empathetic, and flexible. Like Fantz, his role is "informal and self disclosing."

How might June experience therapy with Lazarus? Would she learn to accept his "utterly frank feedback" as non-judgmental? Would she feel manipulated or the focus of much well-aimed and helpful attention?

Fantz sees June as a person rather than primarily a patient. Her role seems to be to help the patient experience herself ("her humanness") fully. Fantz sees herself as a model who generates permission for genuineness. Therefore, she shares important and varied parts of herself with June. Fantz also explains the treatment process to June, which would allow her to ally with the therapist and reduce her anxiety. We can assume that Fantz is seldom the object of sustained negative feelings. In most cases the hostility and anger of the patient are expressed toward someone other than the therapist.

How might June experience therapy with Fantz? June might feel less manipulated. Since the emphasis is so often on choice, will and ownership of feelings, the patient might experience therapy as less restrictive and threatening than either analytic or behavior therapy.

Simon sees his role as making interpretations and connections for the patient. He sees his role as totally non-directive and not manipulative, but he still makes certain demands on the patient. These demands include being on the couch, free association, and a higher frequency of sessions and length of therapeutic treatment. The therapist remains relatively anonymous and does not express personal feelings freely.

What the therapist means to the patient in analytic treatment will depend on the quality and variability of the transference. The therapist is viewed as a model also, but this function is secondary to the transference.

In contrast to Fantz and Lazarus, Simon makes himself the object of strong negative feelings through the transference. Both patient and therapist would have to endure higher levels of anxiety for longer periods than in the other two types of treatment.

All three therapies impose certain obligations or restrictions and all manipulate the patient to some extent. At the same time, all three therapies direct and control the activities of the therapists to some extent. But it does seem as if Gestalt therapy provides the greatest freedom for expression to both therapist and patient during the treatment.

How long does it take for the goals of treatment to be reached and what are these goals specifically in June's case? The behavior therapist suggests that improvement might be evident in the first three months. Lazarus estimates about 90 sessions of individual, group, and conjoint sessions combined. Simon talks of classical analysis extending over three to five years of four or five sessions per week.

The goals of treatment by the three therapists have much in common when related specifically to June's problems rather than to theoretical issues. They all strive for greater self understanding and acceptance, freer communication and relation with others, and increased sexual enjoyment. Simon is more guarded in his prognosis of curing June's sexual difficulties through analysis than either Fantz or Lazarus. Yet all reflect their confidence in being able to help her.

16

Behavior Therapy Approach

The Case of June (II)

MELVYN HOLLANDER, Ph.D.

Behavior therapy is an action-oriented treatment approach which refers to a wide variety of empirically based procedures, derived largely from experimental psychology, and applied in a professional context toward the achievement of specific goals. What separates behavior therapy from most other approaches is its application of the scientific method to treatment. Clinical goals are concrete and systematically planned, and progress is continuously monitored in a quantitative fashion.

Some additional practices and misconceptions of the behavioral approach are worthy of mention. In accordance with the model, there is a direct focus on the maladaptive symptoms (called target behaviors). Simply put, behaviors that are excessive in frequency, intensity, context, or duration are decreased, while deficit behavior patterns are increased (Kanfer and Saslow, 1969). This is not meant to imply that target behavior selection is restricted to circumscribed problems. The behavioral model recognizes the contribution of past events and the importance of a comprehensive assessment of complex interpersonal behavior and cognitions. These sources of clinical data are acceptable provided that they are securely anchored to both observable antecedent and consequent events (Davidson, 1969; Hollander, 1973).

There is a strong emphasis in the behavioral approach on the open and deliberate use of social influence procedures such as verbal reinforcement and modeling to promote desired therapeutic goals. It should suffice to say that the behavior therapist's use of warmth, acceptance and other relationship skills is common, but not apart from the use of deliberate control and planned teaching.

FRIGIDITY AND BEHAVIOR THERAPY

There is sufficient clinical and research evidence to indicate that behavior therapy is a promising treatment for frigidity. Theoretically, Wolpe (1969) has suggested two categories of frigidity: essential and situational. Essential frigidity refers to sexual anxiety and a generalized lack of sexual responsiveness to men, whereas in situational frigidity interpersonal retaliation towards a particular man is the predominant feature. Brady (1966) has distinguished sexual activity without orgasm and sexual avoidance coupled with pain during intercourse as two types of frigidity patterns.

Systematic desensitization has been demonstrated to be an effective technique for frigidity. The first reported use was that of Glynn and Harper (1961). Lazarus (1963) employed systematic desensitization in a group setting with 16 females. The anxiety hierarchies were directly related to progressive sexual contact and intimacy. The use of brevital to promote relaxation in conjunction with systematic desensitization was reported by Brady (1966) in the treatment of five cases of frigidity. Direct training of social skills was found to be more effective than systematic desensitization for the treatment of a single case of frigidity (Kraft and Al-Issa, 1967).

Graded sexual activities and mechanical devices have been

widely used in behavior therapy. Masters and Johnson (1970) have developed a comprehensive treatment program for sexual dysfunctioning based, in part, on gradual approximations of sexual activities. Both Rachman (1959) and Haslam (1965) report the success of a treatment program favoring gradual vaginal penetration with objects of increasing size and diameter. The vibrator machine as a method of conditioning orgasmic responding has been clinically illustrated by Knox (1972) with his treatment of marital couples.

Stuart (1969) has theorized that a lack of reciprocity in positive interpersonal exchanges may offer an explanation for frigidity as it occurs in some marital situations. The treatment embodies the use of negotiated exchange contracts to promote more positive interactions, thereby removing negative interpersonal conditions eliciting frigidity. In a similar vein, Patterson (1971) developed an effective behavioral procedure designed to train negotiation skills in conflict-habituated couples. Conjoint behavior therapy was found to promote major behavioral changes in a frigid wife-impotent husband configuration (Hollander, 1974). The strategies included training in negotiations, behavior exchange programs, mutual assertive training, systematic desensitization, and value delineation discussions.

Although the literature clearly documents the usefulness of a behavioral treatment approach with frigidity, published case histories do not usually include the many important details necessary for a full undestanding of how the behavior therapy was conducted (Cautela, 1967). The major purpose of this paper is to provide such details and offer a look at the manner in which I practice behavior therapy.

BEHAVIORAL DESCRIPTION OF THE PROBLEM

Before examining the methods of behavioral assessment and treatment in the case of June, I think it would be instructive to illustrate a behavioral formulation of the etiology and nature of the problems presented in the case material.

Frigidity: June's self-description and initial complaints suggest several working hypotheses. For one, frigidity has presently taken the form of infrequent sexual intercourse with her husband. Attempts at intercourse have failed to produce orgasm and, instead, have resulted in feelings of anxiety and repulsion. Since June continues to engage in sexual contact with her husband under such aversive and non-physically reinforcing consequences, one wonders what is maintaining her sexual activity. A possible explanation is that by engaging in sex (even if in a perfunctory manner) June is avoiding a still more aversive consequence. This aversive consequence is experiencing her husband's frustration, rage, and disappointment upon his discovering her sexual "inadequacies."

Lack of Assertion: This explanation leads to another working hypothesis. June's frigidity may be the result of much more than erroneous sexual information and specific phobic responses to various forms of sexual activity. In fact, the frigidity may be primarily related to a lack of assertive interpersonal skills which have inadvertently produced a situation of general marital dissatisfaction. Several verbal statements reflected a lack of assertion on June's part. She cannot constructively terminate sexual activity with her husband when it becomes personally aversive and repulsive. She describes herself as incapable of coping with her husband's "domineering" tactics. Although June's husband may, in fact, be physically powerful, it is irrational for June to view herself as totally ineffective in containing his reported emotional outbursts. June's other statements that she has no friends and that she cannot make meaningful contributions to conversations again suggest forms of assertion difficulties.

Avoidance Responses: An entire series of target behaviors reflects escape or avoidance from anxiety-generated situations.

One example is the work situation. June avoids work through premeditated "sick" calls and escapes from the same situation via prolonged lunch breaks. Interestingly, the lunch breaks provide two sources of reinforcement. First, the anxiety of being on the job is temporarily averted. Second, this escape provided an opportunity to engage in such reinforcing activities as viewing "trashy" movies.

Another example of an avoidance pattern is drinking. As reported, drinking serves the function of reducing social anxiety and the anxiety that results from feelings of helplessness during altercations with her husband. Another reinforcing function of drinking is that of removing unpleasant thoughts through physiologically altering her consciousness.

Irrational conditioning anxiety is evident in two other circumstances: being touched on the breasts and falling asleep. The former situation could be one of the earliest aversive links in the sexual activity chain. The latter phobia may be related to June's frigidity problem. Whether due to symbolic or accidental learning conditions, a deviant sexual fantasy currently plays a prominent role in June's sleeping problem. Let us hypothesize that falling asleep is a problem due to general tension and anxiety. The fantasy occurs and then is paired with masturbation, which not only produces reinforcement in the form of orgasm but also creates the relaxing condition necessary for sleep.

Several problems can result from this practice. First, since the age of 13, masturbation reinforced a passive, self-punitive sexual fantasy. It would not be suprising if this practice tended to shape her perceptions of the sex act. Second, the masturbation sequence was used only under near-sleep conditions. Thus, the orgasm has been associated only with a restricted, non-interpersonal context.

Coercive Control: Patterson (1971) theorized that one form of deviant interpersonal control is coercion. In this control pattern, person A resorts to presenting person B with a continuous barrage of punitive experiences which are removed only when person B responds to the demands of person A. Often, person A is ineffective in the use of such positive control forces as affection, encouragement, or attention. This phenomenon may be evident in June's suicidal threats. Failing to terminate marital fights in an assertive fashion, June finds the threat of suicide of sufficient aversion to her husband for him to stop fighting. Unfortunately, June's lack of interpersonal skills results in this "last resort" method of coping.

Past History: June's parents may have failed to provide her with the kinds of opportunities essential to learn self-confidence, independence, and emotional maturity. Her mother saw June as a child "who could do no wrong." If June's retrospective statement is accurate, her mother may have failed to expect responsible behavior from her and may have protected her from the consequences. The relationship with her father prior to beginning menses was good. Thereafter it deteriorated. I am reluctant to advance a sexual inference. Rather, I think June began to be more independent at this time in her life. Independence in June may have been a very anxiety-arousing event to the father. He could have reacted aggressively, which not only caused a deterioration in their relationship but also may have set the stage for June to expect punishment whenever she asserted herself and did not conform to parental expectations.

INITIAL ASSESSMENT INTERVIEW

The initial interview with June would follow a rather standard behavioral format. After putting June at ease, I would encourage her to discuss her reasons for coming to me. Also, I would conduct a brief psychosocial history. As June is feeling more at ease, I would begin to use what I call behavioral probing. This is a simple interview strategy of focusing the discussion on the identification of specific target behaviors, the relevant antecedents that set the occasion for the target behavior problems, and the relevant consequent conditions that maintain them. Through behavioral probing, June would be helped to define her terms with more precision. For example, she complains that her husband had outbursts of rage. The word rage lends itself to multiple interpretations. June would be asked to define the specific manner and contexts in which rage occurs.

Next I would offer June a brief overview of behavior therapy. How I conduct this orientation depends on several factors. Among them are prior treatment and unfounded stereotypes. Often, I find that persons who have undergone years of insight therapy benefit from a fair comparison of approaches. Stereotypes must be examined and worked through. Two common ones are: behavior therapy produces dramatic results in two to three sessions; behavior therapy subjects a patient to the direct, powerful, and unwise control of the therapist.

Assuming that June has had no prior therapy or irrational stereotypes, I would tell her that I plan to teach her more effective behavioral skills and rational cognitions. June hears me emphasize the mutual responsibilities inherent in behavior therapy. I assume major responsibility for the formulation of treatment plans, whereas June assumes major responsibility for practicing the newly learned skill in her day-to-day routine.

No behavioral explanation is complete without a discussion of the meaning of psychopathology. June would probably be reassured to learn that I view her problems as not markedly different from so-called normal behavior. I would tell June that her fears, lack of assertion, etc. result from the same learning processes that produce independence, courage, and determination. She simply failed to learn some desirable skills or she learned rather ineffective ones.

As the initial interview draws to a close, three tasks remain. First there is the important triad decision of who should be treated, how often, and in what context. Would June benefit most from individual therapy or might couples therapy provide more benefit? Should June's husband be seen regularly on an individual basis? Would either of them benefit from exposure to a larger group? I doubt that I could answer these questions in the first meeting. What I would do is ask to see both June and her husband together during one of the future assessment sessions.

Second, June would be given several behavioral forms to fill out at home and mail back before the second interview. Some of the forms are designed to gather general information (Life History Questionnaire and Reinforcement Survey Schedule). The remaining forms are concerned with more specific problems (Fear Survey Schedule, Assertive Questionnaire, Marriage Pre-counseling Inventory).

Third I would ask June to take baseline data (the natural frequency at which an event occurs) on several important behaviors. June would record the frequency with which she has intercourse with her husband. Also she could report on her feelings during lovemaking. Other assigned behaviors to be recorded would include the frequency of drinking, marital fights, avoiding work, and initiating conversations.

FURTHER ASSESSMENT - PRELIMINARY TREATMENT

Three or more assessment sessions would be conducted with June in order for me to complete a functional analysis of her problem areas. I might add that the general process of assessment continues throughout treatment. Assessment data are used to evaluate therapeutic gains and to determine an appropriate time to terminate treatment.

By the time June comes for her second session, I would

hope to have scrutinized the forms that she returned. My guess is that the information derived from these forms would substantiate my judgments based on the initial interview. To briefly illustrate, I imagine that the results would indicate strong fears of rejection, failure, and criticism (Fear Survey Schedule) ; general and multi-faceted assertion deficits (Assertive Questionnaire) ; apathy and over-reliance on the support of others (Reinforcement Survey Schedule) ; marital conflicts in several areas (Marital Pre-counseling Inventory).

The baseline data that June would bring to the next few sessions would give June and me a standard with which to evaluate progress in areas like sexual functioning, marital harmony, drinking, suicidal threats, assertion, etc. Probably by the third session sufficient interview, questionnaire, and natural observation data would have been collected for me to have a reasonable understanding of June's problems. Also, by this time I should be prepared to formulate treatment plans.

I feel that it is important for me to share the clinical information and my judgments with June at this time. I would describe my behavioral formulation of the past and current development of her target behaviors. I would suggest representative behavioral techniques for each target behavior and explain the procedures involved. June would be encouraged to react to my formulations and offer any revisions that seem reasonable to her. This information exchange process highlights the kind of educative, teacher-pupil relationship that I try to create in my practice of behavior therapy. From this standpoint, it is important for me to share my clinical judgments directly with June once sufficient information is available to make those judgments.

June's husband would be interviewed during either the third or fourth session. With June present, I would carefully observe their interaction patterns for clues to marital difficulties. June's descriptions of her husband and his contribution to her current difficulties would be independently evaluated. Let us say that June's husband comes across as a cooperative, impulsive man who lacks mature sexual experiences and knowledge. Furthermore, his social behavior appears to have a negative influence on June. However, recall that the majority of June's problems developed prior to marriage and so the major contributor to the current problems would be June herself. Thus, I would continue to see June individually, but would meet approximately once every three weeks with both of them for marital behavior therapy (described later in the paper).

During this further assessment stage, June is receiving specific behavioral treatment. Surprisingly, one form of treatment is data recording and baseline observations. The research literature clearly points out that self-observation and record collection often result in greater self-awareness, increased objectivity, and sometimes direct changes in objectionable behavior (Bandura, 1969). June would begin to show the gains described above.

The remaining preliminary techniques that I would use are self-control techniques (relaxation training, thought stopping, and coverant control) and assertive training.

I prefer to start by teaching June some basic self-control and assertion skills and like to defer treating the sexual problem, marital upheavals, drinking, phobias, and work aversion to the next stage. Primarily, my rational is to give June some immediate success experiences by applying powerful techniques to relatively amenable problems.

Relaxation Training: June would receive deep muscle relaxation training and would practice this at home on an audio tape recorded during the session. June might monitor her anxiety level in the context of her daily activities. During the first relaxation session, June would learn to discriminate the internal states of relaxation and tension. In the second session, June would discover how to relax deeply in a comfortable seated position. By the third training session, June will have learned to relax in any position and would be using relaxation in general tension situations.

Thought-Stopping: Although June does not appear to be obsessional, she does suffer from suicidal ruminations, preoccupations with feelings of inferiority, and excessive worry over her lack of social and vocational success. Thought-stopping (Wolpe and Lazarus, 1966) is an effective means of distracting and punishing these unproductive thoughts by yelling "Stop" to oneself. June would use this technique regularly and after each application she would relax. Occasionally, she might have to reapply thought-stopping should a thought immediately reappear. If some unwanted thoughts still persist, an external punishment control such as a manually operated, portable shock device would be introduced for daily use.

Coverant Control: Removing negative and irrational cognitions by thought-stopping can be therapeutically augmented by increasing positive self-evaluation. The most appropriate technique for this purpose is coverant control (Homme, 1966). The procedure starts with an identification of some reasonable positive thoughts (e.g., "I am a worthwhile person"). Following this, June would select several reinforcing events such as eating, TV watching, and reading. Finally June practices saying the positive self-evaluative thoughts to herself and then immediately engaging in a reinforcing event. This constant pairing of thought and reinforcement will result in the thought becoming a more frequent evaluative label.

Assertive Training: Only rudimentary assertive skills would be worked on during the preliminary treatment phase. Again, let us speculate that June is extremely shy, non-assertive, and lacking in feelings of self-worth. In June's case it would be essential to begin assertive training with a general discussion of her interpersonal rights, fears of the consequences of self-asser ion, and related matters. Subsequently, representative assertiv problems would be identified from June's conversations. One or more of these problems would be rehearsed, with June portraying herself and me taking the role of a person who causes her social discomfort. After commenting on the positive and negative assertive aspects of her performance, I would model a few assertive alternatives. Finally I would encourage June to model my behavior directly or in her own style.

FURTHER INDIVIDUAL TREATMENT

After approximately four sessions, the treatment tempo is intensified. As for assertive training, June and I would be rehearsing numerous and distinct interpersonal situations (marital, vocational, parental, and friendship, as examples). A video or audio tape recorder would be played back after the majority of role rehearsals in order to gradually shape assertive words, eye contact, voice volume, and gestures. Among her weekly assignments would be the practice of these newly learned skills in "safe," receptive social situations. If motivation posed a problem, I would have June reinforce herself for practicing these assertive assignments. Also, I would be inclined to place June in a four-session assertive training minigroup (Fensterheim, 1972) near the end of treatment. June's goal in this group would be to practice initiating conversations, maintaining other's interest while she is talking, expressing anger, and expressing tender feelings.

Another behavior therapy technique I would introduce in the sessions is systematic desensitization. One of the basic steps in the procedure—relaxation training—would have already been mastered by June. The procedure would continue by teaching June to pair the state of relaxation with imagined anxiety-producing scenes in a hierarchical order. Several distinct fear themes emerged from prior discussions and now would be employed for fear deconditioning. Representative themes would be fears of sexual intimacy with her husband, expressing anger and annoyance with others, job responsibilities, and rejection.

Other themes might be identified as the sessions progress. As an example, some painful historical associations could serve as additional material for systematic desensitization. June's past sensitivity to her father's reactions during menses and the memories of her abortion could well be exerting some influence over her present perceptions and interpersonal behavior and, if so, these themes would be treated.

Other presenting problems such as drinking and sleep disturbances should be ameliorated as an indirect result of assertive training and systematic desensitization. However, if these problems prove to be autonomous, I would be inclined to use a behavioral procedure called covert sensitization (Cautela, 1969). According to this procedure, June would be instructed to imagine an aversive state of affairs (i.e., nausea) following an imagined drinking scene. The same pairing in imagination of maladaptive behavior and aversion would be applied to the "masochistic" sexual fantasy. Possibly I would also urge June to conjure up a fantasy of sex with her husband if she had to masturbate to a fantasy. Theoretically, sexual arousal would be used to reinforce a more desirable heterosexual fantasy.

COUPLES THERAPY

The first focus of conjoint sessions would be the clarification of sexual myths and misconceptions. Sexual information would be discharged in an open and rational manner. Bibliotherapy might be used as an additional method of providing the couple with accurate sexual information and of loosening their cognitions about sex.

Assuming that June and her husband are motivated to sustain the marriage, they would be taught to gradually increase mutual sexual responsiveness (Masters and Johnson, 1970). In a hierarchical manner, they would calmly approach intercourse. Using the sensate focus technique developed by Masters and Johnson, June and her husband would slowly explore erogenous zones without sexual demands. Various components of full sexual expression would be built into the experience over time.

The residual forms of marital dissatisfaction would be approached through still another behavioral strategy called negotiated exchanges (Patterson, 1971). Since the couple complain of frequent and unresolved quarrels, they likely have difficulty discussing personally distressing problems with each other. Accordingly, they would be requested to set aside approximately 10 minutes per evening to discuss problems. A standard time and place for the negotiations would be selected. Beforehand, an agreement would be reached to limit discussions to one problem apiece. Moreover, both parties would understand that the negotiation sessions would have to be terminated if interpersonal attacks occurred.

Once general negotiation skills have been learned, the couple would exchange behavioral requests with each other. June might want her husband to come home from the office with pleasant words for her. He, in turn, might want her to participate with him in weekend sports. Each would decide how they would reinforce the other for compliance with their requests. Several of these exchanges might be attempted during a single week. If this treatment proceeds as expected, the behavioral exchanges would gradually reflect more significant and complex aspects of the marriage dyad.

COURSE OF TREATMENT

Based on prior cases of a similar nature, I would estimate that the treatment would last approximately seven months. During this time, June would be seen individually for approximately 25 sessions, with an additional four assertive group sessions. June and her husband would need approximately eight joint sessions. However, the actual number of sessions could vary considerably. I might be surprised to find that June has made significant progress in two to three months. On the other hand, more treatment time would be necessary if unexpected problems such as life crises or technical misapplications arose.

Within the first four sessions, June would begin to show signs of being more assertive with her husband and fellow employees. There should be a marked decrease in her general tension level and the frequency of self-defeating and suicidal thoughts. Also she would be more aware of herself and her actions as a result of collecting baseline data.

During the more advanced stages of treatment, I would expect that June might be free of her sexual anxieties and be more active in work and social roles. She would also be capable of expressing her genuine feelings as the situations demand. The marriage relationship would be improved in the areas of sexual gratification and communications. June would report that she is beginning to enjoy herself and feel a sense of participation in the social aspects of her life. Drinking would no longer serve as an escape from social confrontations and the sleep pattern would become normal.

When these treatment goals have been met, the therapy would be terminated. To facilitate a smooth transfer from therapy, I would schedule the last several sessions a few weeks apart. Termination anxieties would be dealt with in the final sessions. Also, I would review all of the techniques used and summarize June's progress. When June leaves treatment, she would take with her the knowledge of behavioral self-assessment and would have at her disposal several behavioral techniques. In essence, this may be the primary strength of behavior therapy for June. She would have learned enough self-control skills to cope with unexpected future stresses. Moreover, June would come to rely heavily on herself for support and guidance.

REFERENCES

BANDURA, A. 1969. *Principles of Behavior Modification.* New York: Holt, Rinehart and Winston.

BRADY, J. P. 1966. Brevital-relaxation treatment of frigidity. *Behavior Research and Therapy,* 4:71-77.

CAUTELA, J. R. 1969. Behavior therapy and Self-control. In Franks, C. (Ed.), *Behavior Therapy: Appraisal and Status.* New York: McGraw-Hill.

CAUTELA, J. R. 1968. Behavior therapy and the need for behavioral assessment. *Psychotherapy: Theory, Research, and Practice,* 5:175-179.

DAVIDSON, G. C. 1969. Appraisal of behavior modification techniques with adults in institutional settings. In Franks, C. (Ed.), *Behavior Therapy: Appraisal and Status.* New York. McGraw-Hill.

FENSTERHEIM, H. 1972. Behavior therapy: assertive training in groups. In Sager, C. J., and Kaplan, H. S. (Eds.), *Progress in Group and Framily Therapy.* New York: Brunner/Mazel.

GLYNN, J. D., and HARPER, P. 1961. Behavior therapy in a case of transvestism. *Lancet,* 1:619.

HASLAM, M. T. 1965. The treatment of psychogenic dyspareunia by reciprocal inhibition. *British Journal of Psychiatry,* 111:116-120.

HOLLANDER, M. A. 1974. Comprehensive behavior assessment and strategies for the treatment of marital problems. Paper presented at the 82nd Annual Meeting of the American Psychological Association, September.

HOLLANDER, M. A. 1973. Affect changes in behavior therapy. In DiScipio, W (Ed.), *The Behavioral Treatment of Psychotic Illness.* New York: Behavioral Publications.

HOMME, L. E. 1966. Contiguity theory and contingency management. *Psychological Record,* 16:233-241.

KANFER, F. H., and SASLOW, G. 1969. Behavioral diagnosis. In Franks, C. (Ed.), *Behavior Therapy: Appraisal and Status.* New York: McGraw-Hill.

KNOX, D. 1972. *A Behavioral Approach to Marriage Happiness Counseling.* Champaign, Ill.: Research Press.

KRAFT, T., and AL-ISSA, I. 1967. Behavior therapy and the treatment of frigidity. *American Journal of Psychotherapy,* 21:116-120.

LAZARUS, A. 1963. The treatment of chronic frigidity by systematic disensitization. *Journal of Nervous and Mental Disorders,* 136:272-278.

236   THREE PSYCHOTHERAPIES—A CLINICAL COMPARISON

MASTERS, W. H., and JOHNSON, V. E. 1970. *Human Sexual Inadequacy.* Boston: Little, Brown.
PATTERSON, G. R. 1971. *Families: Applications of Social Learning to Family Life.* Champaign, Ill.: Research Press.
RACHMAN, S. 1959. The treatment of anxiety and phobic responses by systematic desensitization psychotherapy. *Journal of Abnormal and Social Psychology,* 58:259-263.
STUART, R. B. 1969. Operant-interpersonal treatment for marital discord. *Journal of Consulting and Clinical Psychology,* 33:675-682.
WOLPE, J., and LAZARUS, A. 1966. *Behavior Therapy Techniques.* New York: Pergamon Press.

17

Gestalt Approach
The Case of June (II)

JOSEPH C. ZINKER, Ph.D.

I. WHY I SHOULDN'T WRITE THIS ARTICLE

How is a therapist to write a therapeutic process description from three pages of typed, double-spaced material without experiencing the person who is in need of help? It is a devastating feeling to be staring at some descriptive matter on paper, in a position of having to say something meaningful, something creative, something theoretically cogent in relation to that material. It is devastating and difficult. I ask myself, who is she, this June? How does she sit in her chair? How does she walk? She's pretty, but what does she really look like? Where does she show tension in her body other than in her shaking hands? Does she have a tight mouth? What does it mean that she is seductive? Is she charming? Is she hard? Articulate? Does she make herself interesting to another person? To what degree is she able to establish contact with me? Does she look directly into my face or does she glance away? Is she merely nervous or is there some shyness in her?

And then there are those practical questions that a therapist might ask himself. What is her medical history? Has she seen a gynecologist? Does she have pain on intercourse? Is she psychotic? Is there history of psychiatric hospitalization? Does

237

she look medicated? Has she ever been in therapy before? What was her experience in therapy? Has there been a diagnostic workup?

Then too, there are questions about her family. Is she an only child? Is it possible to make contact with her parents to get more background material? Is her husband willing to participate in this therapeutic experience?

Although there is some explication of her difficulties, what are her strengths? What are her capabilities? In what areas can she function well? These and many more questions are significant for me, and even more important is the style, the manner in which this patient would respond to my questions—how she would move, how she would talk, and how much pressure she could take. Would she cry? Would she become hostile? How would she generally respond to the initial interview?

Not having an opportunity to encounter the patient visually, I realize how heavily I rely on the visual mode in my work as a Gestalt therapist. Much of what I do and say depends on how I see the patient from moment to moment.

I often feel like I'm exploring a living sculpture, constantly "working" it and watching its development as it responds to me.

For example, if I think of June as a living, breathing organism, then I can begin to add (however limitedly) some of her described dysfunctions, like her shakiness, trembling, and blushing face. At the same time, she would appear to be muscularly and sensorially frozen in her pelvis, genitals, and her arms and legs (muscular armour components involved in anxiety and conversion states associated with sexuality and with contact pathology in general). The latter description is sheer conjecture of course, since only visual perusal and questioning would give me the concrete data to confirm my hypotheses.

Therefore, as a self-respecting and naturally obsessive therapist, who has inadequate experiential information about this young woman, I should not write this article. My vanity, however, keeps me from quitting and challenges me to do the best I can. What I would like, then, is to take the skeletal description of *The Case of June,* mold a psychodynamically and visually real woman from it, and proceed to relate to her as if she were that person.

II. PERSONALITY, THERAPEUTIC STRATEGY, AND OTHER PRACTICAL MATTERS

A. Personality Reconstruction

To begin with, I would like to give a brief translation of how I conceptualize this young woman from the case history. This conceptualization, hopefully, will then be related to the specific therapeutic methodology to be used in dealing with her problems.

Because I cannot see the patient and explore her background in the spontaneous liveliness of the ongoing therapy, I find myself relying more heavily on her history than I ordinarily would. In Gestalt therapy, historical information is not gathered as such. The person's past reveals itself naturally in the context of her present concerns. In my individual style, however, I like to gather historical information in the first several sessions.

1. HISTORY

I see June as a girl brought up by inadequate parents. The mother, a sexually frightened woman, had a poor feminine identification and probably was not sexually interested in the father, putting him in the position of being sexually frustrated. June's mother used her daughter to ward off the father's sexual approaches. In addition to that interactive possibility, it would seem to me that the mother felt generally inadequate, did not experience her own self worth, and projected onto her daughter her own needs to be a perfect angel. The mother appears to have had little skill in bringing up a child and was unable to help June acquire a sense of self control. Neither did she engender a sense of respect for her own strengths, making it impossible for June to respond to the mother positively.

My guess is that the mother communicated to her daughter a disdain, suspiciousness, and distrust for men. This was especially evident in the way in which the mother handled June's abortion. The father was left out of it, thereby reinforcing June's view that he could not be counted on for love, support, and concrete help in a difficult situation.

The father is a simple man. He was not able to join his wife in helping with his daughter's feelings related to her menses and the consequent sexual guardedness that June experienced toward him. In his simplicity, the father experienced such guardedness as rejection and proceeded to defend himself by attacking his daughter and fighting with her. (This is also his way of maintaining his own sexual excitement in the relationship.) June and her parents were not aware of the causes and effects of these arguments. They merely became victims of a difficult situation that they could not cope with. The father was unable to see that his daughter needed support, love, understanding, and the ability to be heard, all the things, in fact, that adults are able to share with one another without necessarily cuddling and/or sexualizing contact. He, therefore, failed to prepare his daughter for the full range and complexity of future contacts with men.

June appears to be an only child. Without contact with siblings, she has a tendency to be alone. She does not develop skills for dealing with ongoing nitty-gritty difficulties, nor skills which make it possible for siblings to have long-term, satisfying, mutually nurturing relationships. She winds up, therefore, going into the world with a sense of inadequacy and lack of self-worth in relation to her peers, as well as a rather poorly formed self-concept as a woman. She is seeking a father figure with whom she can begin to experience the kind of adult tenderness and understanding that she missed with her own father. Because of her good looks, she has no difficulty attracting older men, and finds herself engaged in sexual encounters which only confirm her reductionistic notion that men are interested solely in sex rather than in what she is all about. She winds up feeling used and unloved, and disliking herself in the process. On repeated occasions she's drawn to older men, trying to work through her conflict with her father. This kind of resolution would require that the men experience her in depth, rather than merely through sexual excitement alone. The difficulty is that June is not aware of her own sense of depth.

2. Physical Components

Chances are good that, when she rejected the notion of cuddling with her father, June turned herself off in the most vital and simple sensory contact functions with people, especially men. She did this in order to handle her increasing sexual urges; she closed off tender sensations in the breasts, created functional anesthesias in her vagina and clitoris, immobilized her legs to tighten inwardly knee to knee. June probably moved her pelvis posteriorly, curving her shoulders forward in order to hide the breasts, and finally constricted muscles in her arms to avoid simple, open physical contact. It is quite possible that she has difficulty hearing statements intended for simple contact or support, rather than for sexual purposes. (For example, her fear of anything sensuous might prevent her seeing very colorful paintings in the office.) If excitement occurs, it is probably experienced as anxiety, with consequent disruption of breathing, causing her to feel shaky, stiff, and flushed. She probably experiences all the classical symptoms of anxiety neurosis and depression. These symptoms reflect the still existing liveliness in the upper portion of her body and it is this obvious, visually-available excitement that is open to the therapist to work with.

I have made an attempt to build a "living sculpture" of June. The description is very "thin" indeed because it lacks a deeper phenomenology of the person. It does not begin to tell how June *experiences herself in the world.* And it is, after all, the person's view of herself that the Gestalt therapist works with. Most of his interventions and creative efforts grow out of the patient's moment-to-moment expression of the self. It is this finely concretized expression with its peculiar individual style which is lacking here (Zinker, 1973).

B. Basic Therapeutic Strategy: Importance of the Couple

Since sexuality in its healthy state is an interpersonal function, I would have to work with June's husband, as well as with June, in order to treat her. I would have to find out what kind of person he is and how he experiences his wife. I would, therefore, spend at least one session a week working with them as a couple, teaching them how to deal with each other, how to fight creatively, how to learn to express feelings to one another, which they are unable to do at this point in their development.

We would discuss the manner in which they get into their sexual difficulty and how they can both acquire skills to work that difficulty through with one another. For example, June needs to learn to talk to her husband about her difficulty without feeling that he will abuse and destroy her. Her husband needs to learn how to control his outbursts, if indeed they are outbursts rather than June's fantasies. He also needs to learn how to listen to her and how to be in touch with his own fatherliness and sense of caring for June as a total person.

Such couples therapy would be indispensable for this case; to leave it out would be a therapeutic disaster. Not involving the husband would cause June to see the therapist as an ideal father figure, the only person who could understand her and satisfy her needs. She would tend to compare her husband unfavorably with the therapist and to reject him even more than she already has. In cases in which the therapist is particularly engaged by her prettiness and by the romantic quality of his role with her, he might even stimulate a final break in the marriage and get stuck with a patient who might then direct most of her psycho-sexual energies towards her relationship with the therapist. The role of the therapist, after all, is to make it possible for June to be a woman, able to enjoy her husband and other men, be satisfied with her work, and experience fullness in her on-going development.

Techniques employed in this portion of therapy would be chiefly behavioristic experiments in which the couple would be asked to practice new contact-oriented behaviors under the supervision of the therapist. Interpretation and advice giving are not considered useful in gestalt therapy. (I will return to the use of the experiment later in the discussion.) June and her husband would be asked to carry out certain experiments at home. These would often relate to safe gradations of sexual contact.

In addition to couples therapy, June would be seen individually (and so might the husband) in order to deal more specifically with her developmental gaps, anxieties, and concomitant character armour.

For the remainder of this report, then, her therapy will be discussed as an individual therapy, highlighting the various Gestalt methods to be used in the case.

A. Exploring June's Range of Awareness

The degree to which June knows herself is not clear, so part of the early therapeutic process deals with discovering how much awareness she has of her own organism as well as of her relationship with the therapist. Therefore, the therapy would explore, for example, the phenomenology of her understanding and experiencing of verbal arguments with her husband, as well as physical contacts. There would also be exploration of her experience of anxiety, and the degree to which she is aware of that anxiety. June experiences severe depression and a desire to escape, leading her to lose herself in "trashy" movies and fantasies of suicide. A major portion of the therapy would involve exploring as well as broadening her awareness of her depression, the way in which she experiences depression physiologically, what it does to her voice, to her postural configuration as she related to other people, to her energy level, to her productivity and to other physical functions.

Exploration of her range of self awareness and the awareness of others will give the therapist a more accurate notion of June's repertoire and capacity to profit from the therapeutic encounter and the various techniques that the therapist may use to help her achieve greater insight into her situation. This exploration in turn will unblock tied up psychophysiological functions. It is from such a base that the therapist will acquire a more complete view of June, which will enable him to gauge the range of his own relationship to her. The specific experimental methodology utilized in the therapy will grow out of his full understanding of her phenomenological world.

B. *Awareness-Excitement-Contact Cycles*

The major portion of the therapy will consist of locating frozen areas of functioning, mobilizing energy around these functions, and helping the patient release them. For example, when June interrupts her need to scream out at her husband, she winds up getting stuck with constricted vocal chords, tightened chest, and shallow breathing. In the aware-ness-excitement-contact cycle, the therapist and the sheltered environment of the therapy office make it possible for her to re-experience the use of her vocal chords, the outraged scream, the resulting sense of contact with her anger and the objects of her anger. The expression becomes an unlocking of the defense and a simultaneous satisfaction of the original re-pressed need. The patient is able to repeatedly experience success in locating and energizing blocked functions, which are made available for fuller exploration and expression in her daily life. These are called awareness-excitement-contact cycles, and they may occur at various levels of functioning.

For example, the patient may become aware of her locked knees. She feels tension in her thighs being drawn together and her knees touching each other. At the same time, she experiences a sense of safety. The therapist directs attention to the legs and asks the patient in what other way she might use her legs to express herself to her husband or her father. She then has a fantasy of using the legs to push the other person away. The therapist encourages her to do so, and, in the process of extending her legs and pushing away the imag-ined person, she becomes more fully aware of her anger. This anger may be accompanied by verbal expressions of resent-ment, and the rest of the session may be spent in pursuing the fuller expression of such feelings and the completion of unfinished situations vis-à-vis her father.

In the meantime, the patient experiences a relaxation in

her legs and a sudden awareness of revivified sexual feelings toward the husband and/or the therapist. The very musculature which was used in the service of resistance (Zinker, 1973) is now used in the service of expression, as well as in the service of the more deeply blocked sexual feelings. As she continues kicking, for example, she begins to experience lubrication in her vagina, a sense of fluidity in her pelvis, and it may become obvious to her that she is again feeling alive and in contact with her own sexual sweetness.

This experience of success, if handled properly, may then be generalized to workable success experiences with her spouse, whom she is again able to deal with at the level of verbalized feelings and expressed sexual needs. The therapist becomes the source of her acquisition of self-awareness skills, which not only lead to cognitive understanding, but to motoric satisfaction and the use of physical skills to get what she needs for herself. The repeated experience of the awareness-excitement-contact cycle, whether it takes place in the areas of sensorial blockage or in the areas of interpersonal contact, gives the patient a sense of inner strength, a sense of personal identity, and a sense of having a range of skills to deal with feelings and interpersonal contacts in the outside world.

C. Experiment

Experiment is a method of Gestalt therapy which allows the patient to practice new behavior in the safety of the therapist's office. The behavior practiced is, of course, directly related to some of the difficulties which the patient may have. In the case of June, the therapist would create behavioristic experiments which would deal with her blockages in tenderness toward men, with her anger toward her father, blockages in the areas of sexuality, sensory receptivity, and muscular expression of anger, tenderness and mourning. Other experiments might deal with ways in which she can talk to her husband, and still others might deal with her relationship with her mother and the values she swallowed whole, resulting in her current need to spit up and work them through.

I have already mentioned an experiment which would deal with her tightened legs, originally produced by inhibiting her sexual feelings toward her father. This is an excellent example of a physiologically-based experiment. Another experiment that June may be attracted to would be an empty chair dialogue with her husband, in which she would simply practice expressing her feelings about her sexual difficulties with him. This kind of experiment might then make it possible for her to address herself similarly to her husband in a living situation.

To further elucidate the use of the experiment, there follows a table giving examples of three experiments that may be used in this case. To further clarify, I refer to location or focus, function, source of energy, and development of experiment is a cooperative creation of the therapist and his patient; it allows the patient to actively explore herself.

LOCATION: The Gestalt therapist focuses on and locates the area of phenomenological interest, as well as blockage, in the patient. He begins with "where the patient is at."

FUNCTION: Usually the content of discussion as well as the location gives a hint as to the organismic function involved.

SOURCE OF ENERGY: In order for the experiment to be successful, the patient must have energy invested in it both psychologically and physiologically. Therefore, it is important for the therapist to pay attention to the source of energy involved in the function and the commitment of the patient to such exploraion.

DEVELOPMENT OF EXPERIMENT: The experiment, which is a concrete attempt to modify existing behavior, grows directly out of the area of blockage, the focus, the function of interest, and the energy needed to express the new behavior. The experiment is a cooperative creation of the therapist and his patient; it allows the patient to actively explore herself.

POSSIBLE OUTCOMES OF EXPERIMENT: Finally the therapist keeps in mind the possible outcomes of the experiment, always allowing for outcomes which grow out of the patient's idiosyncratic experience. One cannot rigidly adhere to a prefabricated outcome and each result has ultimate usefulness.

The experiment makes it possible for the patient not only to work through unfinished situations, but to add the dimension of concretely expressing and seeking satisfaction of needs, as well as making conceptual discoveries of what these needs may be. June not only learns to understand what her difficulties are, but she has a handle on how to deal with these difficulties through the medium of the experiment.

D. Encounter

All of the above transactions take place in the spirit of two people relating to one another. The relationship between June and her therapist becomes a model of how a mature man and woman deal with problems, how one person makes it possible for another to discover his own depth and his own sexuality without reducing the contact between them to a sexual-genital contact. This particular problem is a deep-rooted one for June because she has learned to relate to men only in a sexually reductionistic manner. She needs to find ways of stimulating as well as responding to a variety of interpersonal needs (Zinker, 1974).

As the therapy progresses, June begins to be more sensitive to the therapist; rather than walking in and being determined by her anxiety and discomfort, she is now able to pay greater attention to her visual experience. Various experiments have given her ample opportunity to practice using her senses and she is now beginning to exhibit in the therapeutic situation the varied behavior which is required to make contact with her husband, as well as with other significant people in her life. Walking into the therapist's office, she is able to notice paintings, or plants, or books on shelves, none of which she experiences before. Often, the freshness of her newly-discovered sensitivity strikes her with surprise and amazement. Morover, she becomes more contactful and sensitive to the moods and feelings and appearance of the therapist. In the past he was used only in the service of relieving her anxiety. Now the therapist gradually acquires the characteristic of a person. She is able to see his wrinkled brow, to notice when he might look worried, to ask how he is, to become more curious about his personal life, matters which before had no relevance for her. The relationship between June and the therapist becomes real, so that she is no longer always on the receiving side. The therapist is able to feel more comfortable in expressing his own feelings, and June may feel perfectly natural in responding to these feelings. For the first time in her life she makes a return journey to those early feelings when she felt comfortable and close to her father on those weekends when they spent time together in bed. Because she has learned that her sexuality is a normal by-product of contact with a man, she is able to accept her sexual feelings toward the therapist without panicking or feeling compelled to seduce him. The sexuality becomes merely a psychological lubricant in the encounter between a man and a woman, and takes more complete expression in her deeper and more profoundly satisfying relationship with her husband.

Because June is able to be more fully in contact with her excitement without choking it down, she is less and less anxious. The shaking hands, the trembling voice, and the blushing face begin to disappear, and are replaced by a more energetic, more complete contact with the self, the therapist and

EXAMPLES OF RELEVANT EXPERIMENTS IN WORKING WITH JUNE

Movement from "Location to Experiment" is a Method of Converting a Symptom into Expressed Function

LOCATION (FOCUS) (Blockage in)	FUNCTION (Difficulty in)	SOURCE OF ENERGY	DEVELOPMENT OF AN EXPERIMENT
Hand tremor (Patient: "I feel self-conscious about my tremor.")	General excitation	Breathing and sensation in hands, arms	June is asked to exaggerate her shakiness, supporting each activity with fuller breathing. *SOME POSSIBLE OUTCOMES:* Sensation of shaking; expression of anger; excitation of sexual zones; fuller contact with self and therapist.
Flushing of face (Patient: "Doctor, does my face look red?")	Sexual excitement	Breathing and sensations in face, neck, and breasts	June is asked to look into mirror at her flushing face (or to explore warmth of her face with fingertips). She is asked to "allow the warmth to become fuller and to let it move wherever it wants to. . . ." *SOME POSSIBLE OUTCOMES:* Recognition, identification and acceptance of excitement; fuller appreciation thereof. If flushing spreads, a more comprehensive awareness and appreciation of her sexual excitement in the (male) therapist's presence, without experiencing major anxiety.

Visualization (and general areas of sensation with muscular awareness). (Patient reports seashore fantasy.)	Fantasy life; sexuality— contact with others	Report of seashore fantasy of being bound and sexually used. Energy is generated more fully during acting out of dream

June is asked to tell her "rape" fantasy as if it is happening right now and, after each sentence, to say, "and this is my life, my existence." She says, for example, "I am lying down, completely helpless, and these men are using me . . . and this is my life, my existence." She does this with every part of her dream. She is asked to try to actually physically act out the dream and to observe what happens to her.*

SOME POSSIBLE OUTCOMES:

These are many and complex—and since we don't have prefabricated interpretations of the fantasy, the patient alone can make specific discoveries relevant to her life at her present level of development. Her insights are, however, not merely conceptual, but behaviorally and sensorially supported. The patient not only contacts her own boundedness and helplessness, but also her active involvement of bind-ing, controlling, and the sadistic manipulation of self and others. These are only some of the possibilities, of course. Having taken ownership of some of her own projections in the fantasy, she can begin to play the active demander-manipulator in her sexual relations with her husband. Such breakthrough sexually will also be generalized to other aspects of her relationship with her husband.

---

* Space does not permit detailed description of other exercises used in this experiment.

others. Excessive smoking diminishes and the energy invested in the cigarette is increasingly used for verbal expression and other oral functions.

As the variety of organismic functions become loosened and used for expression, June is able to experience a deep sense of love and appreciation for the therapist. At first, this love is experienced in the form of idealized hero worship, but as June becomes more fully aware of herself and more contactful with the therapist. She begins to experience him as another human being who does not have all the answers, who has his own problems, and who, unlike her original fantasies, is still coping from one day to the next in the trials of living and surviving in this complex world.

June begins to visit her therapist more and more together with her husband. They relate to him, at first, as a wise father-figure, and later as a good friend, and he, in turn, experiences them with increasing satisfaction. He sees himself as a sculptor, who generated enough energy in two people and helped create skillful expressions which allow them to be together in a mutually loving and sexually satisfying relationship. It takes very little time for this couple to part company with the therapist, and for the therapist to see himself as a person who is a consultant to a growing family that may turn to him from time to time in the future.

BIBLIOGRAPHY

1. ZINKER, JOSEPH C. Phenomenology of the here and now. *Gestalt Institute of Cleveland.* Fall, 1974.
2. ZINKER, J. C. Dreamwork as theater. *Voices.* Summer, 1971.
3. ZINKER, J. C. In Loving Encounters: A Phenomenological View. (To appear in Douglas Stephenson's *Gestalt Therapy Primer*, 1974).

18

Psychoanalytic Approach
The Case of June (II)

LEON SALZMAN, M.D.

While it is difficult to discuss complicated issues of treatment with restricted and limited pieces of data, the information presented in the case of June permits considerable speculation.

The patient is a 23-year-old married woman who at the initial interview presented her problem of having difficulty with her husband and being unable to enjoy sex. Her description of being repelled and disgusted when her husband approached her, however, was in marked contrast to her seductive behavior which was reported in the interview. While she was described as being poised and restrained, it is obvious that in addition to her sexual problem she has marked feelings of inferiority and unacceptability, both as a female and an individual. She describes a typical masochistic fantasy which she employs to comfort herself and to help her fall asleep. In this fantasy she can allow herself to enjoy many experiences, including sex only when she is overwhelmed and immobilized so that she has no control over the activity and is unable to resist. Under these circumstances, she is then able to achieve an orgasm and be sufficiently relaxed to fall asleep. She has been unable to "let go" enough to achieve an orgasm unless she has this fantasy which prevents her from resisting. This fantasy is symbolic of her total problem not only with sex, her husband, or her job, but with all other activities in her living.

The brief history which is presented indicates that at an earlier period she had some sexual problem with her father which was terminated abruptly during her adolescence when she began to menstruate. There was undoubtedly sexual stimulation of some kind on those occasions when she was in bed with him, even though there is no specific mention of it in her report. However, her abrupt termination of this activity and her continued career of arguing and fighting with him indicate that this relationship has never been clarified. It would be too easy to jump to the conclusion that this relationship had etiological significance in this patient's marital and sexual problem. However, while the data point directly to an ambivalent attitude towards sex, gender role and her guilt about enjoying herself, it would be premature to presume, without much additional data, that the relationship with her father is the key to her neurotic difficulties.

The data seem to imply that she has some conflict about being a woman and a participant in sex and that she has many resistances and repressions with regard to it. Yet it is clear at the same time that she has considerable interest in it, particularly in a masochistic direction. The conflict over sex is manifested in the contrast between her fantasy, in which she must be overwhelmed in order to succumb and feel released so that she can enjoy sex, and her expressed fear of a dominating and domineering husband who she says may overpower her and injure her. This conflict is notable in that the fantasy is precisely what she wishes, yet overtly she says she is fearful that it might happen.

Her relationships appear to be dominated by a tendency to be irresponsible and to get involved in self-defeating maneuvers which would lead to the brink of some difficulty. This is manifested in her inability to handle her job or her marriage. At her job she calls in late and spends her time watching "trashy" movies, with the inevitability of being found out and perhaps fired.

The patient perceives her mother as being martyred, having worked all her life and resented it. She appears to have taken abuse from the family and her husband. It is clear that her mother also resented her husband's inability to be a success and to be effective in his own affairs. The patient likewise views herself as a martyr who is being abused and taken advantage of by her husband and others. This theme pervades much of her living. It is a typical masochistic orientation which is borne out by her fantasy life.

The masochistic sexual orientation of the patient has some relationship to realistic events, although we must assume that the patient aided and abetted the earliest sexual adventures which were precisely masochistic. The beginnings of her sex life occurred in a relationship with a man 21 years older than herself in which she was overpowered and made pregnant. This resulted in an abortion, which must have been a traumatic event for a 17-year-old who could not share this situation with her parents. Only two months later she took the risk of again becoming pregnant. Her inclination to pursue a dangerous course and not learn from previous experience is highlighted in this sequence. The elements of naivete, immaturity, and pursuing self-destructive courses of action could be safely deduced from this sequence of events. Again, the man was much older than herself and, I would assume, was visualized as overpowering her so that the decision to act was taken out of her hands. Or at least the patient would undoubtedly describe it in this fashion whether or not it actually transpired that way.

The patient appears to be able to cope with her difficulty

only by drinking and withdrawing and satisfies her needs only through masochistic fantasies which require her in some way to be overwhelmed and immobilized. She apparently feels very inadequate with regard to herself and her social activities and berates and derogates herself in her incapacity to function.

On the basis of the data presented, one can formulate this individual's problems in terms of some masochistic character disorder in which the individual requires an overpowering or dominating relationship in order to permit herself some freedom to function sexually and otherwise. In this way she avoids any responsibility for her behavior and can feel abused. Thus, while appearing to be out of control of what happens to her, she actually exerts a maximal control on her living by entering into masochistic arrangements. This type of character structure appears to function only in an atmosphere of anxiety and there is a marked conflict between the need always to be in control and the tendency to want to be forced out of control in order to be taken care of by others. The masochistic solution produces only a minor reduction in anxiety and usually raises and sustains it at a higher level. The formulation of this patient's disorder, therefore, would be crucial in the treatment program since the recognition of a masochistic personality inevitably and invariably would lead to further expectations in the direction of masochistic behavior. One would need to pursue a much more detailed life history in order to elaborate and clarify these tendencies. Her sexual adjustment is only a small piece of the total picture of her character structure.

In the treatment process it would be crucial that the patient recognizes that she believes that she is acceptable only to the extent that she allows herself to be taken advantage of and pushed around by others. Such data would undoubtedly be revealed in the review of her earlier childhood and adolescent years, when she made her earliest attempts to relate to others. We might demonstrate that this continuing pattern was present not only in her relationship with her father and mother but also with friends, both male and female, in the growing years. It could also be demonstrated in her early heterosexual intimacies, both sexual and non-sexual, and finally in her relationship with her husband that brought her into treatment. The key to all such reviews or reconstructions is to focus on the present symptoms and complaints in order to elucidate why the patient acts in the way she does at the present time. The importance of the formulation in the therapeutic process is that our investigations are directed towards facilitating our understanding of how this role developed and how it is sustained, since it is responsible for the maintenance of the present-day unsuccessful and dissatisfying living. The understanding as to how she has come to be the kind of person she is becomes the basis for any potential changes in her living. But for any change to occur, one would have to demonstrate to the patient not only how her present behavior relates to the past but that it is not conducive to successful living in the present.

The problem of control would be of central significance in understanding this patient, since she apparently needs always to be in control and can allow herself to be out of control only under the most pressing and overpowering situations. In other words, to give up control for her means to be utterly powerless and helpless, a factor which plays a primary role in the development of a masochistic defense. This attitude of always being in control makes it extremely difficult to function, since to be in complete control is impossible in ordinary living. Much that transpires in our living is beyond our control and committing oneself to another, whether in love, work or play, requires giving up some control to the situation or the other person. For successful therapy to occur in such people, particularly June, she would have to take some risks and give up some control in her living with her husband, her job, and elsewhere without feeling totally overwhelmed and destroyed. Presently, she suggests that to do so with her husband would result in her being totally destroyed.

In order to get such data and to encourage the patient to take some risks in handling over controls to others, the relationship with the therapist is crucial, because the transference would be precisely similar to the kind that she makes with others in the outside world. Initially, she would present herself as a poor, weak, helpless person who must behave herself or else she will be rejected or deeply hurt. Yet in this attitude there would be a large measure of control of the therapist in the need to dominate him and force certain sadistic attitudes in him. Under these circumstances the patient tends to be a good girl who will accept whatever the therapist says without any disagreements, thus preventing the possibility of an open exploration of her masochism. This kind of authoritative relationship which a masochistic personality generally sets up can become an impediment in therapy because, in order for the patient to abandon her control, she must recognize that the authority is not the great ogre and threat she generally views him to be. To the extent that the patient leans on a masochistic defense as her only source of security, any attempt to make her be independent may be perceived as a threat and an attack. This must be worked through with a friendly helper in order for successful therapy to occur.

Theoretical Considerations about the Masochistic Disorder

Many alternative and frequently contradictory hypotheses have been offered to explain the phenomenon of masochism. Philosophers, theologians and mystics consider it to be natural or logical behavior, arising out of a dualistic view of man. With the advent of a scientific psychology, a more rational and mechanistic explanation was attempted. Masochism was described as a secondary development in dealing with one's aggressive or hostile impulses (Freud). Alexander describes it as the "sexual release of excess excitation caused by guilt." Wilhelm Reich saw it as an adjustive maneuver, designed to deal with disastrous personal or social conditions. Karen Horney also viewed it as an adjustive device, designed to achieve satisfaction by getting rid of one's self. Erich Fromm relates it to the individual's attempt to escape the unbearable feelings of aloneness and powerlessness. Masserman describes it "as an experientially derived pattern of current sacrifices for eventual gains."

There are varying levels of description—some offer a genetic explanation and relate it to instinctual drives, while others view it as a dynamic, adjustive and reparative mechanism. For some, masochism is the inevitable result of the neurotic process, not the cause of it, and, consequently, is always pathologic; others view it as an existential and inevitable accompaniment of human affairs. While it is viewed as an independent drive whose goal is pleasure through pain (fusion of aggressive and libidinal instincts), it is also described as a process for achieving satisfaction where pain and discomfort are unavoidable accompaniments.

Whatever one's conception of the dynamics and genesis of masochism may be, certain elements in the behavior and psychology of the individual are intrinsic to the process and are agreed upon by all. The masochistic performance, however limited or widespread, and whatever its degree of intensity, tends to berate, belittle, or actively destroy the self or part of the self in order to obtain some psychic reward or relief of tension. H. S. Sullivan said it in this way: "A large number of people appear to go to rather extraordinary lengths to get themselves imposed on, abused, humiliated and what not, but as you get further data, you discover that this quite often pays; in other words, they get things they want. And the things they want are satisfaction and security from anxiety. Thus those people who get themselves abused and so on are indirectly getting the other people involved in doing something useful in exchange." (Sullivan, 1953.)

In this process of self degradation, we notice that many issues are served, such as the escape from real responsibility for one's actions, being excused for one's failures, or the capacity for manipulating others to fulfill one's secret needs and obtain a favorable balance of good will. However, on closer examination, we see that in the process of self denial or self degradation, the individual is fulfilling some particular value or set of values, while derogating another value or set of values. Values in this context are not limited to moral issues, but refer to those qualities, attitudes, standards or goals that the individual, for whatever reasons, considers necessary and essential to his physical and psychological survival. These requirements become organized into a code of ethics or personal philosophy of living, and are supported by moral, intellectual, and ethical rationalizations. They have their origins in the life experiences and deprivations of the individual. In their life situations they continually translate friendly efforts at collaboration into situations of threat and abuse.

The theme of unrequited love is played out in an infinite variety of ways, but always with the same result—the feelings of undesirability and worthlessness. At these times the therapist is often unwittingly and relentlessly drawn into being the rejecting parent who either gives too little or at the wrong time. Any activity or lack of activity is viewed as evidence of the therapist's lack of interest and concern.

Freud expressed it in this way: "There are certain people

who behave in a quite peculiar fashion during the work of analysis. When one speaks hopefully to them or expresses satisfaction with the progress of the treatment, they show signs of discontent and their condition invariably becomes worse. ... One becomes convinced not only that such people cannot endure any praise or appreciation, but that they react inversely to the progress of the treatment. Every partial solution that ought to result, and in other people does result in an improvement or temporary suspension of symptoms produces in them for the time being an exacerbation of their illness." (Freud)

The therapist is caught in a double bind, since he's damned if he does and damned if he doesn't. If he attempts reassurance or becomes too active, he is accused of doing too much and of not having confidence in the patient's ability, or of belittling the patient's capacities and, most of all, of exposing his own insecurity. If he is firm and somewhat detached, he is accused of being cold, indifferent, rejecting, and, worst of all, afraid to expose his own insecurity. This is reminiscent of the analyst's gambit, as he attempts to expose the patient's defenses. This tactic, when used by the analyst, frequently annoys the patient and has the same effect on the therapist when the tables are turned. The patient sets up a situation unwittingly, but inevitably, designed to embarrass, humiliate, and ultimately antagonize the therapist and produce the anticipated retribution. If the therapist remains unaffected, he is presumed to be weak and frightened.

The notion of not needing anybody is reinforced by the enormous manipulatory power which resides in the masochistic defense. Others are constantly being pushed, forced, and tricked into fulfilling the patient's neurotic needs. Much of the success of the masochistic maneuver lies in this area and gives us hints about the technical handling of these patients. It should also be noted that the manipulation is almost always indirect and subtle and is communicated in nonverbal ways. To express it directly or overtly would defeat the whole maneuver. The hurt, defeated look and the whining, hopeless tone of voice convey an accusation that demands some action from the other person. The patient tends to convey his demands in a nonverbal fashion while at the same time verbally denying his needs. Consequently, much of the nonverbal behavior has to be examined in therapy in order to explore the false values that are espoused.

While manipulating and attempting to control the therapist, these patients feel superior to and contemptuous of him. They deride what they consider to be the sham values of the therapist. In this way such patients see themselves as people of deep, personal integrity in spite of being rejected or considered undesirable and worthless. Thus, certain values are supported at the cost of personal degradation. The usual notions of dignity, self-respect, and self-esteem have perverted meanings in the masochistic defense.

It is clear that the therapist is caught in the tug of war before he knows it, in his endeavor to help the patient appraise a situation more objectively. The patient attempts to reduce all the events in her life to the notion of her inadequacy and undesirability rather than to investigate the possibility that neurotic patterns are either produced by realistic rejection or by the unrealistic feeling of being rejected. Freud was unduly pessimistic about the therapy of masochism because he seemingly did not fully comprehend the dynamics of this tug of war. The success or failure of therapy frequently rests on the skill of the therapist in handling this situation.

The masochistic defense seems to be a particularly effective way of dealing with certain problems of existence—guilt, helplessness, and powerlessness. Although masochistic behavior often appears to be "unconscious guilt seeking for punishment," it is not clear what is primary—the guilt or the brazen, exploitative, righteously indignant behavior of the masochist. This kind of behavior often produces guilt in response to actual assaults upon the environment. The masochist more often looks like someone who feels cheated, denied, and abused, and is attempting to get justice and compensation for her claims. This may provoke sadistic rejoinders and guilt feelings. The usefulness of this defense in dealing with the feelings of powerlessness depends upon man's continued belief in primitive magic and its power of expiation, and on the human belief and propensity to stimulate another human being to benevolent action by the appeal of helplessness. This has its roots in the prolonged state of helplessness of the human infant and total fulfillment which accompanies it.

The masochistic maneuver is essentially a primitive technique which attempts to overcome weakness and helplessness by a display of utter inadequacy. It is analogous to the behavior of some animals who, in moments of greatest danger, either freeze or present their most vulnerable areas to the enemy. It is a way of dealing with the hopeless despair which man faces in the awareness of his ultimate powerlessness. Its ubiquitous involvement in all human affairs may be understood in terms of the universality of the feeling of helplessness. Masochism is one of the effects of the development of man beyond the bonds of instinctual necessities as he evolved out of the animal kingdom, without adequate tools at his command to deal with the existential problems of loneliness and powerlessness this produced.

Therapeutic Goals

There are long and short term goals in dealing with the masochistic personality structure. In the short term, the individual benefits tremendously by the elucidation of the role that she plays in producing the difficulties in her own living.

This awareness can be extremely useful. For example, in this patient it would be important for her to see that she is revolted by her husband because of her expectations and desires rather than by any particular qualities in him. This may immediately produce marked changes in the relationship, both sexual and non-sexual. It may be that while she resents his domineering attitude, this is precisely what she wishes and is unable to accept. However, the masochistic sexual fantasies may be very hard to eliminate because they are so successful in fulfilling the individual's goals. Yet there can be some substitutions for these fantasies by allowing herself a more aggressive pattern of sex activity and by permitting her huband to be more aggressive with her. One might guess that in her present relationship with her husband he is not domineering in sex—but rather deals with her very cautiously and very moderately because of her verbalized concerns about being hurt, so that he is not as rough as she might like. Actually, then, she might resent his caution rather than his overpowering behavior and it is his cautious approach to sex which might result in her frequent refusals.

Since in the report of this case the patient is described as acting with much control and restraint, one is led to consider how contradictory this is to the way she tells her story with lack of restraint in describing the unpleasant and unresponsive way that she responds to her husband. It is this dilemma that leads me to suspect that she does not actually avoid activity with her husband because he is overpowering, but rather because he is not. Consequently, in short terms this would be perhaps very effective in relieving the situation.

In long terms, however, this would be a very difficult situation for any characterological changes towards her sex and life in general. The treatment of masochistic disorders is difficult at best and unless there were at least 2 or 3 sessions per week, one could not expect a favorable outcome in the long run. On the other hand, excessive frequency in seeing such patients tends to aggravate their dependency which supports the masochistic orientation. Such a patient must endure real anxiety in order to recognize how she does function, rather than the therapist trying to relieve her of all anxiety so that she might achieve the impossible task of being totally independent and always in control. In the course of treatment many factors would emerge which would have to be dealt with. Among them would be:

1. *The notion that this patient sees herself as a victim who has to take punishment from others in order to function effectively.* The theme of unrequited love would be played out frequently, always demonstrating her to be worthless. The therapist may in time be drawn into supporting this view, but actually it would be important for her to see that her failure to fulfill her goals was often due to her inability to assert herself and her needs rather than the unfavorable view towards her.

2. *The maintenance of an anxiety-filled existence.* These people act as if the world is always denying them, ascribing their anger and suffering to the failures of others to fulfill their needs. Consequently, they have numerous techniques for forcing and demanding some kind of benevolence rather than asking for it directly. This must produce a constant state of being uncomfortable and preventing peaceful, non-contentious living. Actually, these individuals need to live in a world which is full of catastrophe and trouble. This patient demonstrates it in some of the reports of her inability to avoid catastrophes by coming late, not being attentive to her job, and participating in self-destructive ways which are derogating and self-deriding, such as her pregnancies. Undoubtedly there were many humiliating and embarrassing situations that she found herself in.

3. *Problems of control.* This is a crucial issue in the masochistic personality disorder because in order to feel secure these people must be in complete control. Yet, being in complete control prevents them from being reasonably dependent upon others. Since such dependencies are inevitable in all human relationships, it is difficult for them to work out any mutual satisfactory living.

Thus the aspects of the therapeutic process which require constant focus are the self-destructive, masochistic tendencies which pervade her living. There would be no particular order in what issues are to be dealt with, but one would recognize that the problem of sex is only one part of the issue and that the clarification of the sexual problem by itself would not be illuminating. This would be particularly true in regard to early experiences with her father in which the childhood play must have stimulated and focused on her maturing sexual capacity, which ordinarily tends to take the major focus of the therapist's interest, especially in view of some of the theoretical preconceptions which prevail. However, in therapy it would be more effective to avoid such issues until they became part of the transference relationship or the patient began to have fantasies about the therapist.

In a case of this sort, the role of the therapist is crucial in helping the patient illuminate both her defensive patterns and her need to be in control of her emotions, to be more expressive or assertive, to prevent confrontation, to always play the role of the martyr and allow herself to be pushed around. This pattern is carried out in all relationships. The therapist cannot allow himself to be used as the partner in her masochistic needs. The therapist in such instances is largely the teacher who must actively demonstrate and help the patient see that there are alternative ways of living, aside from the way she had to live. She must recognize that she is not inferior or helpless, or powerless. The patient's need to focus on her inferiority is a way of tearing into herself, and is designed only to stir up the expected rejections and disappointments. Generally, the patient has sufficient assets that can be focused upon to maintain or encourage a more solid self-esteem. Such focusing allows the patient to abandon some of her reasons for control. Thus, the patient would present herself each hour in a complaining, always distraught, unhappy manner, always in some kind of experience of failure or discontent. This would be the prevailing need to stir up sympathy or feeling sorry for her.

There would be periodic crises in a therapeutic situation in which the therapist would be put in the position of having either to act as some unfriendly critic of the patient's behavior or else would be asked to support her feelings of being victimized by the world. Whatever would develop, she would feel unfairly treated. If the therapist supported her contentions, she could then deride him for being a pushover or sucker and falling for her masochistic needs. However, if he were critical, she could then accuse him of being unfriendly or unsympathetic.

The earlier sex experience was one in which the patient could see herself as being victimized by an older man who took advantage of her and in her ignorance made her pregnant. However her understanding of the role she played in the event might reduce the possibility that it would be used as a prototype as to how she was taken advantage of, with all the associated horror and anguish. This would help her see that she must have played some role in encouraging or flirting with this man, thus allowing him to accost her. Rather than feeling a helpless victim, she needs to recognize the active role she plays in sustaining and participating in such events in which she ultimately becomes the victim. So it is not that she is truly helpless or taken advantage of by others; rather she uses her feelings of helplessness or powerlessness to set up situations which confirm them. This prevents her from asserting herself or seeing how strong her need to be independent is and how much she needs to be in control through her passive-dependent tactics. In this way, therapy proceeds slowly, with much difficulty, to some relaxation of her masochistic tendencies.

BIBLIOGRAPHY

SULLIVAN, H. S. 1953. *Interpersonal Theory of Psychiatry.* New York: W. W. Norton, p. 353.
FREUD, S. *Standard Edition of Complete Psychological Works.* Vol. 19, p. 49. London: Hogarth Press.